MW01601230

RECALIBRATE

BY MATHEW BOWYER

RECALIBRATE

ISBN:
9798296606341

@MathewBowyer5
on Instagram.

Visit:
www.MathewBowyer.com

TABLE OF CONTENTS

Introduction

This book offers a perspective, not perfection. *Recalibrate* was born from chaos — not clarity. It was written in the shadows of federal courtrooms, financial collapse, broken trust, and the uncomfortable silence of accountability. But it was also written in the early morning light of fatherhood, in the quiet hours of reflection, and in the unshakable belief that I still had more to give.

If you've ever felt like your life has veered off track — if you've stood at the edge of a decision that changed everything — I've been there. I lived there. And I wrote this for you.

One thing I've always been known for is being brutally honest. I don't sugarcoat. I don't hide behind polished versions of myself. I've made massive mistakes, and I'll make more. I'm not perfect, and I'm not pretending to be. But what you'll get in these pages is the truth — raw, unfiltered, and real. I lay everything on the line, because I'd rather be judged for who I am than praised for who I'm not.

This isn't a victim's tale. This isn't a redemption arc wrapped in a bow. This is the story of a man who built, lost, rebuilt, stumbled, recalibrated — and chose to keep going.

I don't expect your sympathy. I hope to earn your respect.

So read this with an open mind. Question me. Judge me. Learn from my missteps.

But most of all, use it as fuel to recalibrate your own life when the road gets heavy.

I'm still walking mine.

— Matt Bowyer

CHAPTER 1
Introduction—The Raid

On the morning of October 5, 2023, it became clear that I would have to recalibrate.

Until 9:30 am, all had been progressing normally enough. After an invigorating six minutes of soaking in the 40-degree water of my cold plunge, I stepped into the adjacent sauna, where I sweated for 45-minutes while scrolling through my phone. Typically, I used that alone time to read up on sporting news and lineups for upcoming NFL games. That cold-hot combination helped my muscles recover before another day of jiu-jitsu training.

By 7:30, Nicole and I took turns reading to Kingston, our 29-month-old son.

Francisco, my jiu-jitsu professor, would join us around 9:00. After some coffee, we intended to walk around the local park with Kingston, then Francisco and I would be off to the gym for our workout.

The FBI had different plans.

While I buckled Kingston into his car seat, I didn't hear the agents flanking around us. An entire team of them had parked at the top of my street, plotting a surprise raid on my residence. I didn't hear anyone approaching while I leaned inside the rear of my SUV. Then I heard a voice:

"FBI!"

"Step back from the vehicle, slowly, with your hands up."

As I stepped back and toward them, I could see a swarm of agents, all pointing rifles. When I turned around, red laser beams from the gun sights centered on my chest. They'd already locked Francisco's wrists behind his back and I saw them walking him to the other end of my driveway. Two FBI agents and an IRS agent approached. They had a warrant to search my house, and asked how many people were inside.

"Just my wife, and a handyman," I responded. While they got ready to search, they allowed me to unbuckle Kingston from the car seat. Since I was holding my boy, they didn't handcuff me.

The agents led me to another side of my driveway, so I couldn't communicate with Francisco. Within a few minutes, I watched in disbelief as two agents escorted my wife out of our home, tears falling from her eyes and hands locked behind her back. I'll never forget the look on Nicole's face that morning. They even cuffed the handyman who had been painting inside. The agents kept us far apart so we couldn't communicate.

While I comforted my son, I couldn't help but think about all the changes about to come.

It wasn't the first time that federal authorities had raided my residence.

Almost ten years had passed since the last time federal agents ransacked my house. On March 25, 2014, a team of officers wearing blue windbreakers with block-sized gold initials of their agency seized just under a million dollars from the safe in my home, and another $100,000 that I was carrying in my Cadillac Escalade. Yet that time, it didn't turn out as bad as it could have. After they got their hands on the money, the agents made me an offer I couldn't refuse. Provided I sign a document they called an "abandonment form" releasing any claim to the cash, they would allow me to go about my business, without filing any charges against me. I signed the document, considering myself fortunate.

This time felt extremely different. As I sat helplessly watching Nicole cry, a thousand thoughts collided in my head. I watched as more agents came down the hill, carrying battering rams and shields, as if they expected that they'd have to break in. I counted 26 men, three women, and a dog that the government had apparently trained to sniff for currency and drugs, wherever it was hidden. My business had grown far larger since the last time they disrupted my life. With approximately 1200 clients depending upon me, my business handled between $5 and $10 million in weekly revenues.

Somehow, by the time the agents left, I knew that I'd have a lot less cash on hand. Fortunately, they surprised me on a Thursday, rather than a Monday or Tuesday when I would have had much more liquidity in the house.

Money, however, wasn't at the top of my concerns. I'm in a highly volatile business that both makes and loses money regularly.

Over the course of my career, I'd placed more than $1 billion worth of wagers, some with casinos across the world, and others with global and local bookmakers. It didn't matter whether it was sports or table games, I loved to gamble.

While sitting at a baccarat table in a casino, if I felt the goddess of fortune beside me, I'd wager up to $300,000 per hand. If luck turned against me, I'd drop my bets to as little as $1,000 per hand. Typically, I'd play more than 50 hands an hour. I'd need that flexibility to switch up my betting style, and I'd sit at those tables for four to five hours per sitting. In any given hour, I'd likely wager a cumulative total of more than $5 million. Surviving in high stakes gambling requires the self-discipline to press when winning, and to scale back when the cards aren't going your way.

It's the same in gambling as in life. As I sat on my driveway that morning, I knew that luck was not on my side. I started to question what I could do about the hand I'd been dealt.

In high-stakes games, I played to win, thriving on the action—putting my skill and intuition against the casino's edge, knowing the odds were against me. I could celebrate incredible hot streaks, walking away with seven-figure checks from the casino. On any given day, I also knew that I could lose millions with the turn of a single card, or when a player unexpectedly dropped a ball or missed a shot.

Through gambling, I got to know a lot about human nature over the past couple of decades. People processed fear and greed differently. Those feelings or emotions likely evolved as adaptive strategies over multiple generations. Some people were naturally afraid and avoided what they perceived as being dangerous, while others felt greedy, motivated for the hunt to acquire more. In casinos, I've watched people play while trying to keep a mental accounting. Instead of concentrating on the task at hand, they track winnings and losses as if they're looking at separate accounts. What's worse, their losses obliterated their sense of confidence, weighing far more heavily than any joy they felt from gains.

I didn't have this gene. Losses didn't rattle me in the same way as other people, and gains didn't change my behavior. I relied upon intuition, sensing that I would know when to bet higher and when to walk away. For more than a decade, I felt luck on my side. Then, things began to turn in 2022. Despite a few wins, the losses grew worse.

I had my biggest score in the 2023 Super Bowl, winning $4.6 million when the Kansas City Chiefs upset the Philadelphia Eagles. It's been a steady stream of losses since then, with sacrifices of more than $10 million to casinos, and culminating with federal agents trouncing the inside of my house.

At the peak of my liquidity, I'd packed a chest with more than $12 million in US currency—winnings from an incredible hot streak. But that liquidity didn't include holdings in real estate, crypto, gold bars, and private loans that I'd made in cash to people who might consider themselves unbankable. I had various other assets that I believed were untouchable. For a while, everything seemed to be going right. I left Las Vegas with winnings an unprecedented 17 times in a row, beating casinos out of millions. Besides those rewards, my business brought me a king's ransom in profits every week, allowing me to gradually increase the funds I'd put at risk in Las Vegas.

In my first ten years of high-stakes playing, between the age of 21 and 30, I lost roughly $1 million to Las Vegas casinos, or so I'd estimate. Over the next eight years, I increased my play, and likely lost another $2 million. By 2016, I'd won it all back. At that point, I was 41 and beginning to play bigger stakes than ever.

Several properties had banned me from playing blackjack, labeling me an "advantage" player. They allowed me to play other games, but I was forbidden to sit at a blackjack table. By watching my play, casinos believed that I used specific strategies or techniques. They thought I used my skill to count cards quickly in my head—which wasn't illegal. It just helped to even the odds, giving me a slight advantage. Casinos set out to take people's money—and in the end, with most players, they prevailed. After all, they've got the edge.

Eventually, all MGM properties, including MGM, Bellagio, Aria, New York, New York, and others prohibited me from playing any games, or even entering any of the hotel properties. When the casino manager showed me the numbers, it looked as if we were about even. Those numbers, however, only showed wins and losses from gaming—not the comps I'd received. To keep me playing, the MGM had been covering my costs for years. I'd get complimentary private jet flights, dining, spa, suites, villas with butlers, and all expenses in the casino's clubs as long as I kept gambling. With all the winnings and losses from gaming, we were about even over the years. But the manager showed that MGM had granted perks or comps valued in excess of $2 million, making me a nonprofitable guest, and ending our relationship.

Labels such as "advantage" player or "nonprofitable guest" didn't matter to me. I loved to gamble, and if MGM wouldn't have me, I knew that others would welcome me with open arms.

Routinely, I'd have days where I won or lost more money than some people would earn in 10 years. And that was before I turned 40, in 2015. By then, my primary business had taken off, and being more lucrative in business meant that I could step up my gambling.

I let my hosts in other casinos know that I intended to play for higher stakes. Rather than bringing a few hundred thousand on each trip, I'd bring $1 to $2 million to wager. And I intended to visit Las Vegas regularly.

With that much fire power, the Wynn, the Palazzo, and Caesar's Palace always made me feel welcome. When Resort World opened in Las Vegas, hosts invited me to play there as well. Since I pledged to bring more than $1 million on each trip, and to bring others who would bet as well, the hosts agreed to provide significantly higher comps and more incentivised deals than I'd been receiving before.

Since childhood, I have had a fascination with gambling. As a young boy my grandparents would frequently take me to Santa Anita and Los Alamitos race tracks. My uncle Doug invited me to join him on a gambling trip for the first time when I was only 18. As a teenager, I didn't weigh any more than 150 pounds and I looked young for my age. Doug drove us to Whiskey Pete's, the first casino on the road from California, in Primm, Nevada. Hoping to look older, I wore a suit and tie. When I sat at a blackjack table, the dealer cracked a joke about why I'd dressed up. I told him I was in town for a wedding and stepped in to play a few hands. The ruse worked, as the dealer allowed me to lose the $300 that I'd brought with me. I went to the ATM, withdrew another $300, and promptly lost that as well.

That lesson, however, was only the start of my casino education. When I turned 21, I had an ID to get into the major casinos, which introduced me to the concept of complimentary perks, known as "comps."

It all began with a weekend jaunt that I made to Las Vegas, when friends invited Monica and me to join them for a weekend of gambling. Monica had been my girlfriend since we were 15, when we met in high school. We married young, and she delivered our first daughter, Lauren, when I was only 19. Although our marriage didn't last, together we brought three beautiful daughters into the world, Lauren, Haley, and Brooke, and for that gift, I'll always be grateful.

At 21, both Monica and I looked forward to some fun. When our friends told us that they were going for a weekend getaway, we agreed to join them. I'd been chasing the adrenaline rush of gambling since I was a teenager, and once I turned 21, I couldn't wait to test my skills.

Our friends had set themselves up at the San Remo, one of the seediest hotels just off the famous Las Vegas Strip. Think all-you-can-eat buffets, and well-fed people wearing tank tops and flip flops. We all settled our bags into our rooms, but I told my friends that Monica and I intended to walk down the strip to New York, New York. They agreed to join us, and cheered me on as I sat at a blackjack table wagering bets. Within a few hours, my winnings surpassed $25,000. None of us had made too much money by then, and my friends couldn't distinguish $25,000 from $2 million. It may as well have been all the money in the world. They couldn't comprehend how I could take such risks with so much money.

My casino host Leslie noticed.

She wasn't much older than us, and I appreciated her walking over to introduce herself. She asked if I'd been to the casino before, and I told her that my wife and I had come spontaneously, joining my friends who had booked a weekend at the San Remo. We made small talk for a while, and Leslie listened politely. Then she told me that New York, New York would like to host Monica and me. As a casino host, she'd be responsible for handling all my needs. If I wanted to visit Las Vegas, she insisted that I call her first so she could make arrangements. New York, New York would cover costs for my suite, my meals, and even treat Monica and me to some of the shows, or the fights.

When I accepted her invitation, she insisted on providing Monica and me with a suite for the weekend. She coordinated a driver to take us back to San Remo to collect our bags. As we checked in at New York, New York, she also gave me a player's card, instructing me to use it any time I sat down to play.

When Monica and I went to our room, we couldn't believe our good fortune. The suite dwarfed the size of our entire apartment where we lived in Orange County, bringing us our first taste of Las Vegas opulence.

Once New York, New York accepted me, all the casinos began to send marketing materials my way. That early win of $25,000 hooked me for life. If I wanted to attend a fight, or Monica wanted to see a show, Leslie would take care of everything. I'd simply have to tell her how much cash I intended to bring. From the moment I provided funds to the casino's cashier, the game had begun, and I considered it my job to walk away with more than I came. During that era, when I had less experience, I typically left the casino broke, or with far less money than when I started.

My player's card allowed the casino to track every bet I wagered, and how long I gambled. Based on the time that I sat at a table, the games I played, and the amounts I bet, the casino could rely on mathematical calculations—in the gambling language, it's known as the "theoretical," meaning it's the casino's estimate of how much I would lose over time. Some games, such as Pai Gow, had a higher probability for players to lose; other games, like Blackjack and Baccarat, had more even odds. Every game had a built-in advantage for the house—known as the house's edge. Theoretical calculations determined this edge, representing the percentage that a casino expected to win over the long run.

To keep degenerate gamblers like me returning, the casino would provide perks that equated in value to a percentage of the theoretical loss amounts. For example, my player's card would inform the casino on which games I liked to play, how much I typically wagered, and how long I'd sit at a table gambling. Based on those calculations, it would compute a theoretical loss, known as the "theo." If the casino expected that I could potentially lose $100,000 on a trip, it might provide me with a theo of roughly $30,000—-which I could use to cover the cost of my suite, my meals, or anything else in the casino.

As a 21-year-old, with a baby girl at home, I doubt Leslie appreciated the value of play I would bring to her over the course of her career. Leslie would transition from one casino to another, and she could always count on me to come along with her as a reliable, loyal customer.

Once I made a commitment to bring in excess of $1 million per trip, I moved into an entirely new category of gambler. As a whale, I could pressure my hosts to increase the comps and deals from casinos. By then, I had hosts at every casino that hadn't banned me from playing, including The Palazzo, Cosmopolitan, Venetian, The Palms, Caesar's Palace, Resort World, or the Las Vegas Hilton, which is now known as the Westgate. Each of the hosts agreed to provide me with palatial villas, some spanning as much as 15,000 square feet, complete with private butlers, pools, bowling alleys, golf simulators, barber shops, spas, and enclosed backyards.

A few years ago, after I married Nicole, I figured out how I could make a casino host work more in my favor. In some cases, the casino would employ the host. When I met Leslie, for example, the New York, New York casino employed her. Another option, however, would be for a person to register with the Nevada Gaming Control Board as an independent representative. As long as a person met the appropriate criteria, and a casino agreed and approved, a person could qualify as an independent representative, earning commissions from the theoretical on the amount of money their clients would bring to gamble.

Through the innovative tactic of registering Nicole, we negotiated even better comps. As soon as we showed up, the casinos would provide Nicole with a gift card valued at ranges between $5 and $20 thousand. I'd get complimentary chips valued at up to 5% of the funds I brought with me. Typically, my bankroll for the trip would be $1 million plus. If I lost, the casino would return or discount up to as high as 20% of the deposit or credit line that I had on the trip to gamble.

All those comps kept us on the Las Vegas treadmill. A weekend rarely passed where we weren't boarding a private jet for another weekend of pampering. And as long as my business thrived, I could withstand the losses.

Yet while a team of federal agents swarmed through my house, and I saw my wife in handcuffs, my perspective began to change. I had to figure out how I could shift momentum.

After approximately 60 minutes, the agents allowed Nicole to leave with our son. They also uncuffed Francisco and the handyman, allowing them each to go their way.

Being the subject of their interest, I understood that the agents would have questions for me. When I told them that I wanted my attorney present before I'd respond to anything they asked about my business, they quit asking. They were not arresting me, they said, but neither would they allow me to go inside the house without an escort until they finished searching the premises.

Although I could have left, I chose to stay by the pool while the agents ransacked my house. Occasionally, two or three guys would come outside and attempt to engage. I'd ask about their lives, such as why they got into law enforcement, and how frequently they raided people's homes. When it came to their questions about my work, I let them know that I'd be happy to respond, so long as I had my attorney present.

Mostly, I spent those six hours in the backyard alone with my thoughts, trying to figure out a game plan, or next steps I should take. I didn't know whether the agents intended to charge me with a crime. If they brought charges against me, I wondered what they would be.

» What did the agents know?

» What were they looking to find?

» What kind of exposure did I have?

I was 48 years old, madly in love with my wife, the father of four daughters and our two-year- old, infant son.

» How could I be in a predicament where others had control over my life?

» What steps could I take, if any, to get back in control?

I started to calculate how I could restructure, recalibrate, and began going through the numbers. Considering the high California tax rates, I'd need to earn a minimum of $200,000 per month to generate an after-tax $100,000 my lifestyle required.

If the federal government destroyed my business, how would I meet such responsibilities?

Around 4:30 in the afternoon, the lead FBI agent came outside to greet me. He gave me an extensive receipt of sorts, a few pages detailing what he had taken. There hadn't been any need for the battering ram or shields that they'd brought, as I cooperated fully, providing access to my safes and any locked rooms. At the end of the day, considering cash,casino chips, gold coins, jewelry, and luxury handbags, they lightened my load by about $1 million worth of belongings. Surprisingly, the agents did not confiscate my wine and liquor collection, valued at another $1 million.

But neither did they provide me with any idea of their intentions on next steps.

The money, however, wasn't the worst of it. I've made millions, lost millions, and I'm confident that I'll make millions again. I felt more concerned about what I couldn't control. In their haul of my belongings, the agents carried my computers, iPads, and cellphones. Electronic information stored on those devices would, potentially, open their interest to every person in my network, a network that included professional athletes and celebrities, and some people who lived on the margins, some might call them family men. In any event, I knew many people who would not welcome conversations with anyone from the federal government.

This would be a day of reflection, and projection. I'd have to think about all the steps that brought me here, and the steps I'd take to get to the next stage. My name is Matt Bowyer, and this is my story.

CHAPTER 2
Bookie 'Beyond The Spread'

I held the television remote in my hand while Nicole and I settled into our room, our son Kingston sleeping on my chest. While pressing the arrow key to flip through various television apps, I saw an HBO trailer for a new series on the life of a bookie in Los Angeles.

Within 15 minutes, I changed the channel. Watching some guy pressuring people who welched on bets of a few thousand dollars didn't interest me.

Over the past several years, studios have been releasing more movies and television shows about sports betting. I understood why. Sports betting has been on the rise across the world.

In 2018, the US Supreme Court issued a ruling that authorized states to legalize and regulate sports betting. Since then, people have become much more accepting. During televised games, we see advertisements for FanDuel and DraftKings. Online ads capture our attention. They feature sexy young women enticing men, encouraging them to wager on sports bets. Those ads feature recognizable celebrities from Hollywood and the sports world. For example, it's common to see ads with stars such as Lebron James, Jamie Foxx, and Kevin Hart. It's in our face, every day, a sign of virility—a man on the hunt. Exponential growth has come to sports betting, generating billions of dollars annually.

Despite society's growing appetite and acceptance of wagering on football, baseball, basketball, UFC, and other college or professional sports, some people don't like the formality of structured betting settings. A bigger government means more eyes watching. Ask me how I know. Registered businesses that take bets must comply with Know-Your-Customer (KYC) rules and suspicious activity reports (SARS), requiring people to provide a driver's license, social-security number, and bank account numbers before allowing people to place bets.

People are moving into an era of decentralized finance, as evidenced by the rise of cryptocurrencies. No one wants the government in their business all the time. As President Reagan told us many years ago, nine of the most terrifying words that Americans do not want to hear include "I'm with the government and I'm here to help."

In America, we love our freedom, and people grow stronger when they develop the confidence to sink or swim on their own decisions. We don't want the government watching over us, but as social animals, we want to be around others whom we know, like, and trust. And all of us appreciate personal attention, especially when we're gambling.

It's one of the reasons casinos lavish high rollers with unbelievable perks. They'll do anything to keep players in the game.

A good bookmaker will do the same, making customers feel comfortable, providing services that Las Vegas casinos cannot provide. To place a sports bet in Las Vegas, a person has to show up, wait in line, and put cash on the table to place a bet. If the guy wants to bet $10,000 or more, or if there is any transaction involving $10,000 or more, the casino will require a CTR report—Currency Transaction Report. Gamblers who put $10,000, $100,000, or $1 million on the line do not want to provide details that regulators expect. Yet the casino will enforce KYC rules, requiring the equivalent of a financial colonoscopy. They'll want to know where his money comes from and ensure that a record exists of each transaction. It's too clinical, obliterating the mantra of what goes on in Vegas stays in Vegas.

A personal bookmaker, on the other hand, doesn't give a shit about where the person gets his money. He has total discretion. He can take a bet over the phone or, if he's more sophisticated, through an interactive website he developed. The bookmaker will have a system to keep a running tally. Together, they'll agree to settle up when it's mutually convenient. They might meet on a golf course or over drinks. A dedicated bookmaker will follow the Nordstrom rule of customer service—

doing everything possible to make things easy. He'll pay on time, without question, but he'll be flexible in receiving payments.

The bookmaker will send or receive funds in any and every way that meets the needs of a customer—including cash, wire transfers, cash apps like Venmo, Apple Pay, Cash App, and PayPal, or cryptocurrency exchanges, or take winnings in personal items, like Rolex watches, Lamborghinis, or Rolls Royce automobiles—as I have done. He'll use discretion to adjust the betting line and accept unusual bets, including straight bets, moneyline bets, point-spread bets, over/under bets, proposition bets. And if a customer loses too much, a good bookmaker will create a payment plan, or make arrangements to work things out, considering all past bets and the personal character of the individual in a pinch.

Las Vegas can't provide that attention. Neither can the gangster-style bookmakers of the past, who relied upon violence or the threat of violence to enforce bets.

More sophisticated bookmakers professionalize the process, creating online programs for customers to place bets anytime, on any device. As long as a customer has an internet connection, he can place a bet. I've invested millions to pioneer that process, providing clients with user IDs and passwords, giving them the right balance of anonymity and personal attention.

Regardless of how much time and energy I've spent on creating awesome betting experiences for my customers, life has taught me to deal with the world as it exists. After all, federal agents stormed my house. When they locked my wife's wrists in handcuffs, and marched her out of our home, they sent me a pretty clear message that I'll have to figure out a new strategy for moving forward.

I'm only 49-years-old, in great shape, with an infant son, and four daughters I adore from previous relationships. I've got a lot of life and many responsibilities. Yet I'm getting a message that the time has come for me to start thinking about next steps. I'm no longer interested in running a business that could put the people I care about at risk. Especially since I know that I'm no longer able to keep things quiet.

Illusions of my anonymity shattered a few months after the FBI visited me. In early 2024, I received a certified letter from Tisha Thompson, an Investigative Reporter at ESPN:

> *My name is Tisha Thompson. I am an investigative reporter based in Washington, DC, and I specialize in complex stories relying on anonymous sources at ESPN.*
>
> *In recent days, I have had multiple sources who have connected ... you to a federal probe. I have seen some of the internet chatter relating to the search of your home, which I have confirmed with sources. I have*

also been given more detailed information about your connection to the case that has not been made public thus far.

I very much want to connect with you so you can confirm or deny what I've been told and give your side of the story—so much so that I have flown into Orange County explicitly to meet with you. I hope when you receive this letter, you will contact me so that I can introduce myself to you in person.

How did she get her information? I wondered whether someone had been listening in to my phone calls, or tapping my electronic communications. She had my home address, which I've kept private. Since authorities hadn't yet charged me with a crime, the media hadn't reported on the raid.

Clearly, someone was talking, sparking media interest in my story. If a reporter took the time to fly cross country from DC to California, even before I agreed to meet with her, I was not going to be able to keep my business private.

Before responding to the reporter, I consulted with my attorneys. I wanted their take on what this new development meant.

Who knew what?

I looked up Tisha Thompson on her social media channels. From her Twitter page, I could see that she brought out the sensational—writing about scandals like "abuse in the workforce," suspensions, sexual harassment, and anything woke. Her official bio on the ESPN website says a great deal:

> Tisha Thompson is an investigative reporter for ESPN based in Washington, D.C. ... Thompson specializes in complex investigations that explore the intersection of sports and power, including league and government investigations, sexual assault and harassment, high-profile civil and criminal cases, consumer issues like sports ticketing, and the evolving field of sports banking, including the use of public funding, private equity, hedge funds, cryptocurrencies and other financial instruments."

She made a living by bringing out the sensational. Some people didn't necessarily want to live a fast and exciting life, but they found it entertaining to live vicariously by others who went all out, putting it all on the line, every time. Her interest wasn't in me as an individual, but in the stories I could tell about fascinating people that would increase her viewership. Like the players who pushed themselves hard to be the best in the world at what they did, the reporter wanted her own trophies. She could get them by shattering the lives of powerful people, all in the interest of investigating reporting. "The people have a right to know," she'd argue.

My attorneys agreed that I should listen to what the reporter had to say, then decide whether it made sense to offer any input into her story. Although her letter indicated that my voice mattered, I suspected that she only wanted to bring out salacious details about the glamorous world of high-stakes gambling in Las Vegas, with hopes of gluing more people to watch her coverage on ESPN.

I didn't blame her. We all had a position to play in this game of life. Some people like to be on the field, advancing or falling back by their own decisions and preparations and skills. Others choose a different path. Preferring less risk, gathering their excitement by reading about how others live. A reporter could serve as that bridge, bringing people into the lives of others. She could tell me that my voice mattered, but I anticipated that it would only matter to the extent that it would provide flavor to what she wanted to write about others.

But who was her target?

On Friday, January 9, 2024, Tisha showed up at my house in San Juan Capistrano. The reporter didn't surprise me when she began asking questions about Scott Sibella, the former president and chief operating officer of Resort World, in Las Vegas. I've known Scott for decades, since much earlier in his career, even before he ran the MGM Grand Las Vegas.

Many trips, I'd gamble millions in his casinos. He'd send private jets, lavish me by comping accommodations fit for royalty or celebrities that needed privacy from the masses. Our paths would mix socially, and on more than one occasion, he had to provide me with the same kind of personal attention that I would provide to my clients.

I've never met Robert Cipriani, a degenerate gambler who masquerades as a "philanthropist/activist/gambler," but he trolls online under the handle @robinhood702. Cipriani brought negative attention to many people, including casino executives like Scott Sibella with his inflammatory tweets:

> "Disgraced, LYING Scumbag and Convicted Felon SCOTT SIBELLA is finally out. Everyone knows he's been doing this shit for DECADES! Will others close to the Wayne Nix illegal bookie scandal join him? The answer-a resounding YES!! @VitalVegas @LasVegasLocally."

Recently, Cipriani started to throw my name into the mud.

> "@VenetianVegas execs are very nervous now. They barred Matt Bowyer from play in 2016 because they KNEW he was an illegal bookmaker. Years later, their PD exec Brad Hayslip got Bowyer back in to play at @VenetianVegas. Are the FEDS looking at Venetian now?"

Authorities had charged Scott Sibella with failing to file SARS reports, which stands for suspicious activities or transactions and Scott pleaded guilty to the felony charge in federal court. To soften me up, the reporter began her questions about my Las Vegas excursions, and the perks that various casinos would extend to me. After questioning why various casinos would send private jets to pick me up every weekend, she asked whether or not Scott's charges were related to illegal bookmakers and violations of laws pertaining to money laundering.

The reporter then pivoted with her questions, asking me to speak about my relationship with Shohei Ohtani.

Shohei had become a staple on ESPN, especially since he signed a 10-year, 700-million-dollar deal with the Los Angeles Dodgers. Understandably, fans wanted to know as much as possible about the man who signed the most lucrative contract in sports history. He's considered among the greatest players ever, with some comparing him favorably to the early career of Babe Ruth. Shohei became the first player in the major leagues to pitch seasons with 100+ strikeouts, stealing more than 20 bases, and belting more than 44 home runs out of the park. He won many awards, including the Most Valuable Player Award multiple times. He also is the first player to achieve a 50-50 in a season. For those who don't know sports, it means he smashed 50 home runs, and stole 50 bases—which is extraordinary. No player in MLB history has reached that milestone. Shohei is that rare combination of power and speed. Writers frequently describe him as a unicorn or the best player ever.

The reporter, however, wanted fans to see a different side of Shohei Ohtani.

"Isn't it true that Shohei books his bets with you, and that he currently owes you more than $25 million."

The reporter wanted to know much more than I wanted to share. On that note, I ended my conversation with the reporter and began giving more thought to the next steps I would have to take. If she knew about the possibility of a relationship with Shohei, that meant others knew as well.

With the potential for criminal charges and potential IRS complications hanging over my head, I had to make a choice. Either I could allow the complications of my pending legal predicament to obliterate my peace, or I could recalibrate, figuring out how I could write the next chapter of my life.

I'm about resilience, determined to push through the challenge with my dignity intact. Not knowing how long this process will take, I set my mind on memorializing everything, bringing readers along with me. I'm not under oath as I write these words, so anyone can use discretion to decipher the validity of this story I'll share. Consider it a transparent exercise in personal therapy and introspection. Readers may appreciate this real-time look of what it's like to build a business that processed more than $1 billion worth of sports bets, and then get sucked into the challenges of criminal investigations, charges, and media scrutiny.

One message they'll see is that regardless of how bad things get, we always have the power to pick ourselves up and play another day. We simply need to make a plan, put priorities in place, and work toward building the next phase in our life.

It's something that I've had to do many times before. Those lessons began early, during a childhood that forced me to grow up quickly.

My mother, Linda, raised my brothers and me in Cypress, a Southern California city of North Orange County. I'd describe the first ten years of my life as being superb. My father, Steve Bowyer, supported our family with a bail bonds company he ran with my mom. It seemed to do all right, as it provided us with a nice home and everything a young family could want. I was very close to my mom, who was young and beautiful. She had that kind of beauty that could make other women self-conscious, or uncomfortable if she simply walked into a room.

My dad had been a soldier. When he returned from the conflict in Vietnam, he fell madly in love with mom, marrying her and agreeing to raise my two older brothers and adopting them—Joey and Shawn—as if they were his own sons. They were my mother's sons from an earlier relationship.

I was born on April 4, 1975, and our youngest brother, Andrew, joined us about five years later. The four of us got along well, even though my older brothers resented my father. Despite his promises to my mom that he would love us all the same, he clearly favored my little brother and me, his natural children, which didn't sit well with any of us.

We used to love our time together as a young family. My parents purchased a second home on the Colorado River, located 24 miles outside of Blythe. At least twice each month, my brothers and I would bring friends to join us for the four-plus hour drive to spend long weekends at our river house. We had a dock, a jet boat, jet skis, motorcycles—all the toys that a young kid would take for granted. While at the river house, we'd get to fish, play water sports, or shoot rodents with our BB guns.

By the time I turned 12, my dad's drinking got out of control, which put an end to our happy family. My mom kicked him out. He tried to get it together, but alcoholism is an unforgiving disease. Like all addictions, it causes havoc to a household. No child should have to serve as a therapist to his parents, but in many ways, that's what followed when alcoholism destroyed the home. My dad would call, wasted, trying to talk his way back into our family. As a 12-year-old, I'd have to talk him off the ledge, and simultaneously comfort my mom. I was like a counselor.

People frowned upon divorce back then, and my mom did her best to keep the family together. She was in her late teens when she fell for her first love, but he abandoned her. She didn't want to raise my brothers and me alone. When my dad's drinking got to be too much, she had to put our welfare above her happiness and chose to raise us as a single mother.

I admired her strength, because it sure wasn't easy. My two older brothers were tough, and great fighters. They would do anything to protect us, and like their dad, they had violent tempers. I never had that gene of thirsting for violence. I'd always been a good athlete, and enjoyed the physicality of sports, but I didn't have that mean gene. Even as I grew older, and supplemented my income by collecting on bad debts for other bookies, people on the streets would call me "Tattoo Matt," using my stature to send a message that force would follow if people didn't pay a debt. In the eyes of the weak, confidence is a more lethal weapon than violence.

To hold everything together, my mom had to work multiple jobs. Besides trying to run the bail bonds business, she would supplement her income by selling lotions, cakes, cosmetics, and other beauty products. Despite her best efforts, holding it all together became too much for her.

Out of necessity, I began my life as an entrepreneur after my dad abandoned us for alcohol and life as a single man. From my older brothers, I learned that through hustling, we could earn money to buy treats that our mom couldn't afford. While still in elementary school, I began developing skills in customer service—beginning to appreciate the timeless laws of supply and demand. Kids wanted candy, sports memorabilia, magazines. I'd invest resources to purchase anything that other students wanted, and that could earn a profit.

When I was 12, I saw *Wall Street*, with Charlie Sheen and Michael Douglas. The film fascinated me, inspiring me to earn money. I didn't want to learn by studying books, but by creating my own income streams. By then, I understood how fickle life could become without financial resources. Before my dad went his own way, I thought we were more stable financially. Seeing the stress that my mom went through made an everlasting impression, convincing me that regardless of what it took, I'd have to find my way in the world.

Once I turned 13, I'd become a master of baseball cards, which had real value. I'd buy packs of cards and figure out the value of each. The most valuable cards of the era included Ken Griffey Jr., Nolan Ryan, Rickey Henderson, and Mark McGwire. By working at a baseball card shop and going to shows, I understood which cards had more value, and which cards had less.

That exercise of collecting and trading baseball cards taught me a lot. It also helped me learn more about business. Some cards had more value in the marketplace. Teachers at Bell Junior High tried to impress upon me the importance of learning about social studies, dead presidents, and other useless subjects. Learning the value of baseball cards, on the other hand, could make me money, which I found more useful.

I'd buy packs of cards for $1 or $2, and by attending shows, I could sell some of those cards for $10, or $20. Later, I learned that I could expand my market with a job. A local gas station hired my brother Shawn to work as a cashier. I admired that he was earning a steady paycheck.

I wanted to be like him, to get more regular money that I could count on. But I was too young for any regular business to hire me. The typical local businesses required work permits for people who were under 15. But I found a loophole, with the Orange County Register. They'd let me work on a paper route delivering newspapers, which was okay.

As soon as I turned 13, the Orange County Register considered me old enough to start selling door to door, which was awesome. I started knocking on doors and asking for orders. I learned a great deal about customer interactions through that experience. If someone opened the door, I could pitch. I wouldn't let them close the door without making a sale. I could always weave a story to convert them, pressing them with tales about how I was competing to win a sales contest, and that I only needed five more orders.

"I just don't read the paper," the person might object.

Sensing that they didn't want to disappoint a 13-year-old boy, or shatter him from reaching his dreams, I'd keep pressing. "Here's what I'm going to do for you," I'd say. "I'm going to let you try it out for 30 days. That's it. No big deal. Let me deliver the paper to you for 30 days, then you can cancel. It's free for 30 days. What do you have to lose? After that, I'm going to get your subscription down to only $7—that's less than 20 cents a day to get all the information you need. Now think about that! Think of how that information will help you spot new opportunities. Can you afford 20 cents a day to spot new opportunities?"

You'd be surprised how many people would sign up.

Overcoming objections became my speciality. I signed up so many customers that I crushed all records at the Orange County Register. Every day they'd drop off 125 papers at my doorstep. I'd assemble them with rubber bands and then I headed out into the marketplace as a young teenager. If I saw kids playing out front while I delivered the papers, I'd ask if they collected baseball cards. My knowledge of which cards had value put me in a superior position, allowing me to earn more money by expanding my trading card business.

The Orange County Register brought a highlight of that early adolescence, when I blew through the competition of signing up the most subscribers. I was only 14 years old, competing against kids as old as 18—but none of them had my hustle. I never told my mom about the prize of the contest, but when I won, I surprised her by giving her two tickets for a fully paid trip to Waikiki. She started to cry when I gave her the tickets, and I'll always remember the joy I felt in providing her with a treat that she deserved, but couldn't afford because of the sacrifices she made for my brothers and me. I owe a great deal to my mom. She helped me to believe in myself, to know that there wasn't anything I couldn't do.

Once I began studies at Pacifica High School, I felt like a seasoned money maker. I could buy my clothes and pay my way. Standing only five-feet tall, and weighing only 89 pounds, I developed a native intelligence to push my way through a crowd of bigger kids. Too small for football, I gravitated to wrestling, where the lowest weight class was 98 pounds. Coaches appreciated that I was relentless, like a fearless honey badger, refusing to give up. They promoted me to the varsity team during my freshman year. I went 9 wins and 27 losses, because I was only 14 and wrestling against 18-year-olds. But I learned. My sophomore year, I went 19 and 12.

Life was changing for me in high school, especially when a beautiful, model-type girl enrolled. She was Filipino, the prettiest girl I'd ever seen. Somehow, I convinced her to go out with me, and her family even accepted me—despite my being a tiny blonde-haired, blue-eyed hustler of a kid. We dated through high school, and Monica became a forever-part of my life.

To earn more money, I took a job as a cashier and filling gas at a local Chevron station, which brought awesome opportunities to hustle, sometimes in an unethical way. In fact, as I reflect, it was outright theft. People would give me their Chevron card to charge gas, frequently driving off without remembering to retrieve their card. Never considering the implications of my actions, I'd take those cards to other Chevron stations, inviting friends to join me. I'd earn extra money by filling their cars, and allowing them to pay me half price for the gasoline. I'd also use the card to charge for cartons of cigarettes. Then, I'd take the cigarettes back to the station where I worked, and if people paid cash for a pack, I'd sell them the cigarettes from my inventory rather than the store's inventory.

In retrospect, I know that those activities were wrong. As a 16- or 17-year-old, I lacked the maturity to measure the rightness or wrongness of my decisions. Rather than considering the ethics of my decision, I measured my actions by whether they advanced my economic life. With my own money, I purchased a Mazda B-2000 pickup truck for $3700 and tricked it out with mag wheels and loud stereo systems. I could gamble, wear stylish clothes with the most trending brands, and I stood out with girls. On the side, I started buying weed that I could hustle—which didn't go over well when my mother found out.

I'd learned about marijuana from my older brother, who had been my role model since my infancy. Although I didn't use drugs, many people smoked weed in high school, opening opportunities to supplement my income. That was back in the early 1990s, when the first President Bush made his strong stance against any kind of drug use. He said that drugs presented "the gravest threat facing our nation." My mom took that message to heart, saying that it was unacceptable to sell drugs and she promptly kicked me out of the house when she discovered the weed I hid under my bed.

My close friend, Robert Henderson, invited me to live with him. His mom loved me and allowed me to stay until graduation. After a few months, however, she found my scale and some weed, and ordered me out as well. With enough money to support myself, I appreciated the freedom and rented my own apartment.

In 1993, Pacifica awarded my diploma, but I didn't think that college would be the right fit for me. I'd been carving my own way, earning my own keep. Along with my friend, Vince Murray, I rented an apartment in Huntington Beach. Monica moved in with us, and the three of us started to make our way in life. My friend's aunt ran the gift shops at the John Wayne airport, and I talked my way into a job that began at 6:00 am. I stayed there until my shift ended at 2:00 in the afternoon. From there, I'd drive to Irvine to work in the warehouse of a clothing company, Mossimo, staying from 2:30 until ten. If I wasn't working at the two jobs, I was at the Los Alamitos Race Track, betting on Thoroughbreds and Quarter Horse races.

At a horse-track, betting differs from betting on sports, where experts predict favorites and set lines. With pari-mutuel betting, no one sets the odds in advance. Instead, the participants bet on the race, and as more participants place bets, the odds adjust. Depending on how much people bet on a horse, the odds will change all the way up until the race. After the race, the track will take its cut first, and then pay out the remainder in accordance with the odds for the horse that came in first, second, or third—known in horse-track betting as win, place, or show.

With sports betting, on the other hand, the odds become fixed, locked in at the time a gambler places the bet. The sportsbook, or bookie, sets the odds, and those odds remain constant, regardless of the amount bet, or how many more bets come in. With sports betting, there's also a much wider array of bets, including the moneyline bets, the point-spread bets, the over/under bets, the parlays, the prop bets, and the futures. These bets cover various aspects of the game, not just the final outcome. A bookmaker will adjust odds to balance the books, or manage risk.

I enjoyed any kind of gambling, but I loved to wager on sports, and I understood every aspect of the game. For those who don't understand, I'll share more about the business. It was good for me. It allowed me to squander more than $40 million in losses at casinos and to bookies. If I could lose $40 million and still stand to talk about it, it brings some truth to the old line: "What doesn't kill you makes you stronger."

Moneyline Bet: The moneyline is a straightforward and basic form of sports betting. It focuses on the outcome, requiring the player to pick a winner. It's one of the simplest bets in sports betting, because it doesn't involve a point spread.

When a person makes a moneyline bet, the bookmaker assigns odds for each team, expressed positively or negatively. A positive odds means the team is an underdog. The number represents how much profit to pay the winner. For example, if a team has odds of +200, a $100 bet would yield a profit of $200, resulting in a total payout of $300.

Negative numbers on a moneyline bet indicate the favorite. If a team has odds of -150, the bettor would need to put up $150 to make a profit of $100. If the favorite wins, the winner would receive a total payout of $250.

For betters who place a point-spread bet, that means wagering on the margin of victory in a game rather than just the outcome of the game. The point spread, also known as the "line," or the "spread," is a number set by oddsmakers. The oddsmakers make a more balanced betting environment, giving both teams an equal chance of attracting bets.

To make a point-spread bet, the gambler must select a team. He understands that in order for him to win the bet, the team has to cover the spread. For example, if the game is between the Seahawks and the Raiders, and the line says Seahawks minus 3.5, that means the Seahawks are favored. If the Seahawks win the game by 30 to 27, people who bet on the Seahawks would lose the bet—because the Seahawks did not cover the 3.5 point spread. Since a team cannot win by half-of-a-point, the Seahawks would have to win by 4 points in order for a gambler to win a Seahawks bet. On the flip side, a bet on the Raiders would win if the

Seahawks did not win by at least 4 points, or if the Raiders won the game.

Point-spread betting adds an extra layer of complexity and strategy to sports betting. A bettor must not only predict the outcome of the game, but also consider the margin which the favored team will win or lose.

Another bet is the over/under, also known as the totals bet. It involves a wager on the combined score of both teams in a game. Rather than betting on which team will win or the point spread, a gambler can place a bet on the combined total score. The sportsbook sets a predicted total number of points, goals, runs, or other scoring unit for the game. Bettors can put a wager on whether the total score will be over or under that number. These bets can add excitement to a game, as the gamblers get to root for scores, regardless of which team wins.

A parlay bet is a single wager that can combine two or more individual bets into one larger bet. This type of bet allows bettors to combine multiple selections from different games or events, offering the potential for a much higher payout compared to placing each bet individually. For the gambler to win, all selections must prevail.

To place a parlay bet, the gambler selects all types of bets—known as legs. A person may select the Raiders over the Chiefs by 5, plus take the over, plus take the Rams over the Giants. Each one of those bets is considered a "leg" of the parlay. If the person wins each leg, the person wins the bet, at a much higher multiplier. There is more possibility to win big, but also more risk—because each leg of the parlay bet must come through to get a victory.

A proposition bet is a type of wager that is not directly related to the final outcome of a game or event, but rather, focuses on a specific occurrence, or individual player performance in the game. They can cover a wide range of scenarios, and often involve predicting whether something will or will not happen during the course of the game. For example, a prop bet may be whether Patrick Mahomes throws a touchdown during the first drive. Or whether the Chiefs will choose to receive or kickoff during the first half.

Finally, in sports betting, futures bets are wagers placed on events or outcomes that will occur in the future, typically at the conclusion of a season or tournament. Unlike most types of bets, futures require a long wait time, such as who will win next year's Super Bowl.

I didn't only become a master of placing all kinds of bets, I made and lost millions of dollars with each type of bet over the course of my life. Besides placing my wagers, I booked hundreds of millions each year for other gamblers.

That pathway began soon after I graduated high school, in 1993.

CHAPTER 3

Commodities—From the Trailer to The Trading Floor

Living in Huntington Beach, California, could be a young person's dream. As an 18-year-old with a bias for a fast life and gambling, moving to the beach didn't work out too well. Despite an exceptionally hard work ethic, companies did not pay well to young men without more than a high school education. Getting up at 5:30 am to show up for two separate jobs, requiring me to work until 10 each evening, felt unlike a pathway to misery. I loved being with Monica and going to the race track, but if I wanted a better future, I knew that I'd have to make something happen, or make some changes.

Our living arrangements were about what anyone would expect for three young people who didn't have a good income. I could earn more than my wages from the bets I placed, but gambling could also lead to my losing everything in an instant.

I had a very good friend from high school, Vince, who had moved in with Monica and me. He earned a living by waiting tables in a local restaurant and frequently worked late into the night. When he returned to the apartment, he just crashed on the couch, leaving the television on. Sometimes, he left his pants on the chair beside him. When I saw his pants, if I needed some cash, I'd dig through his pockets while he slept, and "borrowed" any cash tips that he had earned. Those resources would allow me to increase my wagers at the track. I always repaid him, and if I won, I'd give him something extra.

When Monica told me that we were going to have a baby, however, I realized that I'd have to make some changes. There wasn't any way I could support a family working dead-end jobs requiring me to stack inventory for other business owners. If we were going to bring a baby into the world, I understood that I'd have to find an opportunity to grow.

All three of us knew that we'd have to get our lives together. Vince decided to return home so that he could start college. To recalibrate, Monica and I decided that we'd move in with my mom to save money. Given challenges in the market, she lost the home where we had lived as a family. After giving up the house that had been our home, my mom downsized into a two-bedroom, double-wide trailer in Dana Point, where she lived with my younger brother, Andrew.

Andrew was only five years younger than me. When Monica and I moved into the trailer, he was only 13. Sadly, he fell onto hard times. Starting with bad decisions during his adolescence, he got involved with drugs and petty crime. I did my best to counsel him, but at that time in my life, I was just getting started and not exactly seasoned in success. Even though Monica and I crowded the trailer, sleeping on the couch, being there made my mom happy, and she hoped that my younger brother might learn something from me.

As an 18-year-old with a pregnant girlfriend, I already had a lot on my plate. Monica came from a strict Filipino family. Once we learned that she was carrying our child, I didn't have any doubt that I would marry her. We agreed that I'd have to get my life together first, and given that we were still in an era when businesses valued college degrees, we didn't see a lot of options. Monica contributed to our income with a secretarial job, but we knew that she'd have to quit as we got closer to the baby's delivery.

Knowing that it wouldn't be prudent to rely on gambling winnings to support our young family, I went searching for a job. I had to find a steady stream of income. When I moved in with my mom, I didn't have much of anything. The car I owned, a beater, wouldn't fetch $400 at best. The floorboard had holes, and I could see the road beneath the car as I drove. With responsibilities of being a father, I set my mind on making a change, determined to secure a job that would allow me to outperform others and grow. I needed a springboard to start my life.

My springboard came at Chevy's, a Mexican restaurant in the affluent Ocean Ranch shopping center in Dana Point,California. I had to consider my strengths and weaknesses. Being only 19, without experience or a college degree, employers weren't going to see me as an ideal candidate unless I proved myself. I had a lot of confidence that I could earn a high income through sales, but I didn't have the breathing room to build a book of business or wait for commission checks. We'd need resources to pay for Monica's medical needs, and I'd have to contribute to the household expenses of living with my mom.

When I walked in, Chevy's hadn't even opened yet, and I anticipated that a manager would hire me as a waiter. Confident that I had an engaging personality and that customers would appreciate the service I provided, I anticipated that I'd earn nightly tips. That steady income would allow me to contribute to my responsibilities while I launched myself into the next opportunity.

Despite my self-confidence that I could contribute to an exceptional dining experience for every customer, the manager didn't want to take a chance, especially since I didn't have any experience. Rather than starting as a waiter, he suggested I begin as a busboy and then work my way up to waiting tables. Considering myself a grown man, it felt somewhat insulting. Although I considered myself charming and charismatic, he perceived me as being young and inexperienced.

He didn't seem too impressed when I cited the records I broke and awards I won while delivering and selling papers for the Orange County Register. Or maybe that success intimidated him. After all, it must have been a colossal disappointment for a man to have reached the end of his career, in his late 50s, and still be working as a hiring manager in a chain restaurant. Believing that I could do better, I refused to lose confidence and accepted the offer on the spot. I had a premonition that I would launch the next steps in that restaurant, and it wouldn't be as a waiter.

Once I got started, I understood how opportunities would open with exceptional service. Although I may not have worked in a restaurant before, I had experience in facing rejection and overcoming objections. I had knocked on doors and spoke with people who considered me an intrusion into their home. With relentless persistence, I convinced them to purchase subscriptions from me that they didn't want. Then, I'd supplement my income by trading baseball cards with their children, exploiting my knowledge about each card's worth in the marketplace to harness more value out of each trade.

Compared to the ways that I'd earned an income in the past, I considered the prospects of working in a restaurant to be a piece of cake. People were coming in to get served. What could be easier than that? I'd simply have to set aside my predilection for gambling for a while so that I could focus on the job at hand—even if I'd have to start by bussing tables, I had all the confidence in the world that I could step up and shine.

To outshine the hostess, the waiter, and even the manager, I knew what I had to do. Hustling, I'd keep the chips and salsa full, reading facial expressions and body language of each customer so I would know when to converse, or when to smile silently and move on.

Within weeks, regular customers would request seating in my section. Rather than waiters tipping me out with gratitude, on many occasions, they begrudged that some customers tipped me directly. Micky and his wife gave me much more than a tip—they opened opportunities for a new way of life.

For several weeks, they'd been dining regularly in the section where I worked for the evening. Micky always expressed gratitude for my service with a generous tip, sometimes giving me $50. He and his wife made a favorable impression on me and I wondered what they did. He spoke with a British accent and grew up in London, but he was East Indian; his wife, Ishani, was also of Indian heritage. To me, they seemed an exotic couple. I admired the matching Rolexes they wore, platinum with diamond bezels and icy blue faces.

After his meal one evening, while pressing a generous tip in my hand, Micky passed along his business card. "I'd like you to visit my office tomorrow," he said. "I have an opportunity that I think would suit you. Can you be there at 1pm?"

It hadn't been two months since I began bussing tables at Chevy's, and I already sensed the next chapter of my life opening. Micky's card identified him as the CEO and founder of Baron's Worldwide Financial Services, which sounded prestigious. Since he looked to be in his late 20s, only about ten years older than me, I thought this could be a great opportunity.

Wanting to make a good impression, I knew that I'd need some new clothes. I didn't want to work my way out of the opportunity by showing up at the office building in the heart of Irvine's swanky financial district wearing jeans, a t-shirt, and flip-flops. By 9:00 am the following morning, I was in a Marshalls discount department store to purchase a dress shirt, dress shoes, and a pair of slacks—telling the clerk I didn't have more than $150 to spend, all in, shoes included. The girl helping me laughed, but she got me set up.

When I drove to the office, I parked my beater in a covered garage packed with exotic cars, including Aston Martins, Ferraris, and many Porsches. A receptionist greeted me, and walked me through a grid of desks and glass conference rooms, with well-dressed guys, most of whom were younger than 30. I didn't have any idea what they were doing, but they radiated confidence, giving high fives and fist bumps while passing each other as they walked and talked into their headsets, giving off the vibe of the trading floor in the movie *Wall Street.*

I didn't have any idea what they were doing, but I wanted in.

Stepping into his sleek, imposing office, I felt struck by the air of success that surrounded Micky. Despite being young, he exuded an aura of authority and achievement, his desk adorned with awards that spoke volumes of his prowess. On the wall, I saw pictures of his wife, Ishani. They stood in an opulent home, with the ocean and Dana Point harbor in the background. I saw a picture of a sleek boat, presumably his. Micky greeted me with a firm handshake, his demeanor welcoming, yet also commanding as he invited me to sit.

"I've seen your work ethic at the restaurant, Matt. Your charisma and enthusiasm caught my eye, which is why you're here," Micky began, his voice both encouraging and serious. It sounded much more formal than when he sat in the restaurant's booths, while he smiled, laughed, and enjoyed himself as he sipped on a margarita. I felt hopeful, ready to dive into whatever challenges lay ahead, but also a bit taken aback by the seriousness of his demeanor.

"I can't tell you how surprised I was, and how grateful I was, when you invited me here, Micky. I tried to find any information that I could about Baron's Worldwide Financial Services."

"Why not?" his eyes pierced me.

"What?" I didn't know what he meant.

"You said you can't tell me how surprised you were. I asked why you couldn't." He wasn't laughing.

"In all honesty, I don't even know what you guys do—but I'll do anything to learn," I responded, trying to convey my readiness and ambition. I believed in myself and that I could fit in.

Micky leaned in, his gaze piercing, and it sounded as if he'd changed his tone. "So, Matt, why a bus boy? A bright young man like yourself, surely you could have aimed for something more challenging, something with a clearer path to advance. What does that say about your ambition?"

The bluntness of his question caught me off guard. "Well, I didn't set out to be a busboy. I simply needed to get my foot in the door, into a job that would provide a paycheck quickly. From there I expected to advance. I always intended to use the job as my stepping stone. By showing I'm responsible and willing to work hard, opportunities would open." I managed to respond, though I felt my confidence slipping.

Micky's expression was hard to read. "And what about your future? Do you plan to build a life, support a family on the earnings of someone who serves others? What should the choice you made tell me about your self-confidence? What thoughts do you have about your abilities?"

His words felt like a direct challenge to my self-worth, far more confrontational than I had anticipated. I struggled to maintain my composure, realizing that this wasn't an ordinary interview. Mickey kept pushing me, testing to see if I had the determination to persevere.

"Every experience has its lessons. As a kid, I stood out in any job that I've ever had. After high school, it became important for me to start something new. I'm here because I want to achieve more, and I'm ready to work hard for it," I replied, my voice steadier than I felt.

Micky continued to probe, each question a deeper inquiry into my ambitions and the decisions that led me here. Despite the discomfort, I hoped it was his way of testing my resolve, a necessary ordeal to see if I was truly prepared to step out of my comfort zone and strive for more.

The interview lasted about an hour and felt more like an interrogation, or an inquisition. It wasn't anything like the encouraging vote of confidence, or reassurance I had initially felt from Micky's invitation. Yet, it forced me to confront my ambitions and insecurities head-on, a difficult encounter that, in retrospect, perhaps gave me exactly what I needed. As I drove back to my mom's trailer, I felt as if I had bombed the interview.

But I didn't know what I could have done differently. I was who I was. Our backgrounds, and the choices we made, always spoke louder than our words.

Micky and his wife didn't come into the restaurant the next week, but the following week, I felt surprised when his secretary called to invite me in for a second interview. When I got there, Micky said that he had a few follow-up questions. He wanted to know why I didn't try harder in school, and why I hadn't given more thought to my future and attending college.

"I've answered those questions," Micky, I said. "Maybe you should tell me what it is that you didn't get."

"What do you mean," my question took him aback.

"I'm 18 years old," I told him. "High school didn't interest me. Making money interests me. When situations change, a person's got to adapt. As I told you last time I was here, I took a job as a stepping stone. College wouldn't fit me. I wanted to focus my attention on launching opportunities, not collecting credits that would lead to a diploma no one would care about. I'm here because you want me on your team. It's the right decision. You're going to find a hard worker who can both inspire others and connect with your customers, whomever they are. I'll make them feel welcome, just as I made you feel welcome when you visited my restaurant. Isn't that the reason you always requested my section?"

Micky laughed.

"I don't know exactly what Baron's Worldwide Financial Services offers. If you give me a shot, you'll find that I'm the hardest working guy here, dependable, the first to come, last to leave, and quickest independent study that you'll ever meet."

"How much does a busboy make," he asked.

When I said that I earned about $800 a month, he offered to start me at $1,200 a month, but expected 100 percent commitment.

"We've got 50 employees," he said. "You'll be number 51. You'll sort the mail, answer phones, build relationships and then pass along customers to the sales team. We broker commodities, and we've got customers across the country."

I didn't know anything about commodities, but I liked everything I saw. Micky hired hustlers, people who fought for the deals they wanted. The majority of brokers in the firm were young and aggressive, a place where I'd fit in instantly. Young guys with smiles, crushing it. Most in their early to mid 20s, all driving 100-thousand dollar cars, the kind of guys who live on the edge, the kind of guys who liked to gamble. The kinds of guys whose company I enjoyed the most.

Micky had attended college at Long Beach State, but he performed at a higher level than people who had Ivy League degrees. He was smart and ruthless, with a cut-throat business savvy and he'd do anything to succeed. His wife, Ishani, struck me as being the same way. If they brought someone onto their team, they expected the same level of commitment.

Monica sensed the opportunity and she encouraged me. We eventually rented an apartment in Irvine, just down the street from the brokerage firm. We only had one car. Since she might need the car for appointments, or anything else, we had to live close enough so that I could walk from the apartment complex to the office. At 4:45 am each morning, I'd leave the apartment and walk about 600 yards, wearing a suit and tie. I'd make sure that I was always the first person in the office. Dark and cold when I got there, I'd start to liven it up, making myself indispensable.

Most of the guys who worked there had university degrees. But Micky was a maverick, and he'd hire anyone if he thought he could mold him into an asset for the company, an earner. To make real money, a person had to pass the Series 3.

To sell securities in the United States, a person must pass the Series 3 license, also known as the National Commodities Futures Examination. Getting the license didn't require a university degree, but a person had to pass a rigorous exam, covering various financial topics that didn't have any true relationship to selling. If a person wanted to earn a passing grade on the exam, he had to learn about investment risk, taxation, and all different types of securities. I've heard it described as one of the hardest professional exams in the nation.

I've never been a great test taker. In high school, I found ways to get around such burdens, like persuading girls to do my homework or assist with my exams. Micky didn't offer the position with expectations that I'd ever become a licensed commodities broker. As the founder of a growing company, he needed a trusted assistant. I did anything he asked, including sorting mail, sending letters to prospective customers who inquired about our services, or taking calls and warming prospects up before passing them along to the sales team.

That role proved to be an exceptional training ground. By listening to people on the phone, I understood more about what spawned their interest in our firm. As it turned out, we had an outstanding lead-generation service. Ken Roberts authored a popular course that he called *TWMPMM One: The World's Most Powerful Money Manual.* He wrote the course specifically for investors,farmers and other people who wanted to learn about commodities, and how to hedge or make money by trading commodities. The course recommended only three firms, including ours.

I still remember the cover of that book. It had a glossy picture of yachts, a Ferrari, a mansion, which attracted the kind of people we wanted as clients. They wanted to get rich quickly, and they purchased the book that Roberts wrote in order to learn how. It would teach them everything they needed to know, including how to connect with a brokerage firm. Since the book endorsed Baron's Worldwide Financial Services, we had a steady flow of calls every day.

Reading Ken Roberts' book to learn about trading commodities was a little like reading a how-to guide to get rich by speculating in the commodities market. Just because a person learned how to pick a broker and place a trade didn't mean that a person understood the value proposition, or the underlying reason behind a trade, using either technical analysis or fundamental analysis.

Commodities are different from stocks and bonds. Typically, we're talking about commodities when we're discussing raw materials or products like energy, metals, and agricultural goods. In the commodities markets, we create exchanges to trade them, without ever taking delivery. We're providing a service to the businesses that rely upon the commodities, and opportunities for speculators to make money from the trades. Since prices fluctuate, a commodities broker like ours could earn fees from matching buyers and sellers. We're an exchange, a marketplace so that a buyer and a seller never have to meet. As a service, we provide certainty that prices will remain at a fixed point, regardless of external factors, for a specific period of time.

For example, think of a farmer who grows oranges. The price of oranges can go up and down due to many factors like weather conditions, demand for oranges, or anything else. The farmer wouldn't want to invest time and energy to grow a crop of oranges, but find out later that the price for oranges was too low to justify the expense. To minimize the risk, he could enter a contract to sell his oranges at a specific time, for a fixed price, to a juice manufacturer. This way, the farmer would know at the start how much he would get for his oranges, and the juice manufacturer would know how much to pay for oranges. This contract would be a simple form of a commodity trade.

A commodities brokerage, like Baron's Worldwide Financial Services, facilitated the trading of commodities. Opportunities opened for speculators who wanted to buy low and sell high, leveraging market trends and economic indicators to earn profits. Since these types of trades involved both an asset, and time, they were very risky for the speculator—but insanely lucrative for the commodity broker.

Any person who fancied himself ready to speculate with commodities after reading *TWMPMM One: The World's Most Powerful Money Manual* would be a welcome customer at our firm. Our brokers specialized in walking those people through their trades, and they earned lucrative commissions when a customer chose to make a trade. The firm would charge a $95 transaction fee for a "round turn," buying and selling the asset. With that system, many brokers earned commissions north of $100,000 per month.

By partnering with Ken Roberts, Micky built a steady flow of prospective customers. Those people paid for Ken's course, and they attended his seminars or coaching programs to learn how they could make money with commodities. Since Ken's literature promoted our firm, those customers trusted us. They looked forward to opening accounts and funding them with balances from $5,000 to more than $1 million. Once they called us, they wanted to start placing orders, at $95 a transaction. Typically, a customer would place dozens of orders at a time, generating thousands of dollars in commissions in calls that might last 5 to 10 minutes. Within hours, or minutes, those same customers would call back. They'd want to exit the trades, paying the fees once again. Then they'd typically repeat the cycle.

Although I appreciated Micky for trusting in me and giving me the job as his assistant, the more I learned about his business, the more I realized the importance of becoming a broker. I needed to learn everything. As the first-point of contact, I fielded calls from customers and then relayed them to a broker on the sales team. When I made the call transfer, however, I could remain on mute to eavesdrop from the conversation. That live training taught me everything I needed to know about the business. If I ever wanted to earn commissions, however, I'd have to pass the Series 3 exam.

I gathered every pamphlet and manual I could find around the office that would help me learn more about the Series 3 exam. Since brokers had to provide educational and compliance materials, there was a lot I could choose from. I found mock exams that I could use to practice.

Each night, when I walked home, I'd carry those books with me. While Monica watched television, I'd read to learn about investment risk, taxation, equity and debt instruments, packaged securities, options, hedging strategies, and every type of commodities product, such as stocks, municipal bonds, and variable contracts. By creating index cards, I could learn the terms. Monica would quiz me with questions from the mock exam.

I didn't tell Micky that I'd been studying. But about six months after I began working with him, I handed him a stack of index cards. The front side of the card asked a question, on the back, I wrote the corresponding answer.

"What are these?" He looked surprised.

"Pick a card," I said. "Ask me anything."

"If a customer owns 20 contracts for soybean futures, how can he protect his investment?"

"He can buy put options on the exchange," I responded.

Micky went through a few of the cards. As I continued to answer correctly, he asked how I learned. To pass the exam, I told him, a person only had to respond correctly to 70 percent of the questions. I'd been studying every night, on weekends, and during any time I had at work. I consistently scored more than 85 percent. "I'm ready to pass the exam," I told him, but I need a brokerage firm to sponsor me."

"Who's going to be my assistant if you get your license to be a broker?"

I pledged to do everything possible to train the next candidate, but assured him that I'd earn much more money for the firm if I could broker transactions. "Sponsor me to take this exam," I said, "and I'll prove to be the hardest worker, and the highest earner on your floor within one year. I'll build my own book of business and crush through any records that Kevin, or any of your top earners have set."

I was 19 years old.

Before asking Micky to sponsor me for the exam, I'd taken the preparation time more seriously than anything that I'd ever done before. That may have been the only stretch of time since I was 12 that I didn't place a single bet, or play a single game of cards. Instead, I gambled on myself, convinced that if I could pass that exam, I'd eventually 10x my earnings, going from $1200 a month to more than $20,000 a month. From there, I intended to go higher.

Micky stepped up, and I didn't disappoint. I passed the exam and he inducted me into the firm, advancing me from clerical worker to becoming a first assistant for Keith Beever, his top broker. Since I didn't have my own book of business, I'd have to start as a broker's assistant. I'd been answering the phone for several months, so I had an advantage over other new assistant brokers who were starting out at Baron's Worldwide, as I'd built a rapport with many of Keith's customers. It didn't take long for them to bypass him and ask to speak with me directly.

Like Micky, Keith was only about ten years older than me. He had a great work ethic and was tenacious on the phone, always in pursuit of the daily goals that he had set. Micky had taught me lessons on the value of setting daily goals. I learned to write goals on a sheet of paper, and put a picture beside the goal. Then I needed to craft a plan that would show how I would get there. No one else had to see the goals, but showing others the result would provide the self-motivation to work harder.

With a 100 percent commitment to become more successful financially, I followed Micky's guidance. On my desk, I put a photograph of the house I intended to buy. To earn resources that would allow me to purchase the house, I planned to pass the Series 3 exam and I did it. I set priorities, and made a commitment. Until I got my license, I pledged that I wouldn't do anything that wasn't moving me closer toward preparing for the exam. Passing the exam was incidental to the goal, not the goal itself.

I set a goal of earning enough money to buy the house for Monica and me to live in. I set priorities. For that reason, I rarely wagered on sports, on horses, or on cards. I built study guides, anything to move me closer. By writing out index cards, I developed my vocabulary. With a better understanding of the language, I developed confidence that I could pass the exam. Once I passed the Series 3, the National Futures Association issued my license.

I understood that a license itself wouldn't translate into an income. Many people foolishly got degrees and professional licenses for the sake of the certificate. But the diploma or license wouldn't make anyone a star. Too many people celebrate the process. The end game is not to get the license, but to succeed.

Micky didn't have an academic pedigree from Harvard, Yale, or Princeton. But he got the result he wanted, with a $10 million house, and a business that generated tens of millions each year in revenue. With my Series 3 license in hand, I had gone through the process. The time had come to start working toward the results I wanted.

As I look back on my life, it was Micky who gave me my start. After the feds raided my house, he was one of the first people I called. We drove to the Ritz Carlton for breakfast, and I told him all about the raid. He's always been a good friend, pledging to be there for me if I needed anything at all. We went over the past and he laughed while asking if I remembered that old beater car I used to drive when we met, the one with the holes in the floorboard.

"Do you remember the picture of that house you used to keep on your desk," he asked.

I do. It was the house that I grew up in as a child. Once I started working at Baron's, I'd set a goal of buying that house, for sentimental reasons. When I purchased the house, it brought tears to my mom's eyes.

"The house you own now is twice as big as that one," he reminded me. "You can make money, and you can lose money. Always remember that the little steps you take today will lead to the success you enjoy tomorrow."

Micky pulled out his phone to show me pictures of his first car, his first house. He liked to memorialize the progress, to remind himself of what it takes to be successful. "We've always got to connect the dots, to remember what it took to succeed. We've got to do hard things, and we have to do them persistently. Then, we've got to write the next chapter of our life, over and over again."

"Use this time to start writing," Micky challenged me. "Start writing the next chapter now, and when you get through this phase, you'll be more successful than ever."

CHAPTER 4

Dead On Paper, Alive In Purpose

A few months before authorities raided my house, Rebecca, an estate-planning attorney that I hired a while back, made an unexpected call to my wife. Nicole didn't know how to interpret her cautiously probing tone.

"Are you doing okay?"

"I'm doing fine." They didn't interact socially, so Nicole didn't grasp the purpose of Rebecca's call.

"I'm sorry to hear about your loss."

Nicole paused, wondering what the attorney was talking about. After the awkward silence, Rebecca said that she'd heard about my passing.

"What are you talking about?"

"Didn't Matt die?" Rebecca sounded surprised.

"Matt's fine," Nicole said, "He's in the other room. What gave you the idea that he died?"

"He's not dead?"

"No, he's not." She laughed. "He's standing less than 10 feet away from me playing with Kingston, our son. Matt's very much alive."

After expressing relief, Rebecca told Nicole that Social Security had sent her a letter—clearly erroneously—inquiring about my death benefits. Apparently, someone had either mistakenly typed a Social Security number on a form, or attempted to collect death benefits by fraudulently using my identity.

Neither Nicole nor I gave any more thought to Rebecca's call until a few days after the raid, when I started making changes to my auto collection. I didn't want to switch up my vehicles, but since I didn't know which direction the government would take my case, I thought it prudent to downsize, especially after my meeting with my friend Micky. His advice about writing the next chapter of my life was spot on, and I intended to begin by getting rid of some of the dead weight.

Micky had been a car collector for many years. After I started earning higher commissions as a broker with him, I'd picked up his habit of collecting exotic automobiles. Like many young men who began to earn more money, I went through them all. Rolls Royce, Bentleys, Lamborghinis, Ferraris, Aston Martins. For several years, my car of choice had been the Bentley GT Continental Super Sport. I've owned three of them. They're heavy, built like tanks, but super fast and fun to drive.

Earlier in 2023, the Rolls Royce SUV started to gain popularity. I'd owned several Rolls Royce's in the past, but I really liked the newest model.

Every time I saw a Cullinan driving around town, I became more convinced that I should add one to my collection. It was a beast, one that made an absolute and immediate statement. One day, after a series of hands went my way at the Pechanga Casino, in Temecula, California my winnings started to approach $300,000. Typically, I'd keep playing, trying to multiply those gains. Since I'd only been there a few hours, I cashed out, and brought my winnings to a dealership in Orange County. They were happy to take my cash, and I drove away with a floor model of the Rolls SUV, dropping more than $450,000 for the privilege.

But after meeting with Micky to discuss the raid and how I'd navigate next steps, I changed perspectives. The optics of a Rolls Royce and a Bentley in my driveway would not do any favors for my two attorneys, Chris Glew and Diane Bass. They'd try to present me as a candidate for leniency with how authorities charged me. If I had a sentencing date in my future, they'd want to argue for the lowest possible sanction, and I didn't want my cars to give my judge the wrong impression.

A prosecutor could weave a tale about my ownership of a Bentley and a Rolls to portray me as the personification of reckless spending. A federal judge might not look too favorably upon such a description. I remember a funny line from the comic Steve Martin:

> *"I love money. I love everything about it. I bought some good stuff. Got me a $300 pair of socks. Got a fur sink. An electric dog polisher. A gasoline powered turtleneck sweater.*
>
> *And of course, I bought some dumb stuff, too."*

That line from Steve Martin made me laugh, but I didn't want a federal judge seeing me in that way, as a heavy spender.

Expensive vehicles could leave the judge with the wrong impression. I'd want him to think about the totality of my life, how I built myself up from nothing, how I lived as a good father and a good friend, always willing to help others out. If things worked out differently after the investigation, I could purchase any car I wanted.

By liquidating the two vehicles, I raised cash, which I welcomed. Everyone has heard the phrase, "Don't make a federal case out of it." While in the midst of it all, I got to know the true meaning of such phrases.

A federal case was serious, threatening my liberty. To fight, I needed as much liquidity as possible. Still, I would also need a vehicle to get around. Since I didn't have any doubt that I could stay current with payments toward an automobile loan, I set my sights on a Range Rover, as I was partial to British vehicles. No one would categorize the luxury SUV as the type of beater that my friend Micky remembered, but it certainly wasn't as ostentatious as a Rolls Royce.

Although the dealership allowed me to drive off the lot with the Range Rover, the finance manager asked a lot of questions about my identity when I filled out the loan paperwork. Apparently, that problem with the Social Security number lingered. To resolve the matter, I tried working through the bureaucracy, confirming that I hadn't died. I wasted an entire day in a dingy government office to speak with a case manager and show multiple forms of identification. Apparently, he couldn't correct the error on his own. Somehow, my name floated in a government database as a person of interest, and I didn't know how long it would take to get fixed. It led to a problem in mid February, 2024, when a group of security guards took me into custody at the Commerce Club Casino.

For a while, I thought those guards would hand me over to the LA County Sheriff. It wouldn't have been the first time that casino guards tried to put me in jail.

Casinos and gambling were a part of my life. The government may have launched an investigation into my bookmaking operations, but I intended to continue with my livelihood. By gambling 100s of millions over the years, I developed both skills and confidence as a gambler. Truthfully, I enjoyed the feel of hand-to-hand combat that came from betting, putting my wits against the dealer in any casino. Anytime I received an invitation to spend time in a casino, I was in.

In mid-February, that opportunity opened.

While standing on the sidelines as a spectator at my daughter's volleyball game, I got an unexpected call from my friend, Manny. We frequently worked out together and gambled together. He told me that some buddies of his were heading out to the Commerce Club in Los Angeles to check out the local MMA flights; a friend of his had a match in the lineup. I didn't have any cash on me, and didn't want to drive all the way back home for money, so I asked Manny to bring an extra $10,000. I'd repay him at the end of the night—or if I lost, I'd pay him later. We looked forward to enjoying the fights.

I've always been a huge fan of mixed-martial arts. I even got involved myself, ironically, through my ex-wife Monica's husband. We divorced in 2003, but as the mother of my three daughters, Lauren, Haley, and Brooke, Monica would always have a special place in my heart. She and Matt had been married for several years, and we've developed a great friendship.

During the Pandemic, Matt told me that he'd begun practicing jiu-jitsu with an amazing trainer,

Francisco, and he recommended that I try the sport.

Although I'd been physical my entire life, the only training I ever received came from my wrestling coaches in high school. During the craziness of the Pandemic, I wanted to challenge myself. Once I went to the gym, I immediately hit it off with the instructor, Francisco "Chico" Lima.

Besides being an amazing human being, Francisco had charisma and distinguished himself as a Brazilian jiu-jitsu champion. The more I trained with him, the more I liked him and wanted to help him out. He immigrated to the United States from Brazil without many resources. Seeing that his employers at Gracie Barra didn't really appreciate him, I spotted an opportunity. I invited Francisco to partner with me in opening a gym. When he said that he didn't have any savings to put toward opening a gym, I relieved him of that burden. He could put in the expertise, and I'd invest the capital. Since Monica's husband Matt introduced us, I invited him into the partnership as well.

We named our new venture "Rysk Brazilian Jiu-Jitsu," and opened our doors in January, 2022. Francisco did an amazing job of building the business. As the lead trainer and manager, he made every customer feel welcome. Matt handled the administrative affairs. My limited role was to provide the capital, to train regularly, and to invite friends to join.

My sports-betting buddy, Manny, became a regular. Opening that gym was one of the best life-style investments I could make. It provided an income for two people I cared about, and in time, it could potentially lead to a return on capital for me—or it might not. Either way, we built great camaraderie while working out there, and it sometimes carried over to fun nights like I expected at the Commerce Club. When Manny told me that one of his friends would be fighting, I wanted to offer support, and hopefully win some money at the tables too.

Within minutes of arriving in the club, the cashier gave me $10,000 in chips. I played baccarat, seven-to-eight-hundred dollars a hand. With luck on my side and pressing when the tide was my way, the $10k bankroll quickly grew to more than $35,000. My friends wanted to leave the casino for the arena, as it was getting close to the start of the first fight. The casino didn't allow single bets of more than twenty grand, otherwise I would have put all my chips on the table for the final hand. Hoping to cash out for more than $50k, I put down the maximum bet. Unfortunately, the bet didn't go my way, so I dropped $20k. Still, I cashed out for $15,000, enough to repay Manny the $10k he spotted me, and put five grand in my pocket.

Adhering to Casino rules, I completed a currency-transaction report, required for any transaction of $10,000 or more. After clearing out those matters, my friends and I walked to the arena and took our ring-side seats. I loved the adrenaline rush from thousands of cheering fight fans. By being up front, we were close enough to feel the smack of every blow.

After the second fight, I felt a tap on my shoulder. When I turned, I saw several security guards, some standing behind me, others on each end of the aisle. A total of seven.

"Are you Matt Bowyer?" The head guard eyed me, asking his rhetorical question.

"What's this about?" I looked at him, wondering what was going on.

"We need you to come with us." The security guards were polite, but I could see that they weren't asking. Something was wrong, but I had to stay cool. Gambling had conditioned me to keep a stone-cold face, absent of all emotion.

Since we were between fights, I felt kind of self-conscious, as if the thousands of fans were all staring at me with suspicion that I'd done something wrong. Those ringside seats were not the place for me to converse with the guards, so I stood to weave my way out. The guards flanked my side, and my mind wandered to the darkest places, to all that could be going wrong.

What would a group of casino guards want with me?

Four months had passed since the raid. As far as I knew, my attorneys were working through matters with the investigators, but authorities hadn't charged me with a crime. While following the guards into their security area, I anticipated that my legal status must've changed, with the worst thoughts going through my mind.

When we walked into their little detention center in one of the sealed off places of the casino, they asked me to sit down. They didn't respond to my questions about what was going on, telling me that the sheriff would let me know once he got there. I didn't think they had authority to detain me, and as security guards, they couldn't make an arrest. Yet rather than challenge them, I waited cooperatively, observing the dingy office and wondering who would want to work in such a place.

Not wanting to worry Nicole, I didn't call or text her. I simply sat there, curious as to what would happen next. Ten minutes passed, then 20. No one came by to see me. After 30 minutes, I politely told them that I was leaving.

Before I could get out the door, a supervisor intervened. He put an end to my anxiety, telling me that he'd received a report that I'd stolen an identity. The cash-out report I filed triggered something in the casino's computer. "Matt Bowyer is dead," he told me. "We reported the matter to law enforcement, and the sheriff is on his way."

I started to laugh, relieved to know the reason behind the confusion.

"What's so funny," the guard asked.

I explained what had been going on with my Social Security card, and the efforts I'd made to resolve the matter.

Cynical at first, the guard began quizzing me with his series of questions that only I would know how to answer. "What's your date of birth, your grandmother's name, your previous addresses, your mother's maiden name?" Since I responded quickly and accurately, he softened up, realizing that someone had made a mistake.

I'd never live as a scumbag who didn't own his identity. I didn't always make the right decisions, but I always lived with honor, owning the decisions I made.

When I met with Micky for breakfast to discuss the challenges ahead, and he suggested that I start writing the next chapter of my life, I reflected on lessons that he taught me when I first started out. Ever since he opened the doors for me to begin building a career in commodities, I prided myself on being authentic.

Micky was the kind of guy who had an uncanny ability to see into the future, and to create opportunities out of nothing. He saw something in me while I cleared tables in a restaurant. Based on what he saw, he offered me a job, changing my life. Our interactions led to my becoming a licensed commodities trader, and earnings of more than $300,000 per year before I celebrated my 22nd birthday. With that income, I had resources to purchase the house that my mother had lost during a recession. I looked forward to building new memories with Monica, raising our infant daughter Lauren in the same home where I spent my childhood.

Micky's trust in me grew. Despite being one of the youngest guys on his trading floor, my work ethic led to respect from the other brokers and our customers. Sensing me as a valuable asset to his company, he used me as a tool to grow his vision and to respond to changing markets. When he told me to write the next chapter of my life, I understood that he wasn't telling me to do anything that he hadn't done. He was telling me to face the storm head first, with my dignity intact, using the challenge as an opportunity to pivot to something new.

I'd begun working with him in the mid-1990s. When we met, Micky was in his late 20s and he'd already earned millions of dollars. Yet I never got the sense that money drove Micky's decisions. He could easily pivot, just as he was advising me to do after the raid.

Strength came from knowing how to read the hands we were given. Regardless of what happened after the raid, he urged me to push forward. Although we couldn't change the past, we could always put ourselves in a position to seize the next opportunity.

It wasn't long after I began working with Micky that I saw him laying the groundwork for a pivot in his business. When markets changed, he laid out an intricate plan to write his next chapter.

Micky had invested extensively to build a trading firm that would allow young alpha-males to take down hundreds of thousands in commissions each year. The successful business brought many times that amount in profits.

Advancement of the internet, however, threatened to undermine everything Micky built. For every commodities transaction that his company brokered, his company clocked a $95 commission. With the internet, startups were coming on the scene, threatening to revolutionize the way that people could trade financial products. They charged as little as twenty dollars per trade, and offered more services.

Micky didn't whine about the change, and he didn't intend to fight the trend. Instead, he laid out an intricate plan, keeping it to himself, but executing the plan flawlessly.

As his first step, he launched Newhall Discount Brokerage, because he didn't want to disrupt sales at Baron's Worldwide Financial Services, the first company he'd built and where I was employed.

Micky invited me to leave Baron's and to lead the new company, but he didn't tell me his full plan. Despite being only 22, I accepted his offer of setting up the firm. In the new role, I'd have responsibility for hiring, training, and growing Newhall, and in turn, I'd get an override on any commissions earned from the 40 plus brokers I would bring onboard.

Micky's decision to task me with managing his new firm, said a lot about him. He understood that hiring a "professional manager" wouldn't get the job done. He knew that people who worked in professional management might be able to put policies together and ensure compliance. To get a startup off the ground and running, Micky knew that he needed sales. With the rapidly spreading internet, he had to pivot quickly and adapt to a changing world. If he didn't grow larger and faster, other discount brokerage houses would obliterate the company he built.

I hired my older brother Shawn to work as my assistant. He'd been earning several thousand each week as a bookie in Huntington Beach while attending community college, but someone had set him up for a rugged home invasion. A ruthless biker gang broke into Shawn's house, nearly beating him to death, even holding a gun to his head and threatening to kill him if he didn't hand them his cash.

To give him a new start, I invited Shawn to move in with Monica and me. While we set up Newhall, he took the same path as I did, studying to pass his Series 3 so that he could become a broker and a more intricate player in our growing organization.

Just as Micky did, I hired people who were hungry to grow. Within months, we had 25 brokers working with us at the new firm. Shawn and I were always there before 5:00 am, the first in the office and frequently the last guys to leave. We led by example.

While my brother and I worked to build Newhall, Micky was out doing more deals as part of his grand plan. We'd begun Newhall in response to the internet, and in my view, we were doing well as a small, nimble, boutique trading house. By being quick to hire or fire people, and being relentless with our training, my brother and I easily exceeded expectations. We added thousands of new accounts to our trading firm, even though Micky rarely needed to come around.

But Micky's vision extended beyond merely adapting to the changing landscape of the internet. He wanted a complete pivot, to exit the industry entirely, in the most lucrative way possible, so that he could write the next chapter in his story.

To launch his audacious plan, he used me as a tool. While I worked hard to build Newhall, he'd gone out into the marketplace to negotiate the acquisition of a much larger firm, Lind-Waldock of Chicago. I didn't even know about the acquisition until he'd already finalized the deal. He simply told me that he'd bought another business, and he asked me to move to Chicago so that I could run it.

I was 25 years old when I visited Lind-Waldock, which occupied several floors of a towering skyscraper in the heart of Chicago. Lind-Waldock was a massive brokerage house employing more than 600 people, with 150 dedicated brokers. For decades, the trading floor buzzed with transactions of every size. But beneath its impressive façade, Lind-Waldock had become a sleeping giant, bloated with complacent brokers who felt entitled. They were resistant to the winds of change and disruption that the internet would bring to the trading world.

As a 25-year-old maverick, I had earned Micky's trust. He tasked me with the formidable challenge of revitalizing the brokers of Lind-Waldock. I didn't want to leave what I'd built at Newhall, or move to Chicago. Although I could count on my brother to keep Newhall growing, the idea of being apart from my daughter and home life didn't appeal to me. I enjoyed being a young father and appreciated the life Monica and I had built together. We were only a few years out of high school, and Monica and I had a good groove.

At that stage, it didn't really matter what I wanted. Micky had given me my start, and if he wanted me in Chicago to carry out his vision, I didn't see myself as being in a position to hesitate.

Barry Lind, the firm's founder and a legend in the trading industry welcomed me for a preliminary meeting. In his late 70s, Mr. Lind made it clear that he didn't feel any threat from other discount brokers or the internet, which he described as a fad. People would always appreciate the respectable firm he'd built, and he appreciated that Micky understood the value of its reputation. After describing the firm's backstory, Mr. Lind retired with a clear mandate, telling me, "Don't fuck it up kid."

In taking over the firm, Micky held a company-wide meeting to introduce me. He said that he didn't intend to fire anyone, but that he was putting me in charge with a mandate to change the culture. While Micky spoke, I sized everyone up and understood what I was up against.

On first impression, I guessed that I was the youngest person in the room. Most of the brokers looked to be in their 30s, 40s, or 50s, but I also saw several dinosaurs in their 70s. None of them wanted to hear Micky describing me as his best broker, and they didn't show much enthusiasm when he asked them to give me their respect.

Respect had to be earned, and the best way of getting it would be to live by a simple philosophy:

never ask anyone to do anything that I wasn't doing myself. Knowing the seasoned brokers would underestimate me, mistaking my youth for inexperience, I let them know I didn't come in to talk. I knew they didn't have any interest in how I'd built a robust sales team at our office in Orange County. Instead, I planned to show them.

The brokers at Lind-Waldock had grown too comfortable in their ways. Rather than hunting for new business, they relied upon the brand name of Lind-Waldock. They weren't accustomed to the grind of cold calling, and they certainly didn't show any concern for the hard work or threat that lay ahead. Although Micky was nimble, capable of seeing how a rapidly evolving technology would disrupt everything in the financial services sector, most people who worked in financial services had grown fat, lazy, and complacent, expecting that everything would remain the same.

"We're going to meet on Saturday," I told the team. "Before then, I'd like you to go through your book of business. Put a list together of the worst leads you've got. If you think the lead is dead, that's the one I want to see on the list. I'm going to show you how to turn those dead leads into cash."

I instructed the head of Lind-Waldock's IT department to hook up my phone to a company wide speaker system. I wanted those brokers to hear every word I said, and to watch how hard I worked.

When I came into the office for the live training session, I had a stack of numbers on my desk. With each call, I'd demonstrate how to build rapport, how to weave conversations from the mundane to the meaningful, and ultimately, how to convince hesitant leads to place their trust—and their money—with Lind-Waldock.

It was a masterclass in salesmanship and perseverance.

I asked for the worst leads, and that's what they brought me. Without complaining, I dialed dead-end numbers, one after the other. People hung up on me. People cussed me out and told me not to bother them. After each call, I'd follow up with a note, explaining the significance of my message.

"If you dial one number, you might not get through. If you dial ten numbers, you'll have a ten times better chance of not getting through. But dial 100 numbers, you'll get someone willing to listen on the other end of the line. If you do that well, you bring money in the door."

"Bob, how are you doing," I'd say if I reached someone. Its been a little while since we last spoke, (of course we'd never spoken before) "It's Matt Bowyer, from Lind-Waldock. How are things going over in Green Bay, Wisconsin?"

Everything matters during a sales call, including the inflection and enthusiasm of the voice. If we project confidence, the guy pauses, wonders when we spoke before. Generally speaking, he wouldn't want to be rude, saying he didn't remember me. As he hesitated, trying to make the connection of when we last spoke, I'd jump back in.

"Is it cold there?"

Once we got into the call, I'd ask whether he was keeping up with all that was going on with the soybean market.

"The newest agricultural report is coming out next week," I'd say. "You don't want to miss this wave. Take a look at the price predictions. If you see 10 percent of what I'm seeing, you'll understand why we're talking today. You want to get ahead in this trade, Bob, and I can lock you into ten contracts right now that will position you in ways to thank me later. But you're going to owe me a drink later, when I come through Green Bay."

The entire sales team heard me work those dead leads all day. Call after call, only breaking to use the head, without a complaint. Despite hundreds of hangups, I kept dialing. By the end of the day, six people had opened new accounts and placed orders with us, bringing $180,000 in new accounts from three leads that our team had dismissed as being dead.

By putting myself up to their scrutiny, encouraging the entire sales team to listen to every call I made, and to judge me, I changed their perceptions. Although bringing money into the firm felt good, the real success was in showing the sales team what excellence looked like. I'd do anything necessary to bring more money through the door, and if they wanted to keep their careers going, they should show the same level of commitment. I earned respect that way, and through that process, during the first quarter I spent in Chicago, we more than doubled our year-over-year revenue comparisons at Lind-Waldock.

As I labored to build Micky's business in Chicago, he continued on a surreptitious plan that wouldn't become clear to me for several more months. In many ways, I felt as if I were on my own, running a group of alpha males, all of whom needed to keep that adrenaline rush going, even after markets closed. With more disposable income, my gambling increased to amounts that brought more excitement, feeding my needs for a constant rush.

At the offices in Orange County, the other traders got to know me as a guy who would take any bet. At the start of the day, I'd bet on anything— whether the market would go up or down on the day, how many leads would come into our funnel, or which broker would close more sales. Brokering commodity transactions brought me a higher income than I deserved, but the excitement came from the gambling. After hours, I'd continued to feed the rush by going to the horse races, or betting sports. In Chicago, I built that same level of camaraderie, giving everyone the club feel, and carrying on the high-intensity environment that characterized Micky's businesses.

I loved the relationships that I built, but I couldn't wait to get back to my regular routine in Orange County. After six months of commuting to Chicago, I got a reprieve. Micky agreed that Lind-Waldock had turned the tide and had become self-sufficient. Each week, we brought in more accounts and generated higher commissions. With the mission accomplished, we promoted a guy from within to take my place, and by the turn of the century, things started going back to normal for me—or as normal as could be for the type of degenerate gambler I was starting to become.

CHAPTER 5

'The Fight You Don't Train For'

At the time, I felt as if those six months I spent commuting from Orange County to Chicago burned me out. With the weight of potential criminal charges hanging over my head now, and being within striking distance of my 50th birthday, I have a different perspective on the life I lived as a 25-year old kid. All things considered, I had it pretty good ever since I passed the Series 3 exam and began earning commissions from commodities.

Micky's companies paid me generously, putting an end to any financial anxieties. My W-2 wages put me in the top 1% of earners. Every month, I'd get paychecks with gross earnings that hovered between 40 and 50 thousand dollars. Even with deductions of more than 50 percent for federal and California state taxes, I brought home an average of more than $1,000 for every day I worked. With those earnings, I could provide a lavish lifestyle for Monica and our daughter Lauren.

Besides my day job, earnings from my side hustle of booking bets picked up after I joined Micky's sales team. Sometimes my weekly take from those bets exceeded my paychecks—and they came in cash, without the burden of taxes or other withholdings.

I'd been booking bets since high school, but until I started earning real money, those bets didn't amount to much, perhaps a range of 20 to 500 dollars each. As a commodities broker, I worked around single guys in their 20s and 30s, each earning more than 500-thousand per year. They blew their money every week on women, alcohol, nightlife, sports cars, clothes, watches, and gambling. They had enormous sums to wager. And I took all bets.

Those guys loved the action as much as I did. Wherever I worked, I developed a reputation as being the guy who would bet on anything. Whether it was college or pros, football, basketball, baseball, or any sport, the guys I knew placed their bets with me. They counted on me to pay on time, without hesitation. If I wasn't available, my brother Shawn would fill in as my runner. Players understood that I settled up every Monday, and they appreciated my commitment to them.

Typically, before the internet bookies would rent a small office in a rundown area. They'd hire a girl to take calls and write down bets. She didn't know anything about sports or the line, and she'd make mistakes. Sometimes she wouldn't be there to take the call. Customers preferred working with me because action had become my life. My customers knew and understood that I was into the games as much as them, and I'd always take their calls.

Although I took my full time job with Micky seriously, booking bets became a second vocation, requiring at least as much concentration. It paid excellent money that fed my gambling, and I enjoyed bookmaking way more than the commodities business. With sports betting, people enjoyed what they were doing. They understood the action. By selling commodities, on the other hand, I felt more cynical, wondering what value we truly provided. Although we made money for ourselves and for the firm, most of the people who invested didn't know what they were doing and over time, they lost. The business started to rub me the wrong way. Especially after I returned from Chicago. I earned good money, but I started to prefer my bookmaking business to my regular job. Loyalty to Micky kept me on the job, even after my bookmaking business brought in enough money to support me.

Guys I met at the gym, the horse track, and friends I'd made while working in Chicago booked bets with me. By the time I finished my stint of working at Lind-Waldock, I had a steady stream of clients that routinely wagered between five and ten thousand dollars per bet, alternating with winning and losing weeks. Over the course of a season, I'd always come out ahead by several hundred thousands dollars.

For some reason, I thrived on the energy of an action-filled life. My job as a commodities trader required that I begin each day around 4:30 am, but I didn't require much rest after a day at the office. Once the markets closed, I'd head to the gym to power through a demanding weight-training routine, hitting all the major muscle groups during the week. Every day, I'd concentrate on abdominal exercises. Staying in top physical shape boosted my mental acuity and kept me sharp.

Besides the weights, I'd play on basketball teams to get that high-intensity cardio workout. Softball teams weren't as intense, but I played on various teams around Orange County because I enjoyed the competition and camaraderie.

Team sports also proved an excellent feeder for my growing bookmaking business. Profits from taking action covered my gambling losses. Although I had a good feel for the games I played and how they'd turn out, I got a jolt of energy from gambling itself, regardless of what kind of wager I placed.

Micky encouraged us to have that competitive mindset, as it was good for morale in the office. He cultivated a frat-like loyalty, a family. If a person ever spoke badly about the firm or anyone working in his company, he'd fire them without hesitation. He wanted A-players on his team and he demanded loyalty. He understood the value of hiring hyper competitive people. Our guys were needy, always craving attention. They didn't want to be around people who had that soft-underbelly-mindset, people who wanted second- or third-place trophies and believed that fairness required us to placate the losers. We cut the losers and replaced them with eat-what-you-kill kind of guys. If a person didn't go all in on the job and in life, in every way, Micky would cut them as dead weight, knowing their insecurities would pull down his high-performance team. He was ruthless in that way, and I admired him.

Our like-mindedness is one of the reasons we got along so well.

I still remember the time that Micky accompanied my brother Shawn and me to attend a boxing match at the Bellagio, in Las Vegas. Since that first trip where I'd won $25,000 in a session at the New York, New York Casino, I'd become a steady customer for my casino host, Leslie. She could count on my bringing a bankroll of roughly a hundred grand for each of my get-away gambling excursions in Las Vegas. Over time, I began taking most of those trips without Monica. Although I loved my daughter very much, with money to burn, I started to question whether I'd gotten married too young. Las Vegas became my escape from the responsibilities of home life. Since I provided financially, I felt as if I were doing my duty.

When Micky told me about a boxing match he wanted to see, I called Leslie to make it happen.

She hooked me up with Dave, her counterpart at the Bellagio. When Dave learned that I typically gambled $1,000 to $10,000 per hand for four hours or more per day on my trips, he welcomed me with open arms, offering to cover the costs of our suite and expenses. Over the course of a weekend, I could easily turn $100k into many hands of wagers of several million, and walk away either up or down, but always with a commitment to return. The casinos competed for loyalty from a hardcore, compulsive gambler like me.

We'd all seen the advertisements for the Bellagio using Andrea Bocelli in television commercials, and it did not disappoint. The property's majestic, Italian-inspired architecture and mesmerizing fountains impressed anyone who pulled in. We stepped inside to see a bustling casino floor adorned with elegant decor and vibrant lights. Slot machines chimed with bells and dings. Chatter from thousands of guests filled the air. The palpable energy made us feel alive as we walked toward the check-in desk.

Dave had made the process seamless, directing a concierge to tend to our every need. She assured us of our welcome at the Bellagio, and confirmed that the casino would cover all costs on our stay. Wanting to get some rest and make some calls before the evening, Micky took his room key and headed up to the suite. Shawn and I went straight to the casino floor, eager to explore all corners of Las Vegas' newest property.

The Bellagio offered luxurious amenities such as exquisite pools, spa services, and fine dining options, which didn't interest us at all. Neither were we interested in slot tournaments with prizes for the gambling tourists, or all-you-can eat shrimp buffets. Shawn and I went for the more lucrative games of Baccarat, Blackjack,Craps, and Roulette.

After a 15-minute walk to take in Bellagio's vibrant atmosphere, I knew it would be a great weekend. But it wasn't the blend of opulence, entertainment, and hospitality that made my first experience there so unforgettable. It was a fight— and not the professional boxing match that Micky had wanted to see.

Shawn joined a crowd around a Roulette table. He began picking his numbers and placing his bets. I walked to an adjoining area so I could test my skill at Blackjack. By then, I'd developed skills that, in my mind, evened the edge out a bit in my favor. I took a stool at one table, where only one other guy was playing. We didn't talk. He sat a few stools away from me, but after a few hands, I could see that the cards weren't going any better for him than for me while we played.

I laid down $500 to $5,000 per hand, and he alternated his bets between $100 and $200, suggesting a lack of confidence. Within an hour,

I dropped more than $15,000 in chips. I felt okay, anticipating the cards would come my way soon. The other guy wasn't taking his losses too well. Even though I calculated that he was only down a few thousand dollars, I could see it hurt. He kept grumbling, expressing disgust with himself and cards that the dealer released from the shoe.

After growing tired of picking red or black with the purely chance game of Roulette, my brother walked over to the Blackjack table, to check on me and see how I was doing. He didn't say anything, but I felt his eyes on my play. He took a seat between the other player and me, putting a $100 chip down on the circle of the table, indicating he intended to play.

Unprovoked, the other guy moved my brother's chips out of the player's circle. Without looking at my brother's face, the guy gruffly said that he intended to play two hands.

The second I saw that guy put his hands on my brother's chips, I sensed trouble. My brother had a short wick. Ever since childhood, the slightest offense would set him off. He'd been a great fighter in high school, and I learned a lot from him—but he had a temper, and he could be mean when he got into it.

I saw Shawn cock his neck and eyeball the guy, but he didn't say anything. Instead, Shawn walked to the other side of the guy, and stood at another open spot. Shawn put his chips down on the circle, wanting to test his skill against the Bellagio dealer.

"I'm playing three hands," the guy grumbled, and he swatted my brother's chips out from the circle of play.

"Fuck you, dude. Don't touch my chips." Shawn put his chips back in the player's circle.

The guy stood up, raised his voice, thinking he could intimidate Shawn. He picked the wrong guy, and his warnings to stay away didn't go over well.

Rather than responding with words, Shawn smashed him with a head butt, a direct hit on the guy's nose. Blood shot out on the table, and my brother followed up by hooking him with a powerful body shot that curled the guy over. The guy yelled. He was bigger and he tried to grapple with Shawn. They started fighting but it didn't take long before Shawn had him on the ground and started pounding him with shots to the guy's face.

From an adjacent table, I saw one of his buddies running over to get in on the action. I quickly surmised that he intended to help the guy my brother was smashing on the floor. I moved into action, standing up to drill the guy with a solid punch to the guy's chin. That's all it took, catching him off guard. With one punch, he dropped to the floor, shaking from the unexpected power blow.

Shawn kept punching, and people gathered around, some cheering while others were making calls on their flip phones. The dealer screamed, not knowing how to respond to all the commotion. I pulled Shawn off, letting him know that we had to get out of there quickly. A few minutes had passed, and it was only a matter of time before security would come. Besides, Shawn's ferocious temper blinded him to how badly he was hurting the guy on the floor. Chips had fallen to the floor, and the two guys both bled on the plush carpet. After I got Shawn off him, we started walking quickly to the door, which looked to be about a mile away.

We didn't get more than 40 yards away from the table before security guards practically tackled us from behind. Once the guards had us on the floor, they assured us that we weren't going anywhere. They didn't handcuff us, but insisted we walk alongside them as they escorted us toward the security center of the casino.

Knowing my brother's temper, I asked him to stay quiet so that I could try to de-escalate the predicament we were in. When we got into the corridor that led to the security offices, we saw the two idiots we'd taken down. They were holding their faces, playing the victim.

"Look who's crying now," Shawn mocked them as we walked by. "I'll let them know to call your mommy." I nudged Shawn, asking him to be quiet.

I observed the bubble-lens cameras in the ceiling, computer monitors on the desks. Several security personnel were watching those monitors closely. I noticed that they could see what was going on at each table, but they couldn't hear anything.

"Metro police are on the way," the guard finally said. "You can talk to them when they get here."

While we waited, I wondered how I'd get a message to Micky, who'd gone up to the suite, oblivious to the trouble my brother and I had gotten ourselves into. About 30 minutes passed before the officers arrived, but it felt like eight hours. Finally, a detective sat with us, telling us that he'd already spoken with the other guys and they wanted to press charges against us.

The officer seemed cool, ready to listen.

I told him that we intended to press charges, too. We were guests in the hotel, coming to have a good time. "The other guys attacked us, without any provocation. Check out the tape."

"Why don't you tell me what happened," the officer asked.

"As you'll see if you watch the tape, I'd been playing cards. I hadn't said a word to the guy. Then my brother came by to join me at the Blackjack table. No big deal. He put his money down. Without provocation, the other guy started talking belligerently, insulting my brother, telling him to go fuck himself and that he should go find another table."

"I saw the tape," the officer said. "But I couldn't hear any of the conversation. What did the guy say?"

That was my cue. "Go back and listen to the tape," I said, acting as if I didn't hear him say that there wasn't any voice recording. "The guy told my brother that he was going to fuck him up," which wasn't true, but I continued spinning the tale. "He said that he didn't want anyone playing in what he called his lucky spot. You'll see that the guy pushed my brother's chips out of the circle. My brother didn't respond. He calmly walked to the other side and put his chips down at another spot. The guy grew livid, saying he was going to fuck my brother up, standing over him, talking about how my brother didn't know who he was connected to. My brother just defended himself against the incoming attack and verbal assault."

"What about the other guy?"

"The other guy yelled from another table that he was coming over to help. I stood up to defend my brother. We didn't come here looking for trouble, officer. But we weren't going to let two bullies gang up on us for no reason." The officer asked if we were guests at the hotel and I replied yes of course you can all my casino host.

The officer asked us to stay put. He said that he wanted to go review the tapes again.

After about another 30 minutes, the officer came back, saying that he'd spoken with the other two guys. They were from Utah, and they were not guests in the Bellagio. They had to catch a flight back home. If they went ahead and pressed charges, the officer told them, they would not only miss their flight, but they'd have to return to Las Vegas in a couple weeks to attend the preliminary court proceedings. If we agreed not to press charges, the officer said, the other guys agreed to go their own way, and they would withdraw their request to press charges. Everyone could leave and enjoy the rest of the weekend."

"Fuck those guys," my brother said. "They attacked me."

"We can let this go," I told the officer. "We'd like to get back to gambling and enjoying our weekend at the Bellagio."

I think the officer understood. He didn't want to go through the paperwork of filing assault charges for a minor disturbance—clearly, we weren't criminals, setting out to cause a disruption. We went on our way. When we caught up with Micky, he had a great laugh. He loved hearing about that kind of action and said that he wished that he would have been there to see it all. We couldn't have had a better boss, or a better friend.

Although I enjoyed every trip to Las Vegas, I didn't have to go out of town to have a good time. I got a boost by immersing myself into any kind of action—especially where I could put money on the line. If I felt the urge for community play, I'd drive over to the Los Alamitos Race Course.

Anytime I exited the freeway on Katella Avenue on my way to Los Alamitos, I felt that familiar sense of anticipation building. Once in the sprawling parking lot, where I sold programs as a 16- year-old, and I walked closer, I could inhale the faint scent of hay and horses, giving me that invigorating excitement and eagerness. The sound of hooves pounding against the dirt track in the distance added to the thrill of the moment. It wasn't quite the same as walking into a casino, but I loved it.

The grandstand loomed ahead, its vibrant colors and fluttering flags welcomed me in. Groups of people, some of them familiar faces, discussed the races, they all looked animated, alive with anticipation and hope.

As I passed through the gates, I heard cheers from spectators. Vendors were calling out to sell programs and snacks. In the distance, horses snorted as jockeys brushed their coats and prepared for the races. The palpable energy crackled with excitement and possibility.

Some people would go home richer, others poorer, but everyone would have an amazing time in the thrill of the moment.

Making my way to the betting windows, I felt a surge of adrenaline as I studied the racing form in my hand, trying to decipher which horse held the key to my success. When my turn came up, I told the teller that I wanted Bengal Bay to win. I counted out $5,000 in hundreds, and the teller gave me a ticket in return. From the moment I placed my bet, I became a part of something bigger than myself. I was in the game, waiting for a journey filled with thrills, challenges, all packed into the span of a few minutes.

Despite all the cheering and excitement, Bengal Bay crossed the finish line in second place, rendering my ticket worthless. Instead of dwelling on the loss, I tore the ticket in half and started scanning my program to find the next opportunity.

A voice beside me interrupted my thoughts. "Tough break, huh?"

The man extended his hand. "I'm Bobby Calhoun." I guessed him to be about 20 years older than me. His easy smile and relaxed demeanor contrasted with the intensity of the race, and I welcomed the distraction. I shrugged off the loss with a nonchalant grin, my eyes greeting him momentarily, then I continued to scan the program for the next race.

"Always another shot at making it back," I said.

Bobby made small talk. Experienced, he quickly assessed me as a seasoned gambler, understanding the highs and lows of betting. We fell into an easy conversation, like old friends reunited. Two triple-A personalities with a similar energy. Inside jokes came easily to us, even though we'd just met, as we both loved the unpredictable nature of gambling.

We started drinking together as we watched the races, sharing anecdotes from our past wins and losses. He was smart, assuming that if I could easily drop $5,000 on a single horse race, I must bet on sports as well. He started asking my thoughts on upcoming games. As it turned out, Bobby was a bookie.

He didn't go to the race track so much to bet on the races, but to recruit degenerate gamblers into his stable of bettors. I told him about my day job as a commodities broker, but that I also ran a sports book on the side. Bobby had the discipline to run his sportsbook like a business, and he didn't gamble on games. I told him that wasn't me, and that I put money down on my own bets each week. I opened an account with him, and quickly became one of his best customers.

As Bobby and I got to know each other better, he asked how I handled all the action. In that era, 40 to 50 guys had my phone number to book their bets. Some bookmakers used a voice recorder, or hired people who took the bets. I did everything myself, always carrying a small spiral notebook and pen in my inside pocket to take notes. If someone called, they'd ask me for the line on a specific game, and place the bet. I wrote down everything I needed to know, confirmed the bet, and locked it in.

During the week, things weren't so bad. Weekends brought calls all day. My guys were like me. They didn't only bet before the game started. Throughout the game, they'd pile onto the action with crazy bets that made the game more exciting. They'd bet on the quarter, on the half, who would win the toss, or anything that gave them a feeling. I'd take any bet, and my guys loved that about me.

"I'm going to make it easier for you," Bobby said.

He introduced me to Tara, a sales rep for an offshore per-head service in Costa Rica called Datawager or IDS that catered to bookmakers. He said that she could set my business up with a web-based portal. For $35 each week, per client, I'd get a dedicated user ID and password.

As long as the clients had internet connectivity, they could log into their accounts. The bettors would immediately see the line from DonBest.com, a recognized source that covered all games. The portal would show their status and balance. Clients would have freedom to place bets at their leisure instead of having to get through to me on the phone.

Tara set me up with the domain BreakTheBookie.net, which would be easy enough to remember. I gave all my clients account numbers and showed them how to start using the system. For the few clients who weren't too technologically savvy, the service included a 1-800 number that was dedicated to me. If the client couldn't access the internet, he could dial the number, give his user ID and password, and place a bet 24 hours a day.

Tara's company didn't have any interest in the game's outcome. Rather than complicating matters by handling financial transactions, it limited the role to publishing the line and providing a portal that would record every bet, for every account. I could log in any time if I wanted to see the total amount of exposure I had. The system even projected how the weekend would turn out. If I didn't like the way things were going, I could adjust the odds— but I usually just went with the published odds of DonBest.com, assuming the risk.

With only 50 customers, the system cost me less than $2,000 a week, and since it freed up my time, it was worth every penny. That automated system allowed me to go into business-development mode rather than dealing with the tedious task of keeping up with everyone's betting.

My business grew quickly. With the technological advancements, I could suddenly double my client base, and then double it again. Although my friend Bobby Calhoun didn't gamble, he had a good strategy of recruiting at the race track.

Prior to getting access to the new website in Costa Rica, my 50 clients kept me busy enough. I knew those guys from high school, from the gym, from sports, but most of all, from my day job with Micky. With the new system, I could 10x the number of clients I served, without having to sacrifice my commitment to Micky.

To grow my business, I began recruiting agents. They were the best. Many of those guys wanted to get into bookmaking, but they either didn't have the capital on hand, or they couldn't stomach the risk. I made it easier on them.

If an agent signed up a person who would bet with me, I'd take all the risk. The only thing I asked was that they vouched for the person, confirming that he was an honorable guy. If the agent had a friend and trusted him, I would trust the agent's word. The agent could give his client a user ID and password, and the guy could start booking bets at BreakTheBookie.net. The system would keep records of all the actions in a transparent way, updating the balances within minutes of each game. The client would see, the agent would see, and I would see.

I'd settle up on Mondays, and give the agent between 10 and 50 percent of the net proceeds, depending upon the amount of clients, amount the players bet, and the risk involved. Rather than worrying about losses, the agent simply had to do his best to make sure his clients honored their word.

Agents might start off small, bringing one or two friends into the system. As they got more comfortable, they could build their own stable. People enjoyed betting together with friends. During football season, a good agent could earn a side income of more than $20,000 per month, without taking on any risk. And I was happy to pay them—because paying out $20,000 to an agent meant at least another $20,000 a month in additional income for me. Besides, I didn't have to deal with all the players—only my agents.

With my active lifestyle, I didn't have any problems recruiting agents. Besides my workouts at the gym, I became an avid golfer. Southern California is renowned for its exclusive and high-end country clubs, offering a blend of luxury amenities, premier golf courses, and social engagements. Friends and acquaintances would invite me to play at Del Mar, Pebble Beach, Aviara, Bighorn, the Vintage Club. Closer to home, I'd play at private country clubs like Big Canyon, Marbella, Pelican Hill, Aliso Viejo, and

Mesa Verde . Wherever I played, I'd find regulars who happily joined my squad of agents.

The more bets I started to take, the more susceptible I became to people who would try to take advantage. In our world, we'd call it "taking a shot." Desperate people would hang out in country clubs, find a bookie, open an account, and start wagering. I had a reputation for paying winners promptly. A scumbag would take the winnings, but if he lost, he'd disconnect the phone and vanish. For that reason, I had to trust my agents to make sure they knew the customers they brought on board.

Young and affluent, in the best shape of my life, I got to be somewhat cocky in my mid 20s. I was in at the top of my game, working out daily to develop a more intimidating presence. I didn't have too many problems with people who didn't pay on time, but other guys I met in the business had their complaints about dead-beat customers. When they told me about challenges they were having, I'd offer to intervene.

"Why don't you pay me to handle the problem for you?"

The situation worked out well, as I could earn several thousand dollars just by visiting a guy. I may not have been 6-6, or look like a criminal, but I could get the job done. In fact, I'd argue that I was more efficient at collecting because I understood the art of confidence and negotiating. The guy wouldn't be expecting me, but I'd show up at his house. As a strategy, I'd show up at the person's house carrying an insulated pouch, such as a red pizza warmer. I wanted to give off the impression that I was a pizza delivery guy. People might not open the door for a stranger, who wouldn't come to the door if they saw a guy carrying a hot pizza?

When he opened the door, I glared at him. "You have a balance of $50,000. You're late. How do you anticipate handling your balance?"

"Yeah, I'm doing the best that I can," the guy might try explaining, but I could sense that my glare was shaking him as he came up with excuses.

I'd hold up my open hand. "You know what that is?" I'd ask.

He'd look at me curiously, "A hand?" not really knowing how to answer.

"That's a stop sign. It's a sign that this isn't the time for you to talk. It's the time for you to listen. We don't want this to escalate. Our team will definitely escalate if necessary," I'd nod my head while glaring at him.

"But it's not what we want. In fact, we want to avoid escalating at all costs. When you won, we made sure that you'd get your money on time. We know where you're located. Look around. I'm at your house." I paused to let that statement sink in.

"Now when and how can we get this handled? Because if another guy comes, I don't think he'll be as nice."

I could sense the fear, and I understood. I was at his house, or on his doorstep. He didn't want to see this matter go any farther. Usually, the guy would find a way to get the money by the next day. If not, he'd come up with a reasonable payment plan. I started to develop a reputation.

People started to call me Tattoo Matt.

The bookmaking business continued to grow, and I started to enjoy it more than ever. Around that same time, in the early 2000s, the grand plan that Micky had been orchestrating began to reveal itself. While my brother and I had been working to grow Newhall Discount Brokerage, and I'd spent six months in Chicago building Lind-Waldock, he'd been playing three-dimensional chess, without telling anyone. He reorganized all his ventures under a new brand, Main Street Trading. With a record showing rapid growth, and thousands of accounts, Micky liquidated everything, selling it all to a larger firm for nearly $100 million—walking away from the business he built as a very rich man before he celebrated his 40th birthday.

CHAPTER 6

Shohei Ohtani—The Translator and The Truth

I admired Micky tremendously, respected him. By reflecting on his past, recording the present, and planning for the future, Micky disciplined himself to seize or create opportunities daily. He knew how to get ahead of markets.

Discipline opened his eyes to threats, long before they took him under. Instead of complaining about the growing spread of discount brokerage firms, and how they undermined his business with lower commissions, Micky secretly plotted an exit strategy. His innovative mindset that led to planning, prioritizing, and acting catapulted him to a nine-figure net worth. I admired his ability to navigate potential storms into safe and profitable harbors.

When Micky surprised our team by telling us that he had sold his company, my initial thoughts went to the responsibilities of my growing family. Monica had given birth to our second baby, Haley, in 1999. And in 2003, the year that he sold his business to Refco, we were expecting our third daughter, Brooke.

My brother Shawn was in a similar situation to me. As young men, we knew that we'd been earning far more than our peers and we also knew that with market changes, we'd be hard pressed to find other jobs that would pay as well.

Shawn had been rebuilding his life alongside me ever since that group of anonymous bikers broke into his house and robbed him at gunpoint. After Shawn recovered from the robbery, Monica and I welcomed him and his girlfriend, April, to move into the house we'd purchased in Cypress. It was a natural fit. Both Monica and I knew and liked April very much. She had been dating Shawn since high school, so the four of us had that long history. Once Shawn joined me in the brokerage business, and he began building financial stability, he married April and together they welcomed three beautiful children into our lives, Darian, Britney, and Kaya.

Both Shawn and I appreciated the financial stability that had come from our work. We had different personalities, but a profitable working relationship.

Shawn had a forceful personality that would bring his wrath if he believed that people weren't delivering results. He didn't accept excuses or explanations for disappointing performance numbers. If a person didn't measure up to his expectations, and Shawn didn't think the person could rise to his standards, he'd be quick to sever ties. To grow our business, Shawn understood that we needed to process trades.

Rather than yelling or intimidation, I motivated our team by getting in the trenches with them, showing them what I thought excellence looked like on the job. Yelling didn't work for me. But Shawn was my older brother, and I supported him. He took the corner office and big title to let people know he was in charge. The accouterments of power didn't matter to me. My success came from building stronger relationships with customers, processing more trades, and developing people on our team. Together, we made it work, growing Micky's businesses to exceed all expectations.

As Micky's right-hand, I earned at least $500,000 annually in 2003, perhaps $100,000 more than my brother. Besides the income that Micky paid for my contributions to his company, booking bets as a side hustle brought in another 400 grand. Most of that cash went out to casinos or other bookmakers to cover a steady string of gambling losses that characterized that early phase of my career. I had to pay my dues before I could start bringing in bigger dollars. Shawn loved to wager as well, though he never jeopardized his family stability by putting everything on the line— as I frequently did.

Considering the various income streams I'd developed, and the money that I'd earned by working with Micky, I should've had well over $3 million in savings in 2003, when Micky revealed that he had sold his company. But I'd been living on the edge, always gambling rather than investing. I had confidence that new opportunities to earn would open, even if a bad string of losses took away everything.

Still, at only 28, with a growing family, I didn't want to give up on a steady income and benefits that the brokerage business could provide. Although I understood that I could build my bookmaking hustle, with a family, I also thought about insurance and the need to show a taxable income stream.

Like Micky, both Shawn and I understood that online brokerage services threatened the industry over the long term. Yet in 2003, we both believed that if we were to start our own firm, we could squeeze out three to five more years of seven-figure earnings.

Since I had a more substantive relationship with Micky, I told Shawn that I'd reach out for his blessing. Micky had made it possible for my brother and me to build financial stability, and he deserved our loyalty. Neither of us would go behind Micky's back. Even though we were on the verge of losing our livelihood after he had sold his business, we respected him, and considered him a friend. Although we didn't need his approval to go into business, talking with him felt like the right move.

As a condition of buying his company, Refco required Micky to refrain from participating in any aspect of the brokerage business. Yet Micky wasn't the kind of guy to pass up an opportunity. When I asked what he thought about Shawn and I launching a new brokerage business, he didn't only encourage us, but also expected to get a piece.

"You'll make money in this new venture," he said. "I'd like to participate, off the books."

Despite engineering an exit that had made him fabulously wealthy, Micky wouldn't be Micky if he didn't at least try to squeeze more value out of his intellectual property. I told him that Shawn and I wanted to go into business for ourselves, as 50-50 partners.

"You should definitely go after what you want," Micky said, as he leaned back in his chair, bringing his finger to his temple and holding me in a steady gaze. He paused to weigh his next words. "Along the way, I'm sure you'll agree that it's only reasonable to pay a toll for all that I created. I wouldn't be a named partner. How would you recommend that we structure an agreement between us that would be reasonable?"

There wasn't any question that Micky had created a money-making machine. Because of him, both Shawn and I earned more than people who were twice our age. He paid our wages, and for that reason, he had a right to profit from any new business spawned by his ideas and work. Micky's noncompete agreement with Refco prohibited him from being an owner of record, but he clearly expected us to kick up some type of royalty that would last as long as we were in business.

"Consider the lead resources you're getting," he continued. "Wouldn't you agree your relationship with the Guarino group has value?"

He referred to Nick Guarino, founder of *The Wall Street Underground* newsletter. Together, we'd built a relationship with Guarino's firm that resulted in hundreds of highly qualified leads coming into our company. That relationship began when I hired David Rocca, a mediocre broker I hired when we were building Newhall Discount Brokerage.

David was in his mid 50s, clearly at the tailend of his career. He didn't have the energy of the aggressive young men we would typically hire. People came into the business wanting to succeed, but once they acquired their houses, their cars, and their financial stability, they tended to coast, becoming lethargic. By the time brokers had a few decades at a desk, they tended to burn out.

Despite sensing that he was a bit too old for the role, I hired David because of a relationship he had developed with *The Wall Street Underground*. I knew that the newsletter attracted high-net-worth individuals who held contrarian views. In *The Wall Street Underground,* subscribers could read all the negative news they wanted about how the government taxed too much, or how the establishment protected elites at the expense of entrepreneurial, self-made mavericks.

For a fairly large initial fee, readers paid for his newsletter, which he described as research they could use to trade profitably while sticking it to the man.

Guarino understood the emotions of greed and fear. His relentless marketing brought in leads that he turned over to teams of telemarketers. They sold newsletter subscriptions to thousands of people, and they paid Guarino's company high monthly fees for the ostensible value of his research. Every lead in the *Wall Street Underground* database needed to place trades if they wanted to act on Guarino's advice, and up until the time that I got involved, all those prospective leads went to David Rocca.

Once I hired Rocca, I could connect directly with leaders of Guarino's sales team. We formalized an agreement to ensure that our company—rather than David Rocca—would receive the name, phone number, and mailing address for anyone who inquired about the *Wall Street Underground*. Whether those people subscribed to the newsletter or not, their expressed interest in commodities made them a viable candidate for our firm. By taking over the relationship from Rocca, we brought hundreds of highly-qualified leads into our system each month. Distributing those leads to the aggressive brokers we nurtured led to enormous profits for our firm.

Since Micky's company generated the resources necessary to cultivate that relationship with *The Wall Street Underground*, he could rightfully claim ownership of the intellectual property. Although Refco had paid Micky approximately $100 million to buy his company, and would want to keep all leads in house, I had a personal relationship with the Guarino team. As such, I didn't have any doubt that he'd work with Shawn and me. Given all I knew about Micky's obsession with success, I shouldn't have been surprised with his expectation that we'd offer him some form of compensation.

I proposed a compromise. Rather than paying Micky an ongoing royalty as a silent partner, I asked if he'd allow us to make a one-time payment so that Shawn and I could build our own company, as 50-50 partners. He thought about the request for a moment, then smiled, telling me that he had his eye on a Patek Philippe Grand Complication with a perpetual calendar and a black alligator strap.

"So you want us to buy you a watch," I asked.

Purchasing the collectable watch would set us back more than 75 grand, but Shawn and I would have the liberty to launch Aliso Trading Group as our company—with Micky's blessing—which we considered to be worth 10x what we'd be paying him.

Besides covering the costs for Micky's watch, both Shawn and I contributed $100,000 each in working capital to get our company off the ground. Although we anticipated building most of our business through telephone sales, some customers from Orange County would want to come in for face-to-face meetings. To make a favorable impression, we leased a full floor of Type-A office space in a modern building called Techspace. We outfitted the space with sleek desks, computers, trading screens, and an efficient phone system that would allow our brokers to get the job done.

Within two months of opening the door to Aliso Trading Group, our company generated more than $100,000 in monthly profits. I put my desk in the center of the trading floor, inviting all traders to listen and learn as I made call after call, closing deal after deal. They got to see what it meant to work hard and play hard, because I would put in the hours necessary to become the top broker each month—but also had the liberty to get out and play.

With more financial resources, my reputation in Las Vegas began to build. Casino hosts profited by cultivating relationships with guests who would gamble regularly, with increasingly larger amounts. They believed that, in most cases, the gambler would lose over time and the casino would win. As I began to increase the amount I sent to Las Vegas, more privileges opened.

By 2004, casino hosts in every casino knew my name. As the owner of Aliso Trading Group, managers saw me as being a respectable businessman, allowing me to overcome the Know-Your-Customer rules which really weren't being enforced by banks or casinos compliance at all yet. Every new casino welcomed me.

By the early 2000s, the Palms had gained a reputation as a trendy, celebrity-friendly resort. Its staff of stunning women who wore the iconic Playboy Bunny outfits kept its casino full. Managers reserved the "Hugh Hefner Sky Villa," one of the most expensive suites in Las Vegas, for bonafide whales. To get the suite, I'd let JJ, my casino host at The Palms, know that I intended to wire $500,000 for a weekend of play. He'd lay out the red carpet treatment.

Sending $500,000 wasn't quite enough for the casino to send a private jet for me. Those perks wouldn't come until much later. Back then, JJ would send a chauffeur to welcome my arrival at McCarran International Airport. He'd greet me with a warm smile and a firm handshake, then escort me to a Rolls, Bentley, Range Rover, or some other luxurious vehicle to drive me to the casino.

We'd pull into the grand entrance of the Palms, where JJ welcomed and escorted me to the breathtaking opulence of the Heffner villa. On cue, the butler would open the double doors and I'd walk into a spacious living area with plush leather furniture, a wet bar stocked with top-shelf liquor, and a massive flat-screen television. Framed covers of stunning Playboy models and artwork lined the walls. The bedroom featured a king-sized bed draped in luxurious linens, and an expansive marble bathroom included a soaking spa that could comfortably hold several people beside a glass-enclosed shower.

The bow-tie wearing butler showed me all the suite's amenities, including a private gym, massage room, and a private patio with a firepit and a pool that seemed as if it was suspended in the air over the side of the casino. While swimming, we could look over the infinity-edged pool—which provided an incomparable view of Las Vegas—and if we looked up we'd see the tower.

As my friend Bobby Calhoun understood, one of the best ways to grow a bookmaking business would be to frequent locations where people gambled. The race track at Los Alamitos put him in proximity to local gamblers, but staying in the Hefner Sky Villa put me into an entirely different category of gamblers—whales who had the capacity to book six- and seven-figure bets.

In Las Vegas, I loved to gamble, but those trips were also a part of my business-development strategy. While there, the casino would shower me with comps, including meals at the finest restaurants on the property, VIP access to the hottest nightclubs and shows, and preferred accommodations wherever I went. The casino staff treated me like royalty, catering to my every whim. With all that attention, other players noticed, and they could be the lifeblood, or the death knell to a bookmaker's business.

For example, during my time at the Palms, I got to know Walt, a runner for an extremely famous high-roller family who operated out of Las Vegas. Relationships with celebrity clientele led to volatile swings in my business, and even influenced the kind of attention that led to my current problems with authorities. Had it not been for my high-profile clients, the federal government may not have begun a forensic accounting of all my phones, computers, and business activities.

In the spring of 2024, as I wrote these chapters, I couldn't be sure of the total fallout that would come from the government's interest in my business affairs. As Micky advised, I simply needed to recalibrate and write the next chapter of my life. In writing the story that led me into this predicament, I didn't want to write anything that could bring problems for others.

Suffice it to say that in the early 2000s, regulators frowned upon gambling by leaders of some businesses. Rather than placing bets themselves, exposing themselves to Congressional inquiries or unnecessary questions from prying reporters who wanted to trade on their names, high-profile individuals frequently employed runners like

Walt. They could step in to place bets for celebrities and executives who wanted to remain anonymous, but still wager on their favorite sports teams.

The attention I received from casinos put me in proximity to people like Walt, and through those runners, I got to know many of the people they represented, some of whom were well known billionaires. Three brothers, for example, would use Walt to place bets on six to eight games a weekend, with each bet in the range of $250,000.

By placing those bets with the sportsbook at the Palms, Walt could masquerade the identities of his employers, but he didn't stand to benefit much on a personal level. By becoming an agent for me, on the other hand, Walt could supplement his income. On some weekends, the offset of losing bets to winning bets resulted in Walt earning as much as $100,000.

We had a good relationship for a while, but then the unthinkable happened. The billionaire brothers and others hit a hot streak, placing several bets that came up winners during the season. They won about $5.7 million, crushing my bankroll.

In retrospect, I know that I should not have been servicing whales that placed such enormous bets at that stage in my bookmaking career. To handle those bets comfortably, I would've needed a constant liquidity of more than $20 million. In 2004, I didn't have anywhere near that amount of cash on hand. The smart play would've limited exposure by offsetting some of that action, but I loved the gamble and didn't foresee much chance of them winning a complicated NFL hot streak. It felt like free money—until they won.

My willingness to put it all on the line brought me too close to the fire, and that weekend of heavy losses burned me, threatening to undermine my entire bookmaking operation.

To deliver $5.7 million in cash to all my customers, I had to tap into a line of credit I had previously arranged on the house I purchased for my family, take a loan from my brother, a separate loan from our company, and use all my excess cash. Despite all those maneuverings, I was $440,000 short. To overcome that cash deficit, I reached out to Skip and Larry, founders of a well known large sportsbook, in Costa Rica. They'd been courting me for several months, trying to persuade me to join them. I didn't want partners. But at that moment, I didn't have a choice. In exchange for a piece of my bookmaking business, they agreed to provide cash I needed so that I could pay off my debts in full.

Skip and Larry's sportsbook served as a clearing house for sportsbooks all across the world. To pay off the bet, I needed cash fast, and signing up with them would be my only option if I wanted to continue as a bookmaker. If I didn't pay on time, word would spread quickly, obliterating my reputation and ending my business.

When I contacted Skip, he immediately agreed. "We'll float you the $440K you need to cover your loss," Skip said over the phone. Going forward, I agreed to open individual accounts for all my bettors on their website's portal. Basically, I was becoming an agent for them. They'd cover any bet that my players made, and we'd split profits from the juice 50-50—after I covered the $440,000 that I owed.

I hesitated, not feeling great about handing over control of the operation I'd built. But I didn't see another choice.

Despite having earned millions since I began working with Micky, that $5.7 million loss had completely wiped me out. I didn't just lose all my cash, but I also owed money for the loan against my house, and the cash I borrowed from others. Without a bankroll, I wouldn't get to enjoy comped luxury suites in Las Vegas anytime soon.

Feeling desperate, I did what no one should do, taking a shot with wagers I couldn't afford to cover.

Besides setting up accounts for the gamblers who worked with me, I set up a fictitious account on the betting website that Skip and Larry operated, disguising it as an account for the billionaire brothers. Over a weekend, I put everything on the line, placing bets that I didn't have any way of repaying if they went the wrong way. Being the degenerate gambler that I'd become, I couldn't restrain myself from taking the risk—even though I knew that the bets could ruin me.

Surprisingly, the bets went my way. When the underdog Raiders won the final game on Sunday, my fictitious account generated winnings of $1.5 million. Even after the $440,000 that I owed Skip and Larry for the short-term loan, those winnings would clear $1 million—which would be enough to get back in the game.

Later that evening, the caller ID on my phone indicated an incoming call from Costa Rica. When I answered, I heard Skip's voice. "We've got a problem." There wasn't any greeting. "We need you to catch the next flight to Costa Rica. Our man will be waiting for you at the airport." He wasn't asking.

I knew that Skip and Larry suspected me of dishonesty, but I didn't think they could prove anything. I worried about what I'd discover if I flew down there, but I had to go face the problem. The driver who met me at the airport wasn't the friendly type who catered to me in Vegas.

Instead of a suit and tie, the driver wore a camouflage uniform. He tucked an assault-style rifle in a leather-strapped holster that draped diagonally across his chest. We didn't speak as he drove on dirt roads, with dense foliage pressing in on all sides, deep into the Costa Rican jungle.

It was my first time visiting their headquarters, a modern concrete fortress that seemed out of place in all the natural beauty.

As we approached the compound, I saw more armed guards posted at the perimeter, machine guns slung over their shoulders. The driver pulled up to the gate and exchanged words in Spanish with the guards, who eyed me suspiciously. With a nod, they waved us through, the heavy metal gates creaking open.

Inside, even more uniformed men patrolled, their weapons glinting in the sun. It was a clear show of force, meant to intimidate. Accustomed to high stakes encounters, I kept a neutral expression. But I'm not going to lie. I didn't know any of those guys, and as I went in, I felt as if I could be going into Hotel California—where a person could check out any time but never leave.

The escort brought me into an empty conference room, where I waited alone at an oval table for at least 15 minutes. Then the founders walked in. "Tell us about this new account you set up," Larry asked. Specifically, he wanted to hear my explanation of how a new account could generate $1.5 million in a single weekend.

Leaning forward and clasping his hands on the table, Skip jumped in, "The billionaire brothers, right?" His tone made it clear he didn't believe a word of it.

I kept my cool, knowing that I was in the lion's den. Forcing a calm, I met Larry's gaze, spinning a tale about the bets being part of the normal pattern. Yet even I knew that the pattern hadn't been normal at all.

Typically, the billionaires placed bets that allowed them to win big with a complicated mix of parlays, teasers, and straight bets. When I made those bets in the account I set up to supposedly represent them, I placed straight bets and halftime bets. It threw off the pattern that Larry and Skip had come to expect from the billionaire brothers.

The armed guard remained in the room, his presence a constant reminder of the precarious situation I'd put myself in. Skip and Larry relentlessly interrogated me, demanding every detail about the suspicious account. They brought out records, their evidence irrefutable.

"The IP address shows these bets were placed from California, not Las Vegas," Skip pointed out, his eyes narrowing. "And the betting pattern doesn't match the billionaires' usual style. There weren't any parlays or teasers. Your story doesn't make sense?"

I maintained my composure, unwavering, despite their incredulity and cynicism. I tried not to sweat, despite the palpable tension, the air thick with accusation and mistrust.

"You're lying," were the only words that Larry said.

After enduring their questioning for what felt like an eternity, the time had come to force their hand. I leaned forward, meeting their gazes head-on. "You've got three options," I said, my voice steady and resolute. "Option one, I held up my finger. Take me into the jungle and put a bullet in my head. You'll save the $1.5 million you owe, but you'll have to deal with the fallout. People know I'm here."

I paused, letting the weight of my words sink in before continuing. "Option two. Send me back empty-handed. If you do that, everyone in my network will know that your sportsbook doesn't honor its bets, which will shatter your reputation, not mine."

I pressed on, laying out their final choice. "Option three. Pay the $1.5 so I can make my customers whole, and we'll chalk this up to a misunderstanding. The choice is yours. But I'm done with this interrogation. Have your driver take me back to the hotel, or I'll find my own way. But I've had enough of this. I'm ready to head home."

"We don't believe you," Larry stated, without any emotion.

I met his gaze unflinchingly. "You've made that clear. Make a move," I shrugged. "I've told you the truth. But I'm leaving, one way or another. It's your call."

Instead of sending me with an armed guard, Skip drove. "We know you placed those bets," he said, his tone accusatory. "But it's clear you're not going to budge on your story. Just fly home, and I'll discuss this with my partners. We'll decide what to do. Call me when you land, and I'll give you our decision."

The flight home was a blur, my mind racing with every possible scenario. As instructed, I called Skip upon landing. His voice was curt, his instructions precise. "Drive to the intersection of Century Boulevard and Prairie, in Inglewood. Park in the shopping center, near the Target store. When you're parked, call this number and let them know your location. Wait there." He hung up on me.

I followed his directions, my heart pounding as I made the call. Within minutes, a stranger approached, handing me a duffle bag. I unzipped it, revealing stacks of cash totaling over $1 million.

"We're severing ties with you," the man said, his expression indifferent. "We're keeping the $440,000 you owe. Take the rest and lose our number."

And just like that, it was over. I had my money, but at the cost of my partnership with them. As I drove away, the duffle bag remained zipped in the passenger seat beside me. I contemplated next steps in this precarious world of high-stakes gambling.

Those fellas had a right to question the wagers I placed, and I respect their integrity in paying it. Our paths never crossed again, and I wouldn't know how to contact them again if I tried. But as I introspect on the career that led me into the crosshairs of this government investigation, I realize that I'd done the wrong thing. In a desperate maneuver to get back on top, I took a shot. The gamble worked out in my favor, but I'm not proud of what I'd done.

We had to live and learn, pick ourselves up and move on.

Although we went our separate ways, my career continued, allowing me to work with thousands of gamblers. For the most part, people in my orbit were honorable, but there were always some who, like I once did, would take a shot. Sometimes, things went well for them, and sometimes they went badly.

One example is Ippei Mizuhara, the former interpreter for Shohei Ohtani, one of the world's most famous baseball players. That pesky reporter from ESPN, Tisha Thompson, kept digging into my affairs, which somehow led her to Ippei. She visited my house under the auspices of wanting to write a story about my relationship with Scott Sibella, the CEO of Resort World. Yet on March

20, 2024, she and her colleagues at ESPN began publishing stories that would bring Shohei Ohtani into a scandal, questioning his involvement in my bookmaking operation.

The headlines covered wire transfers of at least $4.5 million that Shohei sent. Although Tisha and her colleagues published countless articles to feed the scandal, I refused to participate in their reporting.

As anticipated from the time she visited my house, her coverage sparked a national media frenzy. Television reporters started clustering around our gated community, invading our home life, as if my wife and I would somehow be relevant to the story they wanted to build. Those reporters didn't have details, but knowing the power of a scandal, they published to keep Shohei's name in the news.

Nicole and I did our best to tune out that media noise, but the national attention brought out the kooks. People went as far as calling our home to leave threatening messages, warning us to protect Shohei.

I wasn't in a position to protect Shohei, because I'd never said anything about him. But I kept reading articles, or watching television news reports on national stations, about his connection to "the Southern California bookmaker, Mathew Bowyer."

Those articles fed into the FBI's investigation of me. Through my attorney, they asked me to provide all records of any wagers that Ippei Mizuhara had placed through my website in Costa Rica.

I met Ippei in the same way that I met most people who opened accounts with me—through my prolific gambling. A friend invited me to a poker game with players and coaches for the Los Angeles Angels back in 2021. Poker wasn't my game of choice, but I'd never pass up an opportunity to connect with more professional athletes. For one thing, they're hyper competitive and for another, they had sufficient disposable income that they could wager.

As with celebrity executives in highly-regulated businesses, gambling could be a touchy matter. Major League Baseball rules prohibited players or managers from betting on professional baseball games. The league believed that gambling could undermine the integrity of the sport, as it could incentivize players or managers to intentionally lose games or alter performance for personal financial gain. Athletes who played professional football, basketball, hockey, or other sports had to abide by similar rules.

Rules did not block professional baseball players from betting sports other than baseball.

I went to the poker game in the spirit of meeting like minded people, and that's how I met Ippei. After gathering records to satisfy the FBI request, I saw that Ippei placed his first wager with me on December 3, 2021. It wasn't a big bet—$1,000 on a soccer game in Turkey. He bet on Besiktas, Istanbul to beat Kasimpasa, Istanbul.

Ippei lost the wager, and he lost many other wagers. After reviewing more than 250 pages of records that attorneys had turned over to the FBI, the record showed that he had placed 80% of his bets on soccer games, without a single bet on baseball. From interviews he gave to Tisha Thompson of ESPN, it appeared that Ippei took a shot, betting tens of millions, but Ippei alone wasn't news. To keep advertising dollars flowing, Tisha and her colleagues had to bring Shohei into the story.

And I got wrapped up inside of it all.

CHAPTER 7

Stacks, Scandals, and Silence

As I sit here in April 2024, just days shy of my 49th birthday, the weight of my current challenges continues to press down on me. Coping with challenges and crises has been a way of life, and I'm well suited for whatever comes. Still, the barrage of news seems unrelenting, confirming that I'm going to have to take a new direction.

Ever since Tisha broke her story, journalists have been having a field day with the betting scandal surrounding Shohei Ohtani's interpreter, Ippei Mizuhara. They speculated about my involvement, but they didn't know about what happened. To get attention, journalists published their stories with splashy headlines, such as "Inside the 'very predatory' world of illegal betting that lured Shohei Ohtani's interpreter." That messaging would cast a dark shadow over my reputation, but it didn't have any basis in reality.

The irony is not lost on me. These journalists, in their rush to sensationalize and sell papers, didn't seem to care about the truth. They portrayed bookmakers as being predatory, as if we spent our days pressuring innocent people into gambling away their life savings. Nothing could be further from the truth. Nevertheless, in the spring of 2024, with a series of ongoing investigations, and my freedom potentially on the line, it wasn't the time to try and set the record straight.

That time would come. Until then, I would heed the advice of my defense attorneys, Diane Bass and Chris Glew. They recommended that I keep my head down, avoid the prying questions of reporters, and focus on charting a new course forward.

Fortunately, it wasn't the first time that I had to recalibrate and chart a new course, or as Micky advised, write the next chapter. When the ground shifted, we had to adjust our footing and move forward, sometimes in different directions. I've changed directions many times before, and through this therapeutic work of writing my story, I was beginning to formulate a plan for how I'd emerge on the other side of this experience.

The further reality of my shifting circumstances hit home when I received an unexpected call from Kara, who had been my longtime casino representative at Pechanga Resort Casino. Pechanga didn't have the glitz and glamor of the Vegas strip, but its proximity to my home in Orange County made it a convenient spot when I felt the urge to get away and play for a few hours. Typically, I'd drive east on Interstate 91 at least once each week to play at Pechanga, always bringing a few hundred thousand to gamble.

I'd always stay for several hours, wagering millions of dollars each trip. That level of play made me a favorite of the casino hosts, and Kara oversaw them all. She'd give my wife and me a lot of attention, as she wanted me to play more frequently at Pechanga. "Why travel all the way to Vegas," she'd say, "when you come over for a day." Of course we saw things differently. There was a big difference between The Wynn, The Venetian, or The Aria than Pechanga, in Temecula, California. Over time, I'd guess that my losses contributed more than a million dollars to the Indian reservation.

Kara had always gone out of her way to make Nicole and me feel appreciated, scoring us discounts and comps on the resort's amenities. She once hooked us up with a once-in-a-lifetime opportunity to travel as special guests with the LA Lakers for two of their away games. Pechanga had some type of sponsorship agreement with the basketball team. Their relationship allowed the casino to treat two of its special guests on a team trip, which money could not buy.

The Lakers had exclusive use of a Boeing jetliner that had been modified with only first-class accommodations. It was like traveling in a hotel suite. We got to interact with the entire team of superstars, including Lebron James and Anthony Davis, while they traveled for a game against the Houston Rockets, and then over to New Orleans to play against the Pelicans. Our perk included accommodations in five-star hotels with the team, VIP access to practices, and the best courtside seats for each game. That trip with the Lakers was a testament to the casino's appreciation for my loyalty, and I'm grateful for the memory.

But when Kara called in the spring of 2024, she wasn't offering perks. With all the attention that came my way from the federal government and the global media, rather than vying for my attention, people were distancing themselves from me.

The Pechanga compliance manager had read about the FBI investigation into my affairs, and he tasked Kara with finding out if there was any validity to the media reports. She would have liked me to say that it would all blow over, and there wasn't any truth to it. But lying wasn't in my nature. I leveled with Kara, confirming the raid on my home and the ongoing federal probe.

"Do you anticipate being charged with a felony?" she asked, hoping that I might be able to dismiss the news reports as being fake. But lying wouldn't help. Although I didn't know when, I told her that charges would likely follow, and a conviction for bookmaking could potentially be in my future.

"I'm so sorry to hear that," Kara said, and I could hear the genuine empathy in her voice. She didn't want to lose my business, but she'd also become a friend. "I care a lot about you and Nicole, and I'm sorry this turmoil has come to your life. Unfortunately, I don't have any authority here. The casino has a strict policy against allowing known felons on the property. We're not going to be able to host you anymore."

I appreciated her concern, but it was just another sign that my world had begun to shift in ways that I couldn't control. Since the media had begun reporting on my affairs, casinos from Monte Carlo to Las Vegas had already called to say that I wouldn't be welcome.

The Atlantis Resort and Casino had previously offered to host my family in the Bahamas in celebration of my 49th birthday. Yet in the early spring, my host called to tell me that the casino had to sever its relationship with me. Since my children had been looking forward to the trip, I covered the costs to get away. I could use the excursion to clear my head and prepare for next steps.

I'd reinvented myself several times before, and I knew I could do it again. I'd gone from being a scrappy kid hustling his way through school, to accepting a job as a busboy so that I could figure out how to support a family. While Monica and I bunked on my mom's couch, I landed an unlikely opportunity with Micky, and then went on to build a great career trading commodities.

I knew that I could recalibrate again, but as Micky had advised, progress would begin with reflection. To write the next chapter of my life, I had to consider the many decisions that brought me here.

As I thought about the media's interest in my life's work, I realized that they had gotten it wrong. They tried to tarnish my reputation for being a bookmaker. Yet I wasn't ashamed of the business I'd built. From my perspective, both bookmaking and gambling were far more honorable activities than brokering commodities.

As a commodities broker I paid taxes on a high income, but as years passed, I'd grown increasingly disillusioned by the so-called profession. People who worked in financial services liked to think of themselves as doing honest work. Yet the more I learned about the business, the more it rubbed me the wrong way.

Experience as a broker convinced me that it was a rigged game. The institutions held all the cards, using their inside knowledge to profit at the expense of the little guy. It was all perfectly legal, of course, but it wasn't right for ostensibly trustworthy, regulated institutions to exploit markets in ways that would give professional investment houses an edge over the retail investor.

In contrast, bookmaking seemed honest. There were no hidden agendas, no structured trading systems that engineered an advantage for the house. With bookmaking, it was just two parties, making a wager, each with the same information. In the eyes of the law, I was a criminal, and the media portrayed me as being predatory because people went into debt with the bets they placed. Yet I only provided a service, facilitating those who wanted to add a bit of excitement to the games they watched.

I thought about the media's portrayal of a bookmaker being a villain lurking in the shadows. It was almost laughable. If they wanted to see true predators, they needed to look at Wall Street, to the suited sharks who smiled and shook a customer's hand while they picked pockets with their hidden fees and advanced trading systems. Stories about dishonesty in so-called respectable businesses didn't sell newspapers. It was easier to cast the bookie as being the bad guy, to ignore the hypocrisy that ran rampant in the "legitimate" business world.

Making things legal doesn't make everything right, just as making things illegal doesn't make everything wrong. Over time, there have been many bad laws. As a nation, we should always question whether they made sense. For example, at one time in our nation's history, laws authorized the slavery of human beings. If an enslaved person ran away from a plantation, it would have been illegal for anyone to provide that person with shelter. Did that make it wrong? At another time, laws prohibited women from voting. Were those laws good? In reading about legality, I read that we once had an Alien and Sedition act, which made it a felony to criticize the government, and American prosecutors would put people in prison if they made statements against an administration.

Legislators declared whether behavior was legal or not, but those distinctions didn't always correlate with what was right. It wasn't right to allow financial institutions to rig industries like commodity trading in ways that benefited investment houses at the expense of retail investors. But legislators legalized such conduct. And it wasn't right to criminalize people for wagering on sports. In a free country, the government should trust people to make their own decisions. For that reason, I wasn't ever ashamed of booking bets, regardless of what legislators said.

By 2005, I'd worked for several years as a licensed commodity broker, and I'd had enough. Even though I owned the Aliso Trading Group with my brother Shawn, I knew that the time had come to make a shift. The commodities business had started to feel dirty, and I wanted to get away from it all. I was ready to go full time into bookmaking, as I didn't consider it wrong to work with people who wanted to make an honest bet.

Reengineering my life meant more than changing my career. That would be easy enough. My brother Shawn thrived in his role as leader of the Aliso Trading Group, and he didn't have any intention of changing direction. We were partners in a business that we'd grown, and the numbers gave us a pretty good indication of what it was worth. In exchange for my half of the business, Shawn agreed to give me $1 million minus the debt I owed from that devastating run of losses with my big customers. With my new infusion of capital, I could go all in with my bookmaking ventures.

But as we moved into the early 2000s, I realized that it wasn't only my career that I needed to change. I was 30 years old and feeling trapped. Monica and I had fallen in love when we were 15, before either of us had experienced any aspect of life. With Lauren, Haley, and Brooke, we'd been blessed with three daughters that we both adored. To provide the best life for our girls, we had to be honest with each other. We both knew that what had begun as teenage infatuation evolved into love, but then morphed into friendship. My hyper-fast life had led to us growing apart.

That realization hit me sharply after the unsettling incident in Costa Rica. It dawned on me that Monica was entitled to much more than what I could provide. She needed joy, a partner who would hold her in high esteem and shower her with love. As a 30-year-old man, I had to admit that I wasn't suited for the role. I could not maintain the façade of being the ideal husband for Monica.

Our romance had ignited when we were both 15, in 1990, but by the turn of the century, it had become clear that our relationship would be better as a memory of good times, rather than an illusion of forever. The time had come to acknowledge that, despite our mutual respect and affection for each other, Monica and I wouldn't be going on together as a couple. She'd always be able to count on me for financial and emotional support, but our marriage had come to an end.

Wanting to minimize disruption for my daughters after Monica and I agreed to separate, I leased a 3,000-square-foot house in Huntington Beach. It was close enough to the family-friendly community of Aliso Viejo, so I could see my daughters easily enough. When they visited, we'd only be steps away from the white sand, which they'd enjoy. When they weren't with me, I felt free to explore, indulge, and live for the first time.

Honed by daily workouts and a strict diet that kept me at less than 6 percent body fat, I was in the best shape of my life. I hit the beach, the bars, the clubs, relishing the attention of beautiful young women in skimpy bikinis. Drawn to confidence, a ripped physique, and a man with both free time and cash to splurge, they always responded well, with a smile and a yes. I may have missed out on the experience of frat parties and dating as a young man, but with my new life as a single man in Huntington Beach, I made up for lost time.

I didn't want any day-to-day responsibilities, but that didn't absolve me from family obligations.

When Shawn suggested that we launch a business to help our younger brother, I agreed.

Despite the differences in our age, the four of us grew up close as children. Our oldest brother, Joey, had gone into the Coast Guard and trained to become a boat captain. Shawn and I worked together. But Andrew, being five years younger than me, had been left behind after we all went our way. He fell into a pattern of self-destructive behavior, largely because of drug addiction.

Shawn had taken a family vacation to Lake Havasu, and while there, he splurged on the purchase of a jet boat. Through that transaction, he struck up a friendship with John West, the owner of the boat manufacturer, Ultra Boats. When John told Shawn that he was looking for a new distributor, Shawn wanted in.

As children, we enjoyed our time at our family's vacation property on the Colorado River, and Shawn thought we could recreate that family atmosphere with Andrew. Yet it was one thing to enjoy racing speed boats on the river, and quite another to build a business selling jet boats. Despite Shawn's best intentions, we didn't think his idea all the way through. Instead, we acted impulsively, wanting to recapture that fun from our youth, believing that Andrew would find his way if he had his own business.

Since Shawn and I had been doing so well financially, we naively thought we could put up some cash and everything would work out, creating an opportunity for Andrew. Neither of us gave much thought to what we were doing. Shawn had his brokerage business to run, and once I separated from Monica, I'd gone all in on bookmaking and gambling—and didn't have the time or interest in overseeing a retail boat store. Although we wanted to help our younger brother get his life together, opening a business venture for him to manage proved to be a complete disaster.

It wasn't Andrew's fault. He didn't have the experience or even the stability to manage a store. We set him up for failure by leasing space in a high-rent district, not realizing that Orange County wouldn't be the best spot for a business that catered to people who enjoyed camping in tents and enjoying weekend getaways on the river. We compounded our problem by offering sales of ATVs and Quads, but those didn't sell any better. Within a few months, the rescue mission we wanted to launch for our brother turned out to be a money pit. Contractual obligations required us to keep the store open for a full year, but it was a total disaster, bringing more stress to our younger brother than help.

Fortunately, my bookmaking and gambling business allowed me to move forward, swallowing the losses as another learning experience. Although neither of us cared too much about the money we lost, both Shawn and I felt badly for our younger brother. Drugs continued to be a problem for Andrew, and his addictions led him into numerous challenges with the law. As I confronted my own problems, he was inside a county jail. Like anyone else who followed sporting news, he read about the Shohei Ohtani scandal and called to express condolences for the legal challenges I faced.

My problems were of my own making, yet with each day that passed, I felt more determined than ever to get through.

I've always been well suited to deal with setbacks, and as I transitioned deeper into the bookmaking business, I went through my fair share. Although some journalists characterized bookmaking as being predatory, as I experienced it, we always stood vulnerable to scams and setbacks from people who wanted to take a shot.

After I went into bookmaking full time, Leslie, the first casino host who welcomed me at the New York, New York casino in Las Vegas, gave me a call. She never got involved with my work as an agent, but when another one of her clients, Robert , expressed interest in sports gambling, she reached out.

"I don't know him well," she told me, "but he's a client, and he asked me to introduce him to anyone I knew who might run a sports betting business. I'll give you his number, but you'll have to make your own decision on whether to do business with him."

I appreciated Leslie for thinking of me and gave Robert a call.

Although I typically liked to meet the people who bet with me, or if it was an agent, I wanted them to meet the person. Since Leslie had vouched for him as being a gambler in Las Vegas, I gave him the benefit of the doubt, believing him to be a straight shooter.

After getting to know about Robert's interests during our initial call, I gave him a simple tutorial on how to place bets through my website. He got his account set up with appropriate credentials, and I authorized a six-figure line of credit for him to wager.

While monitoring the site over the weekend, I saw that Robert had placed large bets, basically putting everything on the line. Most all his bets came through, which was unusual, but the way of the business. His wagers netted $88,000 in winnings.

On Monday, I called to congratulate Robert, then asked how he wanted to settle. By making those calls, I gave my players a good-faith showing that they'd always be able to count on me. Some book makers had a habit of hiding from people who won. By calling Robert, I could show my integrity, and give him a sense that if he won, he'd receive payment at a time and manner that was convenient for him. Offering that personalized service differentiated me from sportsbooks in casinos, and gave people a level of comfort in dealing with me.

A reliable gambler appreciated those calls, as my openness gave them a sense that they were doing business with a reputable person. Since we'd typically keep the business rolling, there was rarely any urgency in settling accounts. Yet when I asked Robert how he wanted to settle, he told me that he'd drive down from Fresno to collect his money. After I gave him my home address, he said that he'd be at my house in about two hours.

His response was not only bad form, it was also a huge red flag. When a guy makes the first bet, and wins big, it's understandable that he wants to get paid. But in telling me that he'd drive down immediately to collect, I could read more into his character, or worthiness as a customer. Either he had an urgent need for the money, which wasn't a good sign, considering the amount of credit I'd given him, or he didn't trust me to pay him. Rather than a great start to our relationship, I had concerns that he could be a problem. Yet I owed him the money, so I gave him my address and waited for him.

When Robert showed up, he introduced me to another guy that he claimed was his brother.

That was another bad sign. I didn't invite him to bring anyone to my house, and it was bad form that he didn't come alone. Nevertheless, I opened the door and invited them into my home office. I passed a satchel filled with $88,000.

"Do you mind if I count it," Robert asked.

I glared at him, pissed off at the request. He was in my house, at my invitation, to collect $88,000. Basically, he was telling me to my face that he didn't trust me. Over the years, I'd taken wagers from all kinds of people. Knowing that gamblers sometimes had their own quirks, I waited while he counted out the money, building stacks of $5,000 until he finished.

The next weekend, I monitored the website and saw that he made the same type of bets, putting it all on the line. This time, luck did not favor him and he dropped $114,000.

I called his number on Monday, but he didn't answer. He didn't answer when I called on Tuesday, either. With gamblers, I had to take action quickly. Every day that went by without conversation meant the debt would grow colder. I began looking for information on how to track him down, using Google, calling Leslie, and calling my friend, Toby.

I'd known Toby for many years. We met when he worked at Las Vegas' Treasure Island Hotel and Casino. Sensing that he wouldn't have many opportunities to build a meaningful career, Toby wanted to make a change. When he expressed interest in working as a bail bondsman, I introduced him to my aunt Amy, who ran a bail bonds company and agreed to give Toby a start.

We'd maintained our friendship, and I could count on his help when I ran into problems with deadbeats like Robert. As a bail bondsman, Toby could access software for skip tracing, and he provided me with the home address for Robert in Fresno. Robert had two listed addresses.

The first address took me to a vacant house, but on the second try, I got it right. It was already about 7:00 pm, and the sun had gone down. When I rang the doorbell, a boy who appeared to be about 15 years-old answered the door. I asked if his dad was home.

The kid called for his dad, and within about 20 seconds, Robert showed up. He didn't recognize me and asked how he could help.

"Hi Robert," I said. "It's me, Matt Bowyer. I'm here to collect the $114,000 you owe me."

From his facial expression, I could tell that he couldn't believe I was there, standing on his porch. He turned on the light to get a better look at me. With his son standing by his side, he invited me inside.

Without knowing how our confrontation would turn out, I didn't want to step inside his house, just in case things went the wrong way. "No,

I'd rather have the conversation out here," I told him.

"Give me a minute," he said. "Let me put some shoes on and I'll be right out." I sensed that he wanted to square his son away inside the house, which I understood.

When Robert walked out, I could see a bulge beneath his t-shirt, at his bellybutton. Clearly, he wanted me to see that he had a pistol tucked in the waist of his jeans.

"Look Matt," he said, "I'm sorry that you had to drive all the way up here."

"Why's that?" I asked.

"You see, here's the thing, I place bets, but I don't pay bookies when I lose. That's just the way it goes, and you're going to have to deal with it."

I couldn't believe that he had the audacity to say such a thing. "You should have told me that before you opened an account with me," I countered.

He shrugged. "That's just the way it is. You got beat."

"This isn't going to work out the way you expect," I told him. "Either you're going to pay me, or we're going to have a big problem."

Robert stood about 5-10 and weighed about 185. He looked a little rough, but not like a gangster, and I certainly wasn't going to back down from him.

"The best thing I can do for you," he offered, "would be for you to open accounts for me with other bookies. I'll bet with them, and when I beat them, like I beat you, I'll give you a cut of the winnings."

"That's not the way I work, Robert. The only words I want to hear from you will describe how you're going to pay the $114,000 you owe."

Robert lifted up his t-shirt to reveal his pistol. "I'm not paying you," he said. He then pulled out his pistol and pointed the gun at me. I saw his hand shaking as he seemed extremely nervous.

"In my business, a guy gets to know the kind of people who have guns," I glared at him. "Some people will use them, but others will bring guns around thinking that they're going to scare people. I character you as the kind of guy who wants to scare people. But I've got news for you. I'm not scared."

When he dropped his gaze from my eyes for a second, I knew that I'd broken his spirit.

"Don't look down," I said. "This is your time to think. Think about where I am, at your house, where you sleep, where your family sleeps. Process the reality of your situation. Here's what I'm going to do. I'm going to leave here and drive back to my house. You've got 24 hours to think about how you want to handle this. I won't be calling you again. You've got my number. I suggest you use it. Because I won't be returning here if I don't hear from you. And your next visitor won't be nearly as nice."

As I was driving home, he texted, asking if I'd introduce him to another bookie so that he could put things together.

I couldn't believe he thought that I'd have any role in his charade. "Robert, I don't think you understood. You'll either pay what you owe, or we're going to have a big problem."

The following day, Robert called. "How about if I wire you half the money and we'll call it a day."

"Here's the best deal I'm going to offer you," I responded. "If my bank notifies me within two hours that my account received a wire transfer for $88,000, which was what I paid you last week, I'll forgive the other $26,000 you owe and we'll never see each other again. Short of that, as I told you last night, we're going to have a big problem."

Robert sent the wire, ending our dispute.

As a bookmaker, I accepted that, on occasion, I'd come across guys who would try to get over on me. In those instances, I had to show up, leaving the consequences that would follow up to the person's imagination. Sometimes, a person's imagination of what could happen seemed worse than the reality.

Other bookmakers had a similar, in-your-face approach to anyone who acted outside the boundaries of expected behavior. For example, I didn't know Owen Hansen personally when I began making large bets with him. When the bets I was placing with my friend Bobby Calhoun grew to be too large, he introduced me to Owen, saying he was better suited to handle my action.

Owen had been an athlete at USC who made the football team that won and played for a national title. Following his career with the Trojans, he launched a prolific bookmaking business, which he branded as BetOdog.com. Based on Bobby's recommendation, Owen opened an account for me and on my first weekend of betting, I scored big, winning more than $75,000—which Owen promptly wired to my account.

The following week, on the other hand, had been a disaster. Not only did I lose a ton of bets that I'd placed on his website, the clients who had placed bets on my site had won as well. The weekend would cost me more than $1 million, which was rare, but which happened occasionally.

Unlike Robert , who attempted to hide from me, I called Owen right away.

"Hey buddy," I told him. "The first thing I want to say is that I know I owe you $100,000. I'm giving you my word that I'm going to pay you, and that I'll make it right with you. But I had a bad week. I'll need two to three weeks to put the cash together so I can pay you, but I'm going to pay you in full and make this right."

"That's not going to fly," Owen said.

I listened to his tirade about his paying me on time, and me owing him the money. I was appropriately apologetic, assuring him that I understood his anger. He was right, and I was wrong, I told him, but that wasn't going to change the fact that I'd need two to three weeks to pay him in full.

"We're going to have a big problem," he said.

"If that's how you feel, then we're going to have a problem." I gave him my home address with strong conviction in my tone.

"I'll be there in 45 minutes."

"See you then," I told him.

I laced up my shoes, and sat on the porch waiting for our altercation, not quite knowing how it would go down.

He pulled into my driveway in a white Range Rover, parked, and got out. I sized him up, seeing that he stood about 6-3, and weighed in at about 230 pounds of fury. He wore shorts and a tank top. With all his tattoos, I thought he looked more like a gangbanger than a USC athlete.

I stood up to meet him. "Looks like we're going to dance."

"Nah, bro." He said as he walked over, and gave me a fist bump. "I've never met anyone who had the balls to talk to me like that, giving me their home address. I came here so we could meet face to face. We'll work it out. I think we can do some business together."

That mutual respect led to a lasting friendship that continues to this day.

CHAPTER 8
The California Kid

As I drove north on Interstate 5, the solitude gave me time to reflect on that first encounter I had with Owen Hanson, back when I left the commodities business to focus all my attention on bookmaking, gambling, and beginning a new life after my separation from Monica. The traffic on the Saturday morning drive wasn't too heavy. Instead of listening to music, I used the time to think. Despite the friendship Owen and I had developed after our first meeting, back in 2004, there was a part of his life and business that I didn't know anything about—a part that would lead to his downfall.

In 2014, I got wind that federal authorities had their eye on Owen's business. I'd been playing golf at one of Orange County's pristine courses when I got a random call from Mark Speidel, who introduced himself as a Special Agent with the FBI. His voice was calm but authoritative, with a hint of curiosity that put me on edge.

"Mr. Bowyer, I'm investigating illegal sportsbooks, and I've come across some records that have your name and phone number," Agent Speidel said, his tone measured. "Can you tell me why that might be?"

I felt a flicker of unease, but I kept my voice steady. "I'm not sure, Agent Speidel. I know a lot of people in the sports world, so it's hard to say why my information would be in someone's records."

"Do you know Owen Hanson?" he asked, and I could hear the rustle of papers in the background.

"Sure I do. Owen's a good friend of mine," I said, my grip tightening on the phone. "We play golf together several times a month. That could be why my number is in his records."

Agent Speidel paused, as if considering my response. "I see. And do you know what kind of business Mr. Hanson is involved in?"

I chose my words carefully, not wanting to reveal too much. "To be honest, Agent Speidel, I don't know the specifics of Owen's business dealings. I think he's in real estate, or construction of some kind. We're golfing buddies, but we don't discuss work much. If you want to know about his business, it's probably best to ask him directly."

My answer likely frustrated the agent, but he seemed to accept it. "Alright, Mr. Bowyer. Thank you for your time. If I have any more questions, would it be alright if I gave you a call?"

"Of course," I said, trying to sound cooperative. "I'm happy to help in any way I can."

No one wanted to get a call from the FBI. Ironically, I felt some relief after the call. Special Agent

Speidel didn't appear to know anything about my business or what I did for a living. His questions centered on Owen, and I didn't seem relevant to his investigation, or at least he didn't ask any questions that alarmed me.

The agent didn't tell me to keep his call confidential. Either way, as a friend, I felt a duty to let Owen know that an FBI agent had called with questions about him. Owen listened intently as I detailed the call for him, expecting that he'd use the information as he saw fit.

When I made the call, it didn't occur to me that besides Owen, I had my own exposure, and I should've taken precautions. That changed a month later.

I'd just landed at John Wayne Airport, after a brutal week in Las Vegas, where I dropped more than $500,000 betting on tables and March Madness NCAA basketball games. When the plane landed, I listened to a voice message on my phone, which I didn't expect. It was from Special Agent Speidel, the same guy who had questioned me about Owen Hanson before. Agent Speidel said that he had a few more questions and he asked me to call him back.

Once Rachel, our daughter Sage, and I got settled in the car, I called Agent Speidel back. He told me that he had a few more questions, and that he was in the area. The agent asked if we could meet in person—which I thought was strange.

I felt a flicker of suspicion. Why would he want to meet in person if he just had a few more questions? I already told him that I didn't know anything about Owen's business, and that wouldn't have changed.

As soon as we disconnected the call, my phone rang. I recognized the number. It was my neighbor. When I answered, he sounded concerned, and I could tell something was wrong.

"Matt, is everything okay? There are about a dozen black cars parked outside your house, and they look like law enforcement. The front of your house looks crazy. Your driveway is filled with black government cars, as if they were investigating a bombing!"

In that instance, I realized that Agent Speidel was misleading me—trying to manipulate things. He didn't want to talk with me, or ask me questions. He wanted to lure me into something or other, or catch me. Although I'd taken a big loss in Las Vegas, I still had close to $100k with me, and both Rachel and I were wearing some valuable jewelry. To protect Rachel, I parked my car at a local restaurant, and told her to stay with the vehicle and our valuables. Then I walked to our house.

My oldest daughter, Lauren, was alone at the house. Before I left Las Vegas, we agreed that she'd meet me there, and then we'd go out to spend our afternoon together. While I walked to the house, I called Lauren to check in.

"Hey sweetie, how are you doing?"

"I'm okay." I could tell from her tone that she wasn't okay.

"Are some people there waiting for me?"

"Yes. What's going on?"

I took a deep breath. "It's going to be okay. Let them know that I'm on my way."

I didn't know what would happen.

As soon as I walked into the gated community, a team of agents swarmed me, like bees returning to the hive. They immediately searched me, then cuffed me and escorted me to the front door. I didn't protest at all. Once we got in, they asked where I kept the money, and I told them the safe, which I opened for them. Once it was open, the agents started to unload all the cash I had on hand. They counted out just under $1 million.

To my surprise, Agent Speidel then stepped in to make an offer, which I didn't expect. If I signed an abandonment form to release any claim I had to the money, and if I agreed not to hire an attorney, he said that his entire team would clear out. They'd leave without asking questions, filing charges, or arresting me.

I told him that I would need a little bit of cash to take care of my family. He offered to leave me with a few thousand dollars, and I agreed. I'd simply have to take the loss and move on.

Owen wasn't as fortunate. A few months after the agents visited me, they arrested him, under much different circumstances. The government's press release insinuated that, in addition to booking bets, he led a violent international drug trafficking enterprise.

I knew Owen was a charismatic guy, a fellow bookmaker. He wasn't averse to partying with drugs, but I considered him a friend that I could count on any time I wanted to gamble on sports, or play a round of golf. I didn't know anything about the allegations that he'd been involved with international drug trafficking. The allegations against him kind of shocked me, but I wasn't passing judgment. There had to be more to the story, and in time, I suspected that he'd tell me what was going on.

I understood the importance of law and order, but sometimes it seemed as if things had gone too far. When consenting adults agreed to wager on sports, it didn't seem like the type of serious crime that would warrant a prison term—at least not in my view. With Owen, the consequences would be far more severe.

He eventually pleaded guilty, and the judge slammed him with a sentence that would require him to serve about ten years. Besides losing his liberty, the conviction cost him everything— his properties, his cash, his cars, even his gold. On top of that, he faced a multi-million dollar fine that would hang over his head long after he served his time.

From prison, Owen wrote about how he'd lost everything. I knew him as a high-roller, a guy who didn't think anything about booking private jets, buying exotic cars, or wagering tens of thousands on a single golf shot. With the conviction, he didn't have anything left, and the weight of that loss must've felt crushing.

I did what I could to support him, happily sending money that the prison would put on his books. I wanted to do anything possible to make his time inside a little more bearable. He never asked, but I wanted to help. It wasn't much, but a lifeline. Owen was a big, tough guy, and I didn't have any doubt that he could handle himself while he o served his sentence, but I wanted him to know that he had at least one friend who cared about him.

In early 2024, nearly a decade after his arrest, I got word that his time inside had come to an end. Authorities were transferring Owen from a federal prison in Colorado to a halfway house in Van Nuys. He didn't have anything, so I picked out the latest leisure wear and sent him a care package with some cash to tie him over.

As I made the drive up from Orange County to Van Nuys to see him for the first time in over 10 years, all kinds of thoughts were spinning in my mind. On one hand, I looked forward to seeing Owen and catching up after so many years. I wanted to learn more about what he'd gone through, not only because he was a friend and I was interested, but for selfish reasons as well—as I wanted to learn more about the possibility of what could be in store for my future. I had an undercurrent of unease, a nagging sense that my own legal troubles were far from over.

During those years that Owen served in prison, my bookmaking business had grown exponentially. Had he gotten out a year earlier, I could have done more to ease his transition back into society. It wouldn't have been any problem to provide necessary capital for him to get a clear start with a new business. I'd done that with the jiu-jitsu studio, and with several other businesses. I gladly would have stepped up for Owen, or done something to get him on his feet.

A lingering anxiety clouded my thoughts as I continued on with my drive. The news about Shohei Ohtani and his translator seemed to be a growing scandal, keeping my name in the news, with reporters continuing to hound me for information. Just as they had done with Owen, I suspected that the feds were building a case against me, piecing together evidence from anywhere they could find.

I hadn't forgotten my earlier experiences with Special Agent Speidel. Clearly, the government could be stringing me along again—leading me to believe that we could work through these matters when, in all likelihood, they had their own agenda—and it wasn't about giving me a soft landing. I felt like that character lying strapped to a bed, with a descending blade swinging from a pendulum above his neck. He knew that he had to escape, but while strapped down, he couldn't do anything but wait for matters to play out.

My lawyer, Diane Bass, had warned me that even with her best efforts, I likely would face some sort of criminal charge. House arrest, she said, would be the best-case scenario, but she couldn't guarantee anything, and the uncertainty kept eating away at me. She didn't have any idea whether a judge would penalize me financially, or how much of a fine he would impose. A criminal conviction and the loss of liberty would be tough to stomach. At 49-years-old, I couldn't imagine what it would be like to lose everything. What would I do if the judge required me to forfeit my assets? With a wife, and five children, I had many responsibilities on my shoulders.

As I navigated the streets of Van Nuys, I couldn't help but feel a pang of guilt. Here I was in a $100,000 SUV, pulling up to visit my friend who'd just been released from prison and had lost everything. I pushed down thoughts that I could ever be in his predicament. To break free from the thoughts, I reminded myself that the only allegations against me were of bookmaking, money laundering and falsifying my tax returns by not declaring all my income. It wasn't as if I was facing the type of serious crimes that Owen pleaded guilty to committing—drug trafficking and making terrorist threats

The halfway house, a nondescript building in a grimy part of town, looked more like a warehouse than a residence. It was a far cry from the luxurious lifestyle Owen and I had once enjoyed, a stark reminder of how quickly fortunes could change in this business.

Owen got my text and came out smiling, looking giddy, grateful for the small window of time we'd have together. As he strapped into the oversized SUV, he told me about all the hurdles he had to go through to get permission for a four-hour social pass that would allow us to hang out from 10 until 2. We drove to a nearby Starbucks, and after we ordered, sat down in a quiet place to drink coffee and reminisce about old times.

"It's good to see you brother," I said. To ease his anxiety, I passed him an envelope with $5,000 in cash. "It's not much, but I wanted to make sure you had some walking-around money. I wish I could give you more," I shrugged.

Owen's eyes widened as he peeked inside the envelope, seeing the stack of crisp $100 bills. "Shit, Matt, this is too much. You didn't have to do this, but I sure appreciate you."

I waved off his protests.

"You were the only person I could count on while I was inside. I really appreciate this, and I'll get you back as soon as I get on my feet."

"You're getting out when I'm in the middle of a pinch myself," I told him.

"What do you mean?"

I filled him in on the raid of my residence last fall, the Ohtani scandal, and the potential criminal charges that could be coming.

"Damn, Matt, I didn't have any idea," he said, shaking his head. "I mean, I saw some of the headlines about Ohtani and his interpreter, but I was so caught up with getting out of prison that I didn't read the articles and didn't know that you were caught up in all that."

I shrugged, trying to project a calm that had been missing ever since I started my drive up to see him. "It is what it is, man. We all know the risks when we get into this business."

Owen leaned forward, his eyes intense. "Listen, I know it seems bad now, and these feds ain't no joke. But you're a smart guy, and you don't have the baggage that weighed me down. They'll probably offer you house arrest. Don't ever think that you'll go through what happened to me."

I wanted to believe him, to take comfort in his words, but the gnawing uncertainty remained. "I hope you're right, Owen. I really do. But I can't help but feel like I'm just waiting for the other shoe to drop."

We sat in silence for a moment, both lost in our own thoughts. Finally, I spoke up with curiosity. "I still don't understand how they built a case against you. I mean, the government's press releases about drug trafficking blew me away."

"You and everyone else," he said.

As it turned out, ghost writers and movie studios had taken an interest in Owen's story. Amazon had already begun to develop "*The California Kid: From USC Golden Boy to International Drug Kingpin.*" Mark Wahlberg played a role in producing the documentary, which was scheduled to go on the air sometime around the start of the 2025 football season.

"I'm spending a lot of my time these days working on the movie project, helping writers craft the story of my life. It's surreal, you know? Reading lines of my life that a professional actor will play on film."

I nodded, trying to imagine what it must be like to have a life story that attracted the attention of Hollywood. "That's incredible, Owen. I'm sure it's going to be a hit. But what about after the documentary? What do you see yourself doing once you're released from the halfway house?"

Owen took a sip of his coffee, considering the question. "Well, I don't get out until June of 2025, so I've got some time to figure it out. But I've been thinking about maybe trying to build a career as an influencer, you know? Like Wes Watson."

The name rang a bell, but I couldn't quite place it. "Wes Watson? Is that the guy who did a bunch of prison time and now makes videos about his experience?"

"Yeah, that's him," Owen confirmed, a note of admiration in his voice. "He served like ten years, and he came out totally ripped, like a bodybuilder. Now he's got this whole brand, selling merch and doing motivational speaking gigs. I think I could do something similar, use my story to inspire people and earn some money in the process."

Owen certainly had a compelling story to tell, and with the buzz around the documentary, he'd have a built-in audience. But as I listened to him talk, I couldn't help but feel that something was off.

Here was a guy in his early 40s, starting over from scratch with nothing to his name but a half-formed plan to become a social media star. It was a long way from the high-flying lifestyle he'd once enjoyed, the private jets and exotic cars and six-figure golf bets.

"For now, I'm just trying to help the writers get the story down. I've been sharing everything, including the good times we had."

I imagined audiences would love to watch Owen's story, especially with the possibility of an A-list star like Mark Wahlberg playing his role. When it came out, he expected the documentary to highlight his transition from student athlete, to building a business that put him into contact with professional athletes, celebrities, porn stars, and Las Vegas. I didn't know what he intended to reveal, but when he said that he wanted to include some stories about our past experiences, I encouraged him.

"Use anything you want, anything that will help you get back on your feet," I told him.

"The writers liked the stories about you and Doug Reinhardt," he laughed, "especially about the Escalade."

The mention of Doug Reinhardt's name brought a flood of memories rushing back. Many years ago, Owen had invited Doug to join us for a round of golf at Strawberry Farms, a picturesque course nestled in the rolling hills of Irvine. Doug was a local celebrity who had a role on a hit television show, *The Hills*, which profiled wealthy high school students from Laguna Beach.

Doug was also a gifted athlete with a massive following in Orange County. He had turned down a baseball scholarship at USC to sign with the Los Angeles Angels, but an injury had cut his professional career short. Still, his chiseled good looks and high-profile social life kept him in the pages of celebrity magazines.

As we warmed up on the driving range, Owen and I set our usual wager. We were both big on "skins," a game where each hole had a set value, and the player with the lowest score on a given hole won the pot. If there was a tie, the money would carry over to the next hole, raising the stakes with each passing shot. By the end of a typical round, Owen and I would be settling up bets that often climbed into the six-figure range.

Doug, with his competitive streak still burning hot from his days as a pro athlete, couldn't resist the lure of the action. He had a long history of betting with Owen on everything from college football to the NBA, and he was itching to get in on our game. Never one to back down from a challenge, I agreed to a side bet with Doug: $1,000 per hole, on top of the skins game I already had going with Owen.

From the moment we teed off, I could tell that Doug was a chaser. I'd seen his type plenty of times in the casinos—the kind of gambler who would keep doubling down, trying to recoup his losses, no matter how deep the hole got. During undisciplined moments in my past, I've been in that same situation, trying to make bets to catch up on losses.

When we get off our strategy, we might start with a $100 bet on a blackjack hand, then double to $200, $400, and before long, we're throwing down $4,000 on each hand. We're convinced that luck would turn our way. For guys with deep pockets and easy access to cash, it could work out sometimes. Yet even then, that strategy could backfire. It doesn't take long to reach the table max limit. And that's where a person gets trapped. A gambler can't chase any longer because the casino rules prohibit him from doubling down.

Owen had told me that Doug's father was a prominent businessman. He owned a large frozen food company, and money would never be an issue for him.

As the round wore on, my game was on fire. I was hitting fairways and greens with machine-like precision, and by the time we reached the 17th hole, I was doing pretty good for a guy with an 18 handicap. I'd never perfected the game of golf, but when playing for money, I seemed to play better. For some people, putting money on the line gets them rattled. Their nerves start to eat them up and they can't concentrate on the swing. They can't even breathe well to take in the moment, because they're nervous. For me, the pressure seemed to make me play better. I was used to it, and I used it as an edge.

Doug was in the red to me for $34k. Now, don't get me wrong—for a guy like Doug, that kind of money wouldn't change his lifestyle. But nobody liked to lose, no matter how much they were worth. For some guys, it wasn't about the money at all — it was about pride, about saving face. Losing a bet could feel emasculating. And the more they lost, the more desperate they got to win it back.

That's exactly what happened with Doug. As we stepped up to the 17th tee box, a short par-3 with a tricky green, he turned to me with a wild look in his eye. "Let's go all in," he said, his voice tight with a mix of frustration and bravado. "Double or nothing, $68,000 on this one shot."

I couldn't help but grin. I was already up $34,000, so I didn't have anything to lose. And my swing had been pure all day—I knew I could stick it close. Doug, on the other hand, was letting his emotions get the best of him. His hands were shaking as he teed up his ball, his jaw clenched tight.

"You sure you want to do this, Doug?" I asked, trying to give him an out. "We can just play it out, call it a day."

But he shook his head stubbornly. "I'm good for it," he insisted, pulling out his keys and dangling them in front of me. "I've got a brand new Escalade Hybrid, fully loaded. That's my bet. You win, it's yours."

I had to admit, it was a tempting offer. I'd never driven a hybrid before, and shook my head in agreement as I thought of sporting the new ride. I accepted the bet, and stepped up to the tee.

The 17th hole at Strawberry Farms is a beauty — a short par-3, just 160 yards from the back tees, but with a narrow green surrounded by bunkers and thick rough carrying it over a ravine. It was almost an island green per say. It's the kind of hole that can make or break a round. But even with $68,000 on the line, I didn't feel any pressure.

Doug, still shaking with nerves and frustration, insisted that I hit first. I think he thought it would rattle me. Obviously it's a slight advantage to going second. Going second lets the player address how aggressive to be. It can also backfire, especially if the person going first hits a great shot.

By then, I thought Doug would've been able to see that I thrived when stakes were highest. The bigger the bet, the calmer I'd get. So I stepped up to the ball, took a deep breath, and let it rip.

It was one of the purest shots I've ever hit. The ball took off like a rocket, piercing through the air on a perfect line toward the flag. It landed softly on the green, just a few feet from the hole, and rolled to a stop no more than three feet from the cup. It was literally a tap in birdie. Tiger would have been proud to make that shot.

I turned to Doug, trying to keep the smirk off my face. "Looks like you're going to need a hole-in-one to beat that bud," I said, my voice tinged with false sympathy.

Doug's face turned red. He stepped up to the ball, his hands gripping the club so tightly I thought he might snap it in half. He took a wild swing, and the ball rocketed off the tee — but instead of soaring toward the green, it sliced hard to the right, disappearing into the thick brush that lined the fairway.

Doug let out a stream of curses, slammed his club into the ground, then stomped off toward the cart, muttering under his breath about how he was done with gambling, done with golf, done with everything. He didn't want to bet on the 18th hole.

I almost felt bad for the guy.

Doug didn't have the car with him that day, as he had ridden to the course with Owen. So we agreed to meet up a few days later at the Monarch Beach Golf Club to settle the bet with another round. I got a ride to the course and looked forward to seeing Doug and Owen again. As we played, my game was quite as good as I played at Strawberry Farms, but my game was good enough to stick him for another $12k.

As the valet brought the cars around, I saw him loading Doug's clubs into the back of the Escalade. "Those go in the Range Rover," I called out, pointing to Owen's ride. The valet froze, a confused look on his face.

"But sir, doesn't the Escalade belong to Mr. Reinhardt?" he asked, gesturing to the Cadillac.

I smiled, shaking my head. "Not anymore, it doesn't," I said.

Owen tossed him the keys to the Rover.

I told the valet to load my clubs into the Escalade. "Mr. Reinhardt's clubs will go in the Range Rover with Owen's."

Doug looked like he was about to be sick as I climbed behind the wheel. To his credit, he honored the bet, and we've been friends ever since.

As Owen and I sat there reminiscing, I couldn't help but think about how much had changed since those carefree days on the links. With the legal hammer about to come down on me, I could only hope that Doug would step up and maybe help Owen get back on his feet as he tried to rebuild his life.

In all my years of gambling, I learned that we couldn't count on success forever. You could be riding high one moment, only to find yourself in a hole so deep you couldn't even see the sky. All you could do was keep playing the game, keep pushing forward, and hope that luck would be on your side when it mattered most.

As we continued our afternoon together, the conversation flowed freely. But even as we laughed and joked, I couldn't shake the nagging sense of unease in the pit of my stomach. Looking at Owen,

I saw a man who had once had the world at his fingertips, only to watch it all slip away in the blink of an eye. When I saw him last, before news broke about his arrest, he was young, rich, and ripped, surrounded by a lifetime of excitement. As much as I wanted to believe that my own story would have a different ending, I knew there weren't any guarantees.

Owen and I got to talking about how the feds had started to build a case against me. He wanted to know what initially prompted them to raid my house last fall.

I told him about Wayne Nix. Both Owen and I had a history of gambling with Wayne, another successful bookmaker who ran an online site, SandIslandSports.com. The Oakland A's had drafted Wayne straight out of high school. Wayne never got called up to the majors from the A's farm team, but he made a name for himself as a sportsbook for professional athletes and celebrities. He had a good name as a person who always paid bets on time.

From the grapevine, I heard various stories of how the feds got turned on to Nix. Allegedly, one of Nix's agents got charged with a crime. I heard that the agent bargained his way into a lighter sentence and avoided other personal problems by agreeing to reveal everything he knew about Nix's sportsbook operation. That discussion led authorities to raid Wayne Nix's house in Newport Coast back in February, 2020.

As I've learned, once federal investigators suspect criminal wrongdoing, they start following leads, eager to expand. The Nix investigation may have begun with bookmaking, but it expanded into Las Vegas casinos and the role they played in allowing bookmakers to launder money.

Owen nodded knowingly. "Yeah, that sounds about right. Once they start pulling on a thread, they don't stop until they've unraveled the whole sweater."

"Exactly," I said, leaning back in my chair. "So they started investigating the casinos, which led them to guys like Scott Sibella at MGM and Resort World. And somewhere along the line, they must've found a connection to me."

At the mention of Sibella's name, Owen's eyes widened. "Oh shit, didn't you have some kind of run-in with him back in the day? Something about a cabana girl?"

I laughed at the memory.

Once I separated from Monica and my brother bought my interest in the brokerage firm we started, I had a lot more liberty. I visited Las Vegas more frequently. Leslie, who had been my host at New York, New York, took a position at MGM Resorts International. To keep my loyalty with her, I made the Mirage my casino of choice for the majority of my trips to Vegas going forward.

Since I'd routinely splurge with big orders and big tips during day trips to the casino's pool, I got to know all the cabana girls, who were stunningly beautiful. They survived on the money guys like me would give. A new hire at the pool, Rachel, caught the eye of every player at the Mirage, and even some of the casino bosses. She was a total knockout, who'd recently moved to Las Vegas from Kansas City, Kansas. At only 22 she didn't know anyone in town, but every guy wanted to get to know her.

As a high roller, I got a lot of perks at the casino, and no one objected when Rachel focused most of her attention on my cabana. We started hanging out, even after her shift ended. I invited her to join me at Jet, the hottest nightclub of the Mirage.

We sat in the VIP section, where tables went for $10 to $20 grand each. I saw Scott Sibella at the table next to us, along with several other casino executives, including Ron Elwood. I was drinking, having a great time with Rachel, who was one of the most attractive girls there.

I excused myself to use the men's room, and while I was away, Ron thought he spotted an opportunity to make a move. Besides being one of Sibella's buddies, Leslie assigned him as my backup host. If she wasn't in, I could call Ron to set me up with whatever I needed, like more credit, or reservations, whatever I needed. Yet when I went to the men's room, I told Owen, Ron tried to put a move on Rachel. He said that the casino executives would be hosting a private party in one of the villas, and he invited her to come if she wanted to hangout.

Owen let out a low whistle. "Damn, that takes some balls. I'm guessing you didn't take too kindly to that?"

"Hell no, I didn't," I said, shaking my head. "I mean, I get it, Rachel was a total knockout, but you don't make a move on another guy's girl like that, especially when he's a big player at your casino."

I didn't hear about Ron's move until Rachel and I had gone back to my villa. When she told me that he had hit on her, I got livid.

Despite Rachel's pleas to let it go, I called Ron and said I needed to see him. He likely anticipated that I'd need more credit. I asked him to meet me outside the club, in front of Kokomo's, the restaurant. I intended to have a little chat about respect.

"Oh shit," Owen said, leaning forward eagerly. "What happened?"

"I took a swing at him," I said simply, shrugging my shoulders. "I mean, I was pretty wasted at the time, so I missed his jaw and didn't hit anything but air. But I managed to grab him by the shirt and launch him over the railing into this little stream they had running through the restaurant. It was actually kind of hilarious, seeing him flailing around in the water in his expensive suit."

Owen burst out laughing. "Holy fuck, Matt, I heard about that, but I wish I could have seen the look on his face."

I laughed, enjoying the memory myself. "Yeah, it was pretty priceless. But of course, casino security showed up about two seconds after I got back to my room. They kicked me out, and I had to go check into the Wynn for the night."

Leslie called me the next day to see what had happened. When I told her everything, she said that she was going to set up a meeting with Sibella and his team. He wanted to ban me from the casino, but she didn't want to lose my account and would try to smooth things over. I had some leverage on my side.

"Oh yeah? What kind of leverage?"

"Well, as things turned out, I had a $250,000 balance in outstanding markers with the casino at the time. While Sibella tried to berate me about the raucous I caused in the casino, and attacking one his employees, I told him to do what he thought was best, because I was in talks with lawyers who were about to bring a case against them on

Rachel's behalf for sexual harassment, since Ron was technically an employee of the casino."

Owen's eyes widened in appreciation. "Damn, son, good for you. So what happened?"

"Sibella and his guys softened up as soon as I mentioned the lawsuit," I said, smirking slightly at the memory. "They said they'd discipline Ron and settle my markers for half the amount, as long as I agreed to stay away from the MGM properties for a year. It wasn't ideal, but it beat getting arrested or having to actually hire a lawyer."

For a moment, it felt like old times, like we were just two friends swapping war stories over coffee. But then the reality of our situations came crashing back in, and the laughter died .

"Listen, man," I said, "it's almost 2:00 pm. This thing is almost behind you and we don't want any problems that might block you from getting future weekend passes. Let me get you back."

As we said our goodbyes, I felt a heavy weight settling on my shoulders. Driving back to Orange County, my mind was a tangle of conflicting emotions. On one hand, I was grateful for the opportunity to reconnect with Owen, to offer him some support and encouragement as he navigated this new chapter in his life. But on the other hand, I couldn't ignore the parallels between his situation and my own.

While waiting for the situation to play out, I'd continue reflecting on the past that got me here, going forward one step at a time.

CHAPTER 9
Damage Report

Following my divorce from Monica, back in the early 2000s, I didn't intend to begin a second family. I'd been enjoying a bachelor's lifestyle, commuting between Orange County, Las Vegas, with frequent gambling excursions to casinos around the world, from Monte Carlo to the Bahamas.

Rachel, whom I began dating after my divorce from Monica, quit working in the casino so she could accompany me on most of my gambling trips, which were always fun. We especially enjoyed our trips to Atlantis, the resort and casino on Paradise Island.

By getting Rachel away from Las Vegas, I could lavish her with the high roller's life. Upon our arrival at Atlantis, my host would usher us into a sprawling suite overlooking the crystal-clear, translucent waters of the Bahamas, at the Cove, a high-roller enclave at the Atlantis resort. More of a penthouse than a room, my suite in Atlantis had floor-to-ceiling windows, a private balcony, and a butler at our beck and call. Each day began with a lavish breakfast spread delivered to our room, and for dinner, if we didn't dine in our favorite restaurants, Nobu and Carmines, a private chef would prepare gourmet dishes from around the world.

As we walked through the buzzing casino floor, I heard the familiar bells of slot machines chiming and cards shuffling, contributing to the electrifying experience that got me in the mood to gamble. Staff greeted me by name, expecting that I'd put millions of dollars on the line over a weekend.

Rachel and I had a great relationship for several years. On November 20, 2010, we celebrated the birth of my fourth daughter, Sage. We did our best to raise Sage together, but it soon became clear that we were not on a path as a couple that would last forever. Although we've found our balance, and we get along great now, our initial separation endured some rough patches. I'm grateful for the mother Rachel has been to our daughter. For the past several years, I've provided resources so they could live near my home in San Juan Capistrano; Sage spends half the week with me, and half the week with her mom.

Sage is now 14. Since kindergarten, she's been attending the prestigious St. Margaret's Episcopal School. Seeing Sage excel has been a profound experience. As a child, I went through public schools in Orange County, and the contrast from St. Margaret's couldn't be starker. The school she attends looks more like a university than a primary school, with a picturesque and expansive campus that spans 25 acres. From pre-kindergarten to twelfth grade, the students get to study in modern classrooms with state-of-the-art facilities that cater to a wide range of academic and extracurricular activities.

Among its notable facilities, St. Margaret's has a performing arts center and the DeYoung Family Math and Science Center. The performing arts center includes the Hurlbut Theater which supports the school's strong emphasis on music, dance, and acting. Additionally, the campus includes two gymnasiums and athletic fields, reflecting the school's commitment to fostering community and wellness among students.

From the first time I walked onto the lush green fields, I wanted Sage to attend school there. By participating in parent-teacher nights, I got to know the other parents, many of whom led lives that were very different from mine. They worked as physicians or business leaders, and they wanted their children to get the best educational opportunities—which both Rachel and I wanted for Sage. She has grown into a capable young athlete and scholar, giving me high hopes for her future.

Over the years, she's grown close to her classmates, participating with them on the track team, and also on the volleyball team. I've been honest with all my children, sharing all that was going on since authorities raided my house. But once the news cycle began its relentless coverage of the gambling scandal that included Ippei Mizuhara and Shohei Ohtani, it hit my children hard—especially Sage.

Newspapers, magazines, and television stations were relentless in their coverage of the case. Sage began asking whether it was possible that I'd have to go to jail. My older children, Lauren, Haley, and Brooke, were all in their 20s and they were mature enough to cope with the predicament I'd placed my family in; my son Kingston was only three-years-old. But Sage was in the seventh grade, a time when everything seems to have life-changing implications. She worried how my problems could potentially spill into her life.

"Dad, are they going to kick me out of school because of you?"

No parent wanted to hear a child ask such questions. But I'd put myself in this situation, and I would have to deal with the fallout. Rather than lying to her, or sugarcoating my problems, I told her the truth.

"It's possible. I don't think I'll go to prison, but I can't really tell what's going to happen. One thing I can promise is that we'll always be a family, and we'll get through this challenge together. I'm going to do the best that I can."

I hoped that I'd be able to find a solution that would keep Sage at St. Margaret's. Tuition costs alone exceeded $45,000 per year. With all the extras, I'd been paying much more than that annual tuition since she was in kindergarten. Further, I had three other daughters and a son I had to support. Those expenditures didn't bother me when I had a seven-figure weekly cash flow, but those days were likely gone. When it came to earnings, I didn't have any idea what to expect going forward.

In April of 2024, I boarded a flight for Utah with Rachel and Sage so she could participate in a club volleyball tournament with some of her teammates from St. Margaret's. They were striving to advance their national ranking. As I made the flight, I wondered how the coaches and other parents would react to the news about my case. It would be the first time that I'd seen any of them since the stories began to break, describing me as the bookmaker associated with the Shohei Ohtani scandal.

After settling into the hotel, we joined the team for a big meal the school had coordinated at an Italian restaurant. About 50 people joined us in the private room, with coaches, assistant coaches, parents, and all the players. I felt a huge elephant in the room, so I decided to address the matter head on with the coaches.

"I don't know whether you're aware of it, but my name has been in the news a lot."

"Oh yes, we've seen them," one coach said. "We're sorry for what you're going through."

"Some of the reports are true, some are not. The truth is, I've been a bookmaker, and I got into some trouble. I'm dealing with it, but I want you to know that the troubles have been bothering Sage, consuming her. I wanted to apologize for the distraction."

The coaches thanked me for being candid. "We appreciate your honesty. Don't worry about Sage. She's in good hands at St. Margaret's and we'll look out for her."

When the bill came for the entire meal, I paid it, grateful to have support from the St. Margaret's community.

After flying home, I only had a day before my wife Nicole and I would take off for the Bahamas for a much needed family vacation. Had I known that ESPN would break a national story that kept my name in the news, I would not have been going on the trip. Sometimes, it's hard to back away from our previous decisions.

Despite my precarious financial situation, I wasn't about to disappoint my family. Nicole and I had already invited our son's nanny, Esthere, to join us. Kingston was only three and although he had joined us on countless trips to Las Vegas, he'd never been on a real vacation. We looked forward to watching him play on the white sand, and swim in the clean, warm waters of the Bahamas. We also invited my daughter, Brooke, who would join us with her friend Alex, from the University of Oregon. I booked a penthouse suite, which included a connecting suite for Booke and her friend.

Besides our family, my friend Ryan Boyajian hit me up with a request to join us for the Bahamian vacation.

I'd met Ryan more than twenty years earlier, when he worked as a mortgage broker. He helped me secure financing for a house I wanted to purchase. We'd become friends through the process, even though I was astounded at the fees he charged to coordinate financing. Ryan hadn't been a gambler when we met, but when he learned about my business, he started to get excited about betting on sports. His growing string of losses more than replenished what I'd overpaid in mortgage origination fees.

Ryan also began to accompany me on my trips to casinos. I gave him pointers on how to win at table games such as Baccarat and Blackjack. But giving pointers to someone didn't mean a person would develop the skills to play at a high level. Like most people who spend too much time in casinos, Ryan lost money. Besides being a friend and part of my entourage, my trust in him meant that he could be of service as well.

I introduced Ryan to the casino hosts that looked out for me, and they set him up with his own credit lines. He wasn't at any risk. Although he had to sign for the credit lines, we had a mutual understanding that I was bankrolling him. It was kind of like a money-management system, allowing me to circumvent the table limits. I'd bet to the limit, and then I could instruct Ryan on how to bet. If his bets went the wrong way, he knew that I'd make him whole. Plus, he'd get all the comps, as if he were the man—which he liked.

This arrangement benefited us both.

With an insatiable appetite to gamble, and an ability to use profits from my bookmaking business to cover losses, I could make up for any amount that I lost, even the losses that accumulated on Ryan's credit line. The more we gambled on his account, the more the casinos would lavish comps for perks he could use in the casinos. It didn't take long before the casinos considered Ryan a high roller, and he was the kind of guy who craved that kind of attention.

Like anyone else who'd experienced it for the first time, Ryan appreciated the accommodations. Our relationship grew closer, as did our business arrangements. If he needed cash, I would step up to help him in an instant. Likewise, if clients wanted to send funds through a major bank, Ryan would willingly step up to accept those funds on my behalf. I needed to have that kind of arrangement because all the major banks, including Wells Fargo, Chase, and Bank of America had fired me—telling me to get my money out of their institutions. He'd do anything necessary to get those funds back to me. That arrangement would later bring Ryan some complications.

When I told him that I'd booked a vacation for my family to celebrate my 49th birthday in the Bahamas, he asked whether I'd mind if he and his girlfriend, Jennifer, could come along with us.

Ryan and Jen loved the sun and getting away. We lived in the same gated community of Orange County. Nicole and I enjoyed hanging out with them. Once the story broke about my case, Atlantis prohibited me from gambling there. Yet I could count on Ryan to help out. He didn't have any problem with the casino, so I told him it would be great for him to join us. Based on our long betting history, he had established a large credit line. We'd find a way to use those resources for our mutual benefit—again, no risk to him, only upside, because if the bets went the wrong way, he'd be able to count on me to cover.

For the past few years, Ryan had begun to appear alongside his girlfriend on the *Real Housewives of Orange County.* The popular reality show offered a look into the dramatic lives of several women who resided in the affluent, gated communities of Orange County. Besides showcasing shopping sprees, plastic surgery, gossip, and lavish lifestyles, the producers were on the constant lookout for people in crisis. Those stories would make the people more relatable to viewers.

Jennifer and my wife Nicole had been friends for several years. With Nicole's stunning good looks, the producers saw her as a natural candidate to join the cast of the show. Once they learned about the privacy of our elaborate home, with its resort-style backyard, they started pitching us with the idea of participating.

Although Ryan enjoyed the Hollywood spotlight, and Nicole would've been great on the show, it wouldn't be a good fit for me. As a bookmaker, being on a popular television show could potentially complicate my business.

Things had changed with the breaking news about Shohei Ohtani wiring $16.2 million to "an associate" of an Orange County bookmaker. Once the television producers learned that Ryan Boyajian had been the recipient of millions in wire transfers from Shohei Ohtani's account, they saw the potential for a new story line. They liked the idea of high stakes gambling, and began courting Nicole even more to join the cast, anticipating that my upcoming legal proceedings would bring more of the drama they liked. Gossip would follow, as the women would speculate about what it's like to date a Vegas high roller who was also charged with a crime. We'd be like a car fire on the highway. Millions of viewers could watch as our life potentially blew up in flames.

Ironically, the idea started to make sense. If the feds were going to freeze all my accounts and put me out of business, it might've made sense for Nicole and I to consider signing with the Bravo network. In exchange for a salary that I anticipated would eventually exceed $1 million per season, cameras could follow us around. The publicity could potentially boost Nicole's line of women's athleisure wear, Coco On the Go, which was already spreading across the country with sales from her internet store and wholesale locations.

While in the Bahamas, we intended to discuss more about the pros and cons of signing with the Bravo network. Ryan told me that he intended to use the trip as an opportunity to propose to Jen, which would of course bring out the paparazzi to cover the reality television stars.

Before we headed out on our trip, Nicole surprised me with a birthday dinner. We pulled into the circular driveway of the Monarch Beach Waldorf Astoria Hotel, where I thought it would be the two of us. The attentive valet staff greeted us warmly, opening the heavy doors of our Mercedes AMG G Wagon, then whisking it away. Nicole and I strolled hand-in-hand through the grand entrance, the soft ocean breeze carrying the scent of saltwater and the gentle rustle of palm fronds. I looked forward to a quiet evening as we walked into the resort's opulent lobby, with its gleaming marble floors and elegant chandeliers.

We walked through the lobby to Bourbon Steak, the premier restaurant at the Monarch. It's rich, dark wood paneling and plush, comfortable seating gave the restaurant a sophisticated ambience. Modern art pieces added a touch of contemporary flair to the refined setting. Floor-to-ceiling windows offered stunning, panoramic views of the Pacific Ocean, the sunset casting a mesmerizing orange glow across the water.

The maitre d Lyle escorted Nicole and I into a private dining room, impeccably set with crisp white linens, sparkling glassware, and flickering candlelight creating an intimate and celebratory mood. Nicole had invited 30 of our closest friends and family for the celebratory dinner.

The culinary journey began with the first course, an artfully plated selection of seasonal appetizers that showcased the chef's creativity and commitment to using the finest, locally-sourced ingredients. As the meal progressed, each dish was a testament to the skill and passion of the Bourbon Steak kitchen. From the melt-in-your-mouth, butter-poached steaks to the innovative side dishes and decadent desserts, every bite was a revelation of flavor and texture.

Throughout the evening, the attentive staff ensured that every guest's needs were met, their glasses never empty. The sommelier expertly paired each dish with the perfect vintage from Bourbon's extensive wine list, enhancing the already memorable dining experience. As the night drew to a close, Nicole and I shared a quiet moment, taking in the stunning ocean view and reflecting on the incredible evening - a truly unforgettable birthday celebration filled with love, laughter, and the finest cuisine.

Early the next morning, our entire crew headed to John Wayne Airport for a direct flight to Nassau. Once onboard the plane, flight attendants greeted us warmly, doting on Kingston. The flight was smooth and comfortable. As we approached Nassau, Kingston pressed his face against the window in awe of the turquoise waters below.

It was early evening when warm, humid air greeted us, the sound of steel drums playing in the distance. After gathering our luggage, we made our way to the Atlantis resort. Within a few minutes, the towering pink spires of the Royal Towers came into view, rising majestically against the backdrop of the crystal-clear Caribbean Sea. At the grand entrance, an attentive staff with warm and welcoming smiles made us feel at home.

As a paying guest, my arrival wasn't quite the same as the first time I treated Nicole to a visit. We'd begun dating back in 2015, when I was 40 and she was 28. After several years of leading a bachelor's life, with millions of dollars to splurge, I started to long for something more permanent. I had a client, Mike Imech, who was engaged to a beautiful woman. Mike had been a client and friend for several years. He frequently traveled with me, always bringing his fiancee. They looked so happy and in love. I asked her to introduce me to a friend. From her phone, she showed me a picture of Nicole, and I wanted to hook up. Once I got Nicole's phone number, I started calling. Nicole didn't answer, so I left her voice messages, letting her know that I wanted to meet.

Since Mike and his fiancee had been part of my entourage, they knew that I always traveled first-class, and that casinos pampered me. Like Ryan, Mike even became a surrogate gambler for me, getting his own credit line and placing bets as I directed him. If the casino gave me a limit of $100,000 per hand, I could count on friends like Ryan and Mike. They'd stand on either side of me and bet along with me. As strawman gamblers for me, they got to experience the same benefits of first-class accommodations. Anticipating that Nicole would have heard about our legendary trips, it surprised me that she didn't return my calls.

In pursuit, I went to the Coyote Grill, in Laguna Beach, where Nicole was waitressing. Although she didn't appear interested in me, I was intrigued with her. I asked the hostess to seat me in Nicole's section. When she said that Nicole hadn't come in yet, I offered to wait at a table by myself. I'd buy everything on the menu if I had to, I said, determined to meet her.

She walked into the room, more stunning than the photograph. Reluctant at first, she warmed up and agreed to a date. From that first moment, we hit it off. Nicole came into my life when I was hitting my stride, with my business growing bigger and more profitable than ever.

With more money, I began upping my play, bringing $1 million or more with me on all gambling jaunts. I'd also make sure that friends like Ryan and Mike had money to play. With Nicole by my side, I felt as if I was winning more—but unlike other women who had accompanied me, the money didn't impress her.

A self-made woman from Orange County, she began her studies at Saddleback College, then transferred to the University of Southern California. After earning her degree, she worked in healthcare, then saw an opportunity to become an entrepreneur.

She waitressed at Coyote Grill while simultaneously building an ath-leisure apparel company for women, Coco on the Go. To give her business a boost, without her knowledge, I'd go onto her website and place large orders of leggings and tops for my customers so they could give them away, promoting Nicole's business. She would tell me with excitement of how quickly her business was growing, and I smiled silently, happy to be helping my girl. Of course I always had an angle. The more her business boomed, the more time she'd have to spend with me. I always congratulated her, and I was happy for her success—and mine. Despite the private jets and profligate spending, Nicole respected the value of a dollar and tried to reel in my spending.

This trip we took to the Bahamas, on a commercial flight, was the first time that I'd be paying for a vacation. Rather than being escorted into the resort with a personal host, concierge, and butlers, we went through the process as a regular guest—albeit guests who'd booked the penthouse suite. Alex, Brooke's friend from the University of Oregon, thought the adjoining suite was over the top, but I missed white-glove service that I'd grown accustomed to receiving any time I stepped foot onto a casino property—but that was before the FBI raid, and before my name hit global headlines, and before casinos from around the world joined together in banning me from gambling.

While Nicole got everything set up in our suite, Ryan joined me in scoping out the casino, searching for the best place to start our ruse. In Atlantis, he had a $150,000 credit line. I intended to gamble his resources to recover the costs of our trip. Our surprise dinner at Bourbon's had set me back by nine grand. The hotel had charged $70,000 to my credit card for the penthouse and incidentals. By the time we got back home, I anticipated that I could burn through $100,000. Since none of that would be comped, I intended to replenish my bankroll at the tables, using Ryan's credit.

Staff in the casino would recognize me, which made playing there impossible. The best spot for us would be one of the smaller casinos in the pool area. It didn't have a Baccarat table, which was my preference, but at least I'd be able to sit beside Ryan, guiding him while he played Blackjack. Rather than a birthday celebration, I thought of the trip as a working vacation, and expected to go home with money in my pocket, as I'd done many times before.

As the sun began to set on our first day in the Bahamas, our group met at Carmine's, the resort's famous family-style Italian restaurant. I loved the aroma of garlic, tomatoes, and freshly baked bread. The restaurant's rustic decor, with its exposed brick walls and wooden beams, created a cozy and welcoming atmosphere. The staff, dressed in crisp white shirts and black aprons, welcomed us with warm smiles and led us to our table.

We started with appetizers, grilled shrimp, fried calamari, and caprese salad. For our main courses, we dined family style, with large plates of chicken marsala, eggplant parmesan, and rigatoni alla vodka.

The conversation flowed freely. Ryan and Jen told us about their experiences from their latest adventures on the Real Housewives. Nicole and I knew that Ryan intended to propose to Jen at some point during the vacation, and we expected the paparazzi to snap photos of them. Brooke and Alex shared tales of their college experiences at the University of Oregon. Kingston, ever the energetic three-year-old, entertained us with his infectious laughter and boundless energy. We capped off our first night with a few scoops of gelato, followed by a stroll along the moonlit beach, the sound of the waves and the distant music from the resort's bars creating the perfect backdrop for our first night in paradise.

The next morning, Nicole, Kingston, and I woke early, eager to explore the wonders of the Atlantis resort. The sun, already high in the sky, cast a warm glow over the lush landscaping and the sparkling pools that dotted the property.

We made our way to the beach, the soft, white sand squishing between our toes. The gentle waves lapped at the shore, their rhythmic sound a soothing backdrop to the start of our day.

Kingston and I splashed in the crystal-clear, turquoise waters, the temperature of a warm bath.

After a morning of beach fun, we walked to the poolside cabanas at the famous Cove, where I met up with Ryan to start our gambling adventure. While we played at the tables, Nicole walked with Kingston from one pool to the next, exploring the Mayan Temple Pool, the waterslides, Poseidon's

Pool, and the Rapid River. Later, we intended to take him to The Dig, an elaborate network of underwater chambers and passageways that showcased the resort's incredible marine life.

Ryan began tapping into his credit line, signing markers for $25,000 to start. We had a hard time getting into the groove, as coaching him on how to play a hand wasn't as easy as I anticipated. We had to be cautious so staff wouldn't notice that we were working together, and that didn't work out so well. We won a few hands, lost a few hands. Within a few hours, we'd blown through the first $25,000 and he signed for another. The pattern continued, dropping another $50,000 before the end of the day.

Previously I wrote about my friend Doug Reinhardt being a chaser, doubling down on bets in an effort to recoup from losses. As we returned to the pool the following morning, I began playing as if I were a chaser rather than a professional gambler. With the restrictions hanging over my head, we had to do the best that we could to recover our losses. But things weren't going our way, and they went from bad to worse when Diane, my defense attorney, sent me a text message.

Her text said it all. "In 30 minutes, the Department of Justice will issue a press release on Ippei Mizuhara. It's not going to be good. Call me. It could jeopardize everything."

Despite the gambling losses, we'd been enjoying our vacation. Diane's text put a damper on everything. The press release didn't only implicate me, but Ryan as well. The gambling debts exceeded $40 million, and Ryan's bank account had received more than $16 million in wire transfers toward those debts. When we looked at the wire transfers, they came from Shohei Ohtani's bank account. The press release didn't only mention me as a bookmaker, but alluded to Ryan as my associate.

According to Diane, with media reports about multi-million-dollar payments, her efforts to negotiate a sentence that would include home confinement could evaporate. She suggested that I consider selling our home, or raising cash to repay $16 million that Ippei had wired to pay gambling debts.

I couldn't let news about the case dampen the mood, and insisted on powering forward. It was just another battle, one that I had to get through. I've learned many lessons from gambling, especially on how to remain stoic during challenging times. I pushed news from Diane out of mind and continued working with Ryan through the table games, losing, winning, and losing again. At one point, we'd drawn out his entire credit line, nearly depleting it. We'd begun with well into the six figures, but losses had brought us down to as low as $16,000 in chips at one point. We then hit a small streak, and before it was time for us to check out, we built the account back up, but I still owed $70,000 on the account when our vacation came to an end. I've had worse, but also better in my time. Just part of the game.

After checking out, as we drove back to the airport for our flight home, I started doing mental calculations to assess how much I'd dropped since turning 49. With gambling losses, the vacation had cost me close to $150,000. Somehow, I'd have to build my cash reserves so I could repay Ryan the $70,000 I'd dropped in Atlantis.

At customs, another fiasco. In the Bahamas, US Customs maintains a checkpoint for Americans returning home. As the subject of a criminal investigation, I anticipated additional scrutiny. Nicole, Esthere, and Kingston walked ahead of me and passed through security without any problems. Pulling up the rear, I handed my passport to the agent. He scanned the document, and as expected, he sent me into a backroom for additional screening. The homeland security officer makes a person feel like a two-dollar hooker—no offense to two-dollar hookers! He began interrogating about how long I'd been in the Bahamas, about whether I was transporting anything I needed to declare. I responded politely to his questions.

He did not return the favor.

"How much cash are you carrying?" He asked.

"I have $640 sir."

"That's it?"

"That's all I have."

"You're supposed to be some kind of high roller. Are you sure that's all you got?" His tone is rude and abrasive.

"Sir, I told you that I have $640. That's all I have."

"What about the rest of your party? Are they smuggling your cash for you?"

"I'm traveling with my wife, our three-year-old son, and our nanny. Together they have a total of about $6,000."

"Do you know that cash structuring is a federal crime?"

"I know exactly what cash structuring is, sir. What I don't know is why you're being so rude. I've responded to all your questions, filled out all your forms. We're not carrying more than $10,000, and I'm not obligated to report anything further."

"You must think you're someone important. Sit down and park it for a while, I'm calling all your luggage up for inspection." He then made me call Nicole, Esthere, and Kingston so they could return to customs.

His insolence made me so angry that I wanted to smack him. Once my family returned, he confined us all to a small space, ordering us not to move. I was fuming. Once our luggage arrived, he slowly and meticulously opened every case and started to rifle through our clothing, as if he suspected our family of smuggling drugs.

"What's this?" He pulled out a shell from son's suitcase.

"It appears to be a seashell."

"What are you trying to hide inside of it?"

"I don't know, maybe there's a crab in there?"

"Are you trying to be a wise ass?"

"Sir, may I ask you a question?" I couldn't remember when I'd been so angry, and he could see the rage in my eyes, even though I tried to keep my tone civil. "Why are you being so disrespectful? I've been polite to you, but you continue to harass me. Did bullies pick on you while you were growing up?"

Nicole did her best to calm me down.

A supervisor came by to calm things down. He was kind, as if knowing his subordinate was a dick. He grabbed my identification. "I see you're from Orange County. You seem like a nice guy. I used to live in Anaheim. What do you do out there?"

"I'm a partner in a jiu-jitsu studio."

"Oh yeah," he said. "I've done some training."

"Great! If you're ever out there, come by and see us for a free session." I gave him a card at my gym, then turned to his subordinate. "That goes for you as well." I invited the weasel to come visit us at our jiu-jitsu studio, which he may have taken as an unintentional veiled threat. I would have liked to have gotten him on the mat, and told him that I'd be happy to offer free lessons.

The supervisor chuckled.

"These guys are alright. Let them through."

I would've loved to have grappled with him.

We made the flight, and on the entire way home, the predicament I was in kind of hit me. Fortunately, we had comfortable seats on the Jet Blue airlines seated in their mint first class, which allowed us to recline and sleep. When I got home, I had a call waiting for me from Ryan.

"I got a call from the casino," he said. "I've got to come up with all the money I owe by Tuesday."

Another crisis. Another opportunity to overcome.

CHAPTER 10

Reputation Rehab

Life is filled with complications, like walking a high wire. Our challenge, regardless of age, is to continuously balance and walk to the next opportunity.

At 49-years old, I reflect on the different stages I've had. Growing up in Orange County, I had a normal childhood that groomed me for the life I'd eventually lead. When my father abandoned our family, I had to step up and do anything possible to ease my mother's burdens—it couldn't have been easy for her to raise four adrenaline-filled boys as a single mother. Challenges of youth helped me to learn the importance of developing an insane, self-directed work ethic, how to sell, overcome objections, and serve customers well.

It didn't matter whether I was signing up customers for the Orange County newspaper, figuring out how to support a young family, or building a million-dollar sales force in the commodities business for my friend Micky. Those experiences influenced the growth of my bookmaking business, going from neighborhood bets with my close friends, like Mike Greenberg, to developing relationships with people who were household names, such as Pete Rose, Leonardo

DiCaprio, and Shohei Ohtani—directly and indirectly.

The different stages in life bring challenges. They feel like waves rolling in, one after the other. We can't fight or ignore those challenges. We've got to roll with them, confident in our skill to stay afloat and breathe, regardless of what comes. There will always be more waves, and it's our job to swim through them in the best way we know how.

I know how to work hard, how to keep my cool, and how to gamble. When I face waves, I rely upon those skills, knowing they'll get me to the other side.

When we returned home from our trip to the Bahamas, on the evening of Tuesday, April 16, another wave came my way. Before we could unpack, my buddy Ryan called. He told me that the casinos had given him notice. They required payment in full for the outstanding balance of his account, which hovered around $300,000.

If he didn't clear the balance, the casino managers told him, they would "drop the marker."

When issuing a credit line, casinos require the gambler to sign a document, known as a marker, which authorizes access to a bank account. Usually, a gambler would be in compliance if he paid all debts to the casino within 30 days. The casino could simply use the marker to tap into the bank account. If the account didn't have sufficient funds to cover the debt, the casino would report the gambler to law enforcement for theft, or fraud.

Ryan didn't have anywhere near $300,000 in his bank account. I owed him the money and he had reason to expect me to do whatever was necessary to cover the debt.

Another wave, but nothing I couldn't handle. The pressure may have rocked others, but it wasn't anything that would set me back.

When Nicole and I went to bed, I had other challenges on my mind. My attorney, Diane Bass, had scheduled a meeting with prosecutors who were continuing to investigate my case. I was scheduled to meet with them through a video call the following day, on Wednesday, April 17. Further, I'd charged about $80,000 on my wife's American Express card. These were the waves I'd have to swim through, but they weren't going to keep me from a good night's sleep.

As men, we always have a job to do. We have to take care of our family, doing the work that we've been trained to do. Some men put on a suit and tie, they go from their home, to a car, to a cubicle, and work, like the job I did when working for Micky. Others work in professions, construction trades, retail, or run businesses that provide services or products to customers.

Since becoming a bookmaker, I've dealt with risk. That's been my job. It's the way I've gotten through life. On the morning of Wednesday, April 17, I wouldn't lie in bed with a pillow over my head wondering what I had to do, or wait for anyone to give instructions. I had to get up and go to work. My work may not have required me to leave my home, but I had trained for many years to complete such work, and I had all the confidence in the world that I could get it done.

After the morning rituals with my wife, which was one of the best parts of my day, playing with our boy Kingston in our room while sipping coffee, I dressed in athletic wear then walked to my home office. As I walked by our massive, stunning aquarium that spans the length of the wall leading into my office, I admired the vibrant, fluorescent fish, in a kaleidoscope of colors. They darted and weaved through intricate caves and rock formations, creating a mesmerizing display of underwater life. The vision flashed me back to the translucent waters of the Bahamas, where we swam in more pleasant waves for the past week.

In my office, I felt at home, with the rich, warm tones of dark hardwood shelves that line the walls. Nicole and I have remodeled many of the rooms in our home, giving it a white, beachy, resort feel. Since the sophisticated backdrop of the office felt masculine, with its solid carvings, I kept it as is. In the center, a sturdy desk commanded attention. Built in shelves lined the walls, with a treasure trove of memories, showcasing trophies that commemorate significant casino winnings.

Alongside the triumphs, I framed mementos from unforgettable outings with professional athletes and celebrities, their signed bats, basketballs, and footballs serving as tangible reminders of extraordinary experiences. Perhaps the most striking piece was a framed ticket, displaying an astounding $4.2 million winning bet I placed on a Super Bowl. In the center of it all, was my real trophy, a photograph from my wedding to Nicole, at the famed Pelican Hill resort, in Newport Coast.

I unlocked a drawer to confirm the cash I had on hand. With only fourteen stacks on hand, I wouldn't be able to resolve Ryan's obligation to the casino. Each stack included $100 bills, totaling $10,000. I had another $3,000 that I found in a jacket. With only $143,000, I couldn't satisfy the debt. But I knew one way to grow it into more.

As I settled into my chair, the glow of multiple computer screens illuminating my face, I began my daily ritual of scouring the internet for the most promising bet. I navigated the keyboard to take me through a maze of websites covering sports, statistical databases, and insider forums. Each click brought me closer to the golden nugget of information that would bring the highest prospect for a profitable wager.

By scouring the sea of data, analyzing past performances, injury reports, and weather forecasts, I could hone in on the game I liked best. The numbers swirled in my head as I mentally calculated odds and probabilities. I liked Reid Detmers, the young left-handed pitcher for the California Angels. The Angels were set to face off against the Tampa Bay Rays, a team that had struggled in the past when Detmers took the mound. I delved deeper into the specifics of his performances, noting his impressive strikeout rate and the Rays' lackluster batting average against left-handed pitchers.

As I cross-referenced this information with the current standings and head-to-head records, I decided to bet on the Angels, and more specifically, on Detmers. The Angels were underdogs in this game, which only made the prospect of a bet more enticing. The higher the risk, the greater the potential reward.

With a few more clicks, I confirmed that the Angels had a solid bullpen to back up Detmers and that the Rays' star hitter was mired in a slump. Every piece of the puzzle seemed to fall into place, pointing toward a profitable opportunity.

I had a small challenge in placing the bet. Diane had scheduled a video call with prosecutors for mid afternoon. That meant I wouldn't be able to get away to place the bet. I knew scores of bookmakers, but they wouldn't want to take a

$140,000 bet on a random single baseball game, which meant that I'd have to place multiple bets with individual bookmakers.

Given that Ryan needed the money urgently, I decided to place the bet in Las Vegas. Although the casinos had banned me from playing directly, I could use one of my reliable runners, Brian.

Brian, a gambler who had one time been a betting client, became a trusted runner for me after a family tragedy. He stepped into the role a few years ago, after my brother died.

My brother, Shawn, who had been my best friend and my partner in the commodities business, eventually had to close down the business. His lead source had moved on, and without leads, the business wouldn't stay afloat. Sales people had to depend on commissions, and without leads, they didn't have a prospect of selling. During the best of times, people found it hard to work for my brother because they didn't appreciate his harsh management style. Without leads, his temper grew even worse. I got into a fist fight with him once in the office, which severed our relationship for several years. He lost everything, including his house, and relocated to Arizona, where he tried to resurrect his career by selling cars.

Shawn and I went through several years without speaking, and then he surprised me with a phone call. After we patched things up, he told me that he really wanted to make a change because he hadn't been getting any traction. The only job I could give him was as a runner. I trusted him implicitly, and tasked him with settling accounts for me, delivering or retrieving cash from my clients.

I was happy to welcome him back into my life, and to give him an income stream that would get him back on his feet. All seemed to be going well for him, until he suffered from an unanticipated medical condition that led to his sudden death. A series of fires in California led to bad air quality. That fire pollution had never bothered him before, but in 2018, it was really bad.

We played a round of golf one day in November, and by dinner he started to complain about being short of breath. Later that night, while he lay in bed, he called 911. While talking with the operator, the lack of oxygen going to his brain led to cardiac arrest and he died. It took us all by surprise. I'd been speaking with him daily, and to me, he seemed completely healthy. I couldn't believe that I lost my brother and best friend. His sudden death took a real toll on me, as it was by far the most tragic loss in my life.

When Shawn died so suddenly, I invited Brian to step into the role. Brian had been working as an Uber driver, earning a decent day wage for driving people around. As a runner, he could triple his income. And when I needed to place a quick bet in Las Vegas, I could send him on his way, trusting him to place the bet correctly. If the bet proved a winner, I trusted him to bring me the proceeds.

I called Brian by 7:00 am to let him know that I needed him to drive over to pick up my cash so that he could get on the road to Las Vegas. The instructions were simple. I wanted to put all the money on the Los Angeles Angels to beat the Tampa Bay Rays. He had to get to the casino by early afternoon in order to place the bets on time.

With $143,000 to bet, I had to structure it into two separate wagers. The casino had placed a limit of $50,000 for a single money line bet, with even odds. Odds makers considered the Angels underdogs. Believing in their potential to win the game, I placed $50,000 with even odds, meaning that I stood the potential to double my money.

As soon as we placed that first bet, the casino changed the odds, to -105, making the Angels a slight favorite. With the changed dynamics, I'd have a different context for making the bet. I didn't have a limit at the new price, so I could place the remaining $93,000 on the Angels. For every $105 wagered, I had the possibility of winning $100. Calculating the risk and potential return, I felt confident in my choice.

As long as the Angels won, the second bet could potentially bring me back $181,582, not quite double my money, but close.

I wouldn't be able to watch the game, because of other obligations. If the Angels came through, I expected Brian to bring a total of more than $280,000, getting me closer to the $300,000 I would need to cover Ryan's obligations. Of course, if the Angels lost, Brian wouldn't come back with any money—and I'd have higher waves to swim through. I put the matter out of mind, taking matters one step at a time.

A video call with Diane and the prosecutors came next on the agenda. With all the press, their interest in Shohei Ohtani had grown by a magnitude of 100. During my earlier proffer, when the investigators reviewed records showing the millions that had come from Shohei's account, they didn't have many questions. When I told them the truth, that the bets were mostly on soccer games, they seemed to have lost interest. Once the news broke that Major League Baseball had launched an investigation, the prosecutors wanted more information. Ippei's press release did not do me any favors.

The government released a trove of information, including 70 pages of text messages between Ippei and members of my team. Prosecutors asked me to elaborate on the various people who worked for me, including the agent Ippei spoke about, my friend Mike Greenberg.

I would've liked to have kept Mike's name out of these proceedings. He runs a small business and doesn't need the complications of a government investigation. No one does. We grew up together, discovered a love of sports together, hung out together. He's a complete family man, running a business that employs more than 40 people.

As a gambler, he frequently came across people who wanted an easier way to place bets. Most of those people bet relatively small sums, a few hundred dollars per game. Cumulatively, those small accounts led to tens of thousands in profits for us both each year—which helped us a lot when we were in our 20s.

Through acquaintances, he came across a whale. Out of respect for his family and career, I'll keep his name anonymous. Let's call him John. John's real name is as recognizable as Shohei Ohtani, because people know him as being part of one of the world's most recognizable business families. I'm not saying it's Elon Musk, but you get the picture. He was a BSD in the world of finance and commerce.

A friend of Mike's married into the family of John's wife. For the purpose of this story, we'll give her the name Sheila. Through that relationship, Mike met John. When John learned that Mike could hook him up with an account to place bets easily, it was a simple conversation to set him up with a user ID and password for my website, AnyActionSport. com.

Anticipating his ability to pay, I started John with a total limit of $100,000, giving him the liberty to bet up to $10,000 per game. Quickly, I could see that John had an appetite to play. As I would describe myself, I'd categorize John as a degenerate gambler. He couldn't get enough, losing wager after wager, playing any game, betting on any sport. He'd bet every week, every hour if he found a game. Repeatedly, he'd reach out asking that I increase his credit line.

John was truly a nice guy who had won the gene lottery—being the son of a billionaire, and going on to create his own career with enormous success. Until Mike hooked me up with the Ippei/ Ohtani account, John had bet as high as any of my other high-net-worth clients.

I never considered a guy like him as having an addiction to gambling. He played, he lost, and he paid. At least that was the case for several months. I'd only met him one time, when I flew to New York to settle up on a $2 million debt I owed him. We met at the new Starbucks Reserve, in Chelsea. By the time I got there, some of the games John had wagered on came back as losers. Those new losses meant that I only had to pay him $260,000 to settle, in real time—but I'd been prepared to pay him the full $2 million had he not lost.

Eventually, John placed bets for $100,000 per game. They caught up to him. Within a relatively short span of time, he owed me more than $9 million. Somehow, his wife, Sheila, discovered the amount he owed. Out of the blue, she called me, upset that I'd "let" him gamble with me. As far as I knew, I provided him with a service that he wanted. We were both consenting adults. No one twisted his arm, or even pressed him to bet. Like him, I was also betting. In fact, if his bets had gone the other way, John would've been celebrating $9 million in winnings—but I don't think my wife Nicole would be calling to chastise John.

John's wife was primarily concerned about whether he was in any danger. I assured her that, although the amount was large, these were friendly wagers. John wasn't in any danger. I took him to be a man of his word, just as I was a man of my word. She asked if I'd speak with his attorney.

That was the first time a client's wife had ever called to advocate on behalf of her husband. I agreed to take the call from the lawyer, who told me that he wanted to settle the matter quickly. He wanted to know if I would agree to settle John's $9 million debt with a wire transfer for $6 million.

"I tell you what," I said to the attorney, "why don't you ask John if he would've accepted a $6 million dollar payment from me on a $9 million dollar balance if he had won the bets that he placed. Then let me know what he says."

"You sound like a reasonable person," the attorney said. "This debt is causing John some family problems. I'd like to put it behind us. As a personal favor, I'm asking you to accept a $6 million payment."

I paused for a moment, considering the predicament. I could have continued to haggle with the attorney. But what was the upside? We didn't have a written contract. Ultimately, we trusted each other. With millions on the line, however, trust only goes so far.

"If the $6 million hits my account before close of business today, we'll consider the matter resolved."

"Just one more thing," the attorney said.

"What's that?"

"I need you to promise me that you won't take any more bets from John."

Although I agreed to the condition, it really changed my opinion of things. John wasn't an imbecile. He was a college graduate, and a sophisticated gambler. He ran a multi-billion-dollar business that was known across the world. He didn't strike me as the type of guy who would welch on a bet. But that's the game.

The money hit my account that afternoon. I happily passed my buddy Mike the percentage that we had agreed would be fair for him, and I was glad to know that I played a small role in changing his life in a magnificent way. I walked away with millions, but all that cash got lost in the shuffle.

With my winnings and losses in casinos, I could have multiplied those winnings into $10 million, or turned into a big fat zero.

Either way, I'd be at it again.

Although Mike brought many gamblers, he didn't hit the big time again until he met Ippei. That relationship began because of Mike's friendship with David Fletcher, who played second base and shortstop for the Angels. David had attended Cypress High School. He and Mike hung out, which got Mike into the inner circle of many players with the Angels organization. As my agent, Mike took on many clients, including Colby Schultz, who had played in the minor league teams of the Kansas City Royals, and had been trying to make his way into the Major Leagues.

Once Ippei spoke with investigators about his relationship with Mike Greenberg, David Fletcher, and Colby Schultz, they wanted to hear what I had to say about them. I didn't have anything to offer that they didn't already know. Mike had been my friend from childhood, David had gone to a high school near us, and we got to know Colby because he liked to place bets, and as an agent for me, Mike could set them up with my booking operation.

That was it.

They asked about the commissions that I paid, and I showed the numbers—which could go up to 50% of the net winnings I took in.

Those responses seemed to satisfy prosecutors, and despite Diane's dire warnings about my facing more severe sanctions, the home-confinement deal we'd been working toward seemed to remain intact.

Still, I understood that many more waves had to come.

After my call with Diane, I didn't want to get lost in bad thoughts about what could potentially happen. A gambler like me knows how to push those kinds of thoughts out of our head. I chose to focus on what I could control. While my buddy Brian drove over to Las Vegas to place my bet on the Angels, I had to suit up for a softball game that evening, which I looked forward to playing.

Our team celebrated the victory with Pizza in Newport Beach. As I stood in line to order, I glanced at my phone, disappointed to see that the Tampa Bay Rays were up 4 to 2. Such is life. Nothing I could do about the game. Rather than dwell on the score, I sat down with my friends to enjoy a great night. I didn't look at my phone again until I closed the door to my SUV, getting ready for the drive home. I had a text from Brian. Miraculously, the Angels pulled out a victory, scoring two runs in the top of the ninth inning, and bringing in a 5-4 victory. The casino paid him out, and he was driving back to my house with more than $282,000.

Ordinarily, I'd take that $282,000 and double down. In this instance, loyalty to a friend meant that I'd use the funds, along with the rest that I'd scrape together, to make sure Ryan had the resources to resolve his debts with the casinos. Because that is what friends were supposed to do.

And husbands were supposed to take care of their wives, which is what I looked forward to doing the next day, on Friday, April 19, 2024. Nicole's birthday would be the following week, on April 22. She'd been going through a tremendous amount of stress, all because of the problems that I brought into her life. Even though we'd just returned from the Bahamas, I wanted her to enjoy a place that could bring her some peace—and there wasn't any better place than the Calamigos Ranch in Malibu.

One of my favorite clients, Hugo Marquez, was also a close friend. Several years ago, he told me that his brother, Val, headed operations at the 250-acre resort property and recommended that I treat Nicole there. Ironically, a criminal charge had been hanging over Hugo's head for longer than eight years—and he'd yet to put it all behind him. I hoped that Diane would succeed in resolving my case, but from watching Hugo, I knew it could drag on.

The first time Nicole and I visited Calamigos Ranch, about six years ago, we felt as if we were stepping into a different world. We were only about an hour outside of Los Angeles, but tranquil, natural beauty had replaced the city. Val set us up for a memorable stay.

True to Hugo's word, Val welcomed us with open arms and shared the rich history of the ranch, which began in 1937. The founder, Grant Gerson, described himself as an old cowboy with a vision for a unique rustic experience in Malibu. In developing his business, he had established principles I deeply admired: Reverence, Loyalty, Honesty, Self-reliance, and Sportsmanship. These weren't just words to him; they were a way of life, guiding principles for everything that happened at Calamigos. He said that he'd always be reverent to God, Loyal to country, family, and friends. He'd be honest with himself and his neighbors. He'd be self-reliant, not depending on the government or society to care for him. And he'd always be a good sport, whether he won or lost at anything. Those were principles I could get behind.

It was clear from the start that our visit to Calamigos would be something special.

Val had arranged for Nicole and me to stay in one of the ranch's beautiful bungalows. Nestled among the lush greenery, our bungalow was a haven of peace, with a private patio surrounded by nature, offering us a serene place to relax and connect. The interior was just as impressive, blending rustic charm with modern comforts, and the outdoor rainfall shower was a delightful touch that truly made us feel at one with the surroundings.

But the highlight of our visit was the private dinner Val had coordinated for us on a vineyard. As we walked hand in hand to the dining area, the beauty of Calamigos unfolded before us. The grounds were breathtaking, with whimsical chandeliers hanging from giant oak trees, vineyards stretching into the distance, and little waterfalls that added to the magical atmosphere. The Vineyards, where our dinner was set, was nestled in our own private canyon, surrounded by majestic waterfalls and vineyards. It felt as if Val had designed the intimate setting specially for us, with the soft glow of lanterns and the stars above adding to the romance of the evening.

The meal itself was a culinary delight, featuring ingredients sourced directly from the ranch's gardens and paired with exquisite wines from the local vineyards. We'd never forget the fragrance, the sounds, or the beauty of the experience.

During our stay, we also had the opportunity to explore the private beaches of Malibu, courtesy of the Calamigos Beach Club. A short drive from our bungalow, the Beach Club offered a slice of paradise with its mid-century restaurant lounge, private walkway under the Pacific Coast Highway to the sand, and attentive staff who set up beach chairs and sunshades for us.

Since that first trip six years ago, we have returned a few more times. I once hosted a birthday party for Nicole, inviting several of her friends. This year, given all the stress I'd brought, I thought it would be great to surprise her again. I called Val, and he coordinated reservations for Nobu in Malibu.

From the moment we approached the valet stand, we saw the unmistakable aura of exclusivity, with gleaming sports cars and polished vintage models lined up like jewels. The valets moved with practiced grace, handling each vehicle with the care befitting their high-end pedigrees.

Stepping into Nobu, the atmosphere was electric yet understated—a hallmark of true luxury. The restaurant's design seamlessly blended modern chic with subtle Asian influences, creating an environment that was both inviting and impressive. The panoramic windows offered breathtaking views of the Pacific, setting the stage for an unforgettable dining experience.

The clientele of Nobu Malibu was a who's who of Hollywood and the business elite. The last time we visited, we had spotted John Legend and Chrissy Teigen enjoying a quiet dinner. Their presence had added a special sparkle to the evening, but it was just a typical night at Nobu, where the extraordinary was ordinary.

This visit was no different in terms of star power. As Nicole and I sipped on our wine, a buzz swept through the restaurant. Leonardo DiCaprio and Martin Scorsese, accompanied by two other gentlemen and three bodyguards, made their entrance. The bodyguards, clad in sharp suits and discreet earpieces, scanned the room with an air of casual vigilance. Their presence was a silent testament to the stature of the men they protected.

Despite the usual blend of celebrities and influencers at Nobu, the arrival of DiCaprio and Scorsese created a palpable shift in the room's energy. Guests pretended to focus on their meals, but the allure of such iconic figures was undeniable. When two young fans approached DiCaprio for an autograph, he politely declined, emphasizing his desire to enjoy a private dinner. His response was gracious, yet firm, underscoring the delicate balance celebrities must maintain in public spaces.

Seizing the moment, I penned a quick note to DiCaprio, introducing myself and hinting at the intrigue surrounding my involvement in the Shohei Ohtani betting scandal. We'd previously had a brief encounter when we sat ringside at a UFC fight, which provided a thin thread of connection. Handing him the note, I introduced myself, banking on the slim chance that he might remember me, and he nodded. Nicole watched, amused and impressed by my boldness, as I navigated the delicate social waters of approaching a star of DiCaprio's caliber.

Returning to our table, Nicole's curiosity about my ease with introductions sparked a deeper conversation about ambition and the necessity of facing rejection. It was a trait that had served me well, from winning her heart to navigating the complexities of my career.

Our dinner took a dramatic turn when two overzealous patrons began heckling DiCaprio, loudly invoking "Armenian Power" as they advanced towards him. The situation escalated quickly, but the bodyguards were faster. With precision and decisiveness, they intercepted the hecklers, escorting them out of the restaurant before any further disruption. The swift action of the security team allowed the evening to resume its rhythm, with the remaining guests whispering about the excitement but gradually settling back into the serene ambiance of Nobu Malibu.

As we finished our meal, the earlier drama faded into the background, leaving us with a story to tell about our night among stars and guardians at one of Malibu's most illustrious dining destinations. We returned to our bungalow at Calamigos. The following morning, we walked to the beach club and enjoyed the breeze from the salt water, appreciating the rolling waves. She thanked me for the getaway. When we returned to the ranch, her parents and five other couples joined us. I'd invited them to stay the weekend with us to celebrate Nicole's birthday.

As always, Calamigos gave us the tranquility we needed to recalibrate and recover, and prepare for the next waves—I knew they were coming.

CHAPTER 11
Locked Up Abroad

Diane Bass, one of the defense attorneys in my case, told me that we're moving closer to a plea agreement. Nothing's definitive, she said, but we're expecting prosecutors to recommend that instead of imprisonment, I should serve my sanction under a term known as home confinement—meaning I'd have to stay in my house unless a probation officer authorized me to leave. The sentence, she expected, would last about a year.

Personally, I'd rather settle this matter by paying a fine in a civil proceeding—without a felony conviction. Although I'm not a decision maker and don't have any say in the matter, my bookmaking operations only involved consenting adults. A financial penalty, similar to the money I forfeited the first time federal agents raided my house, would feel like a more appropriate response to the charges against me.

Unfortunately in our nation's criminal justice system, law enforcement officers have a hammer, and every problem looks like a nail. In my view, we lock too many people in prison, and those people serve sentences that are far too long. Again, I know that it's not my call.

Diane tells me that if I get home confinement, I should feel grateful. Given the continuous barrage of media attention, she repeatedly warns that I shouldn't take anything for granted. Even if the prosecutors recommended home confinement, the sentencing judge would make the ultimate decision.

Whenever she reminds me that imprisonment remains a possibility, I think of my family. Rather than dwelling on matters that I'm not able to control, I turn to happier thoughts, such as my son's upcoming birthday, on May 27, 2024. Kingston is turning three. Nicole planned a party, and we're expecting several toddlers to celebrate with cake and celebrations at our house. We've got to keep some sense of normalcy around us.

At every opportunity, I try to take my mind off these complications hanging over my head. It feels as if I'm balancing myself on a tightrope. Each step is precarious and uncertain. Typically, I'm confident in everything I do. Yet in this case, I'm dealing with many unknowns. Too many people are making decisions that will determine how and when I get to the other side, and what I'll have when I get there.

I remember all the great times with Nicole. From the beginning, she became my good-luck charm, bringing me the best of luck. With her by my side, I had the best winning streak ever, leading to winnings of more than $12 million, which I kept in cash. I stored it all in tightly wrapped bundles of $10,000—all packed neatly in a large chest. Although I had other assets, such as crypto, real estate, stock, and collectibles, a huge stash of US currency can make a person feel secure.

What I'd do to reverse some past decisions, as we could use more liquidity now.

When I drove over to meet her at Laguna Beach's Coyote Grill, back in October 2015, I didn't plan on finding the woman of my life. I'd been involved in two long-term relationships previously, one with Monica and a second one with Rachel. Although I'm grateful to those women for bringing our daughters into the world, neither relationship brought the chemistry we'd need to build a life together, or even sustain a marriage. I expected that I'd be single for the rest of my life.

With Nicole, I was only looking to have the kind of fun that keeps a young man alive. My bookmaking business had been taking off, thanks in large part to my friend Anthony, whom I'd nicknamed Mighty Mouse because of his stature and powerful personality. He had moved to Orange County in 1993, trying to get away from the cold weather from his hometown of Buffalo, New York. After a few months of working as a waiter in Newport Beach, Anthony pooled $2,000 together with two friends to launch a food-delivery service, catering to local businesses. Their business grew quickly, providing him with a good income stream.

We hung out together, watching sports and gambling. When we met, I still worked for Micky, selling commodities and booking bets on the side. As Anthony's income grew, he started betting more, getting out of control, losing way more than he won. Over time, his debts accumulated. I didn't mind carrying a balance for him, even when his debts grew to exceed $600k.

As a bookmaker, I would see many clients go into debt. They were adults, in the game for excitement and presumably, they liked to sink or swim by the decisions they made. No one twisted their arm, or pushed them into anything they didn't want to do. As long as they weren't trying to rip me off or scam me, I didn't mind carrying them when they lost.

Their debt became another type of asset class for me, and I'd look at it in the same ways as another business owner would look at receivables. He'd like to collect, but sometimes he'd have to exercise patience.

Anthony's debts accumulated over time, but he made regular payments. When he'd win an occasional game, we'd deduct his winnings from the balance he owed. We had a great time together, and he'd frequently join my entourage for excursions to Las Vegas.

In 2015, around the time that Nicole came into my life, Mighty Mouse struck gold when a publicly traded company acquired his food delivery business for $44 million. As an equal partner, he walked away with more than $10 million. His payday brought an unexpected windfall for us both, because once he got his money, he paid off the entire $600 grand that he owed. Had I not allowed him to keep betting, I wouldn't have gotten such a big pay day.

Besides paying me off, Anthony suddenly had as much free time and liquidity as I had. Time and liquidity are not a good combination for a gambler who cannot exercise self-control. Within a year of selling his company, Anthony had gambled away his entire bankroll from selling his company. Worse, he'd also gone into debt with the casinos, because he tapped into his multi-million dollar credit lines and lost that as well.

Even after he lost his money, Anthony hung out as a central part of my entourage, joining my friends Mike Imech and Ryan Boyajian on regular gambling trips. Although they all liked to gamble, each of them had a regular career. Mike worked at a golf club, and Ryan earned his living as a mortgage broker. At least twice each month, they'd join my trips to Las Vegas, where we'd gamble and have a great time.

On each trip, we'd bring well over $2 million, most of it mine. Casinos would always send a private jet to pick us up, ensuring that our arrival would be nothing short of spectacular. I remember the first time I invited Nicole to join us on a flight, thinking she'd be impressed by the gesture. To my surprise, she declined, preferring to drive from Los Angeles with her friend Leita. Nicole valued her independence, and I admired those virtues in her.

Before arriving on her first trip, Nicole and Leita had stopped at a convenience store to purchase a cooler and their own alcohol. I got a kick out of her gesture, seeing that she didn't intend to get sucked into the trappings of my lifestyle.

When she called to ask how she could find me once she got to Las Vegas, I gave her an address to the private entrance for the villas at the Mirage. The valet escorted her and Leita to the discreet entrance, with a bellman carrying her belongings, including the styrofoam cooler. When the butler opened the door, Nicole walked in, awed by the opulent surroundings, which differed from ordinary suites. The high ceilings and glass walls that led to a private patio and shimmering pool made the villa more like an extravagant mansion than a hotel room. She charmed me by smiling demurely as she looked down at her cooler. The butler took the edge off by offering glasses of Crystal.

I'd entertained many women in such settings, and they were invariably dazzled by the attention and opulence the casinos lavished upon me. But Nicole was different. Her reservation, humility, and independence set her apart. The longer we spoke, the more impressed I became with her intelligence and business acumen. She'd graduated from USC, studied abroad in Spain, and worked as a waitress while she built her apparel company, Coco-on-the-Go. She was special, in more ways than I could describe.

Nicole and her friend Leita fit in easily with my friends Anthony, Ryan, and Mike. For the first time, I had more fun teaching her how to gamble than playing my own hands. I made a deal with her. I'd give her the chips to get started from my stack, and I'd coach her along the way. Losses would go against my account, but she'd keep all the winnings from the hands she played. The more time I spent with her, the more we both won.

We developed a fabulous relationship, one that I'd never had before. No one could fault me for going after her the way I did. What single man wouldn't look forward to a brief escape with a stunning, 28-year-old beauty? Although I didn't have expectations when we began, as we spent more time together, our connection grew deeper. We became inseparable.

The stars aligned during those good times, not only with my casino winnings, but also with my bookmaking business. I didn't only get more agents who would bring business my way, some of my best players began referring their high-roller friends.

John, for example, had been an excellent customer for several years. By profession, he'd done well for himself developing real estate. As a speculator, he purchased vacant land in some of the most glitzy, gated communities of north Los Angeles, such as Calabasas, Hidden Hills, and Thousand Oaks. After purchasing the raw land, his company built luxury homes that sold for a premium. It was a good business, with steady income, but John also enjoyed the thrill of immediate gratification. Every week, I could count on him to bet at least $500,000.

As a successful businessman, John didn't waste time on small talk. We depended on each other to settle accounts regularly, without problem. But during all the years that I'd been taking his bets, we never socialized. He surprised me with a call, saying he had a potential new client, because he was kind of secretive in making the introduction.

"She's going to be high maintenance," he said.

I told him that wouldn't be a problem.

"She's also kind of high profile."

After several years of betting together, John knew of my discretion, and I told it wouldn't be a problem.

"She's had some problems with bookmakers in the past," he said. "It might be best if you drive up to play a round of golf with her husband and me."

Many of my clients could be problematic, and I didn't mind at all. I told him to name the time and I'd drive up.

We agreed to meet at the Sherwood Country Club on Saturday morning at 8:00.

I looked forward to the long drive from Orange County to Thousand Oaks, in North Los Angeles, on a crisp Saturday morning. The early sun promised a great day. I'd never played golf with John before, and the prospect of meeting his high-profile client added an air of mystery to the morning. Since he said the client would be a woman, I thought about bringing Nicole. In the end, given John's call for discretion, I decided to make the trip alone.

I drove into the Sherwood Country Club, flanked by lush greenery and immaculately manicured lawns. The elegant entry led to a grand clubhouse that looked like an image from the pages of *Architectural Digest*, or *Town and Country* magazine, the kind of place where the wealthy came to relax, away from the prying eyes of the public.

A valet parked my car, and I made my way to the entrance. Stately trees and blooming flowers lined the path, adding to the club's serene ambiance. I saw John waiting near the entrance to the clubhouse, looking every bit the part of a successful real estate developer. He waved me over with a reserved nod.

"Morning," I greeted him.

He shook my hand firmly. "Glad you could make it."

We walked together toward the first tee, the conversation light and casual. I was surprised to meet one of the most recognizable athletes in the world. In his sport, he was as recognizable as Shohei Ohtani was to baseball. People knew him as being not only a phenomenal athlete, but also a great business leader and also an owner of a professional sports team—I'll leave it to the reader to guess who. For the purpose of this story, we'll call him Jordan. Jordan approached us, casually adjusting his golf glove, his expression polite but reserved.

"Jordan, this is my friend Matt, whom I told you about," John said.

"Nice to meet you." Jordan extended his hand.

His demeanor composed, Jordan didn't say much, but his presence was commanding. Dressed impeccably, he looked every bit the athlete he was known to be, with a quiet intensity about him. We didn't discuss gambling at all during the outing, which I suspected was part of the plan. Before allowing John to introduce me to Jordan's wife, the player wanted to get a measure of me.

The course itself was breathtaking, with rolling fairways and pristine greens framed by the natural beauty of the mountains. Every hole presented a new challenge. Jordan's skill with a golf club didn't surprise me, given his athletic prowess. He moved with an impressive, practiced ease, each swing calculated and precise.

Throughout the game, Jordan spoke politely, offering the occasional tip on my swing or a nod of encouragement. He wasn't a big talker. John and I exchanged a few words here and there, but I understood that I was only there for Jordan to size me up, to observe, not converse.

By the time we reached the 18th hole, I felt as if I had passed the unspoken test. Jordan gave me a slight nod as we finished the round. John and I shook hands again, and he nodded in silent acknowledgment that things had gone well.

"Thanks for coming out," Jordan said as we parted ways.

"Anytime," I replied, knowing that this was just the beginning of whatever John had planned.

As I drove back home, the day replayed in my mind. The next step came with a joint text that John sent to connect me with someone who was close to Jordan. To protect her identity, I'll call her Amber.

I wouldn't say Amber was a star, but she had some notoriety because of her relationship to one of the most famous athletes in the world. I understood the need for secrecy. On occasion, I crossed paths with both her and Jordan in high-roller rooms at casinos, but we'd never met or spoken. A few years back, a gambling controversy brought her some unwanted attention. Although it wasn't national news, in my line of work, I kept my finger on the pulse of problems that other bookmakers faced.

The trouble started in 2006, when federal authorities busted a large-scale sports betting ring. Unlike my business, authorities claimed that a bookmaker had worked closely with figures known to be involved with organized crime.

When investigators go after bookmakers, they pull on every thread, trying to get the name of everyone involved. Once reporters learned that Amber had bet with the bookmaker's operation, they began writing stories that would inevitably mention Jordan—knowing that would sell more subscriptions. They tried to, threatening his clean reputation. The whispers and speculations about Amber being connected, even indirectly, with notorious crime figures did not serve Jordan well.

Although authorities never charged Amber with a crime, her association with a gambling ring brought intense scrutiny. During interviews, Jordan had to field questions from reporters about gambling investigations, maintaining composure while showing his support for Amber. I admired him as a stand-up guy.

I didn't blame John and Jordan for being cautious about the introduction. They needed to minimize exposure to the kinds of problems Amber had experienced before.

I connected with Amber, and opened an account for her. With most clients, I'd use a runner to handle the interactions and transactions. With high-net-worth and high-profile clients, it was best to give them my personal attention.

As John had warned, Amber required a lot of maintenance. For the next four years, she'd typically gamble $100,000 weekly. We'd settle any time the account reached $50,000—whether I owed her or she owed me. Amber liked to settle in cash, but given her history, she always wanted to meet discreetly, in a random parking lot, or at a gas station; while filling our tanks, she'd hand me a bag filled with cash. She'd complain when she lost, whining about how the game had gone the wrong way, and press me to give her a discount. I did my best to keep her happy. She'd say that she planned to quit betting, but like most gamblers, it's easier to talk about quitting than to miss out on the excitement of the next game.

Amber introduced me to her friend, Kevin Washington, the scion of another billionaire family. His father, Dennis Washington is well known for his impressive business career. In 1964, he borrowed $30,000 to lease a piece of earth-moving equipment, which he used to build Washington Construction. He grew his company into one of the largest contractors in the world, completing projects in mining, railways, highway construction, marine transportation, and more. Kevin, on the other hand, was in the inheritance business, not quite the type of honorable, self-made man as his father.

Based on Amber's recommendation, I opened an account for Kevin, giving him a $100,000 credit line. In his first weekend, he lost $75,000—which he wired to my account the following day. At her request, I provided Amber with a commission. Given her high profile and history, she surprised me by asking for a cut from the payments that Kevin made to me. By accepting those payments, she became like one of my agents.

As time passed, I got to know Kevin as the type of person who shouldn't gamble at all. Not only did he chase bets, he lacked discipline or self-control, as if totally incapable of restraint or indulging in vice. If he were at a table stacked with a pound of cocaine, I'd expect him to try to snort it all; in a room with 50 hookers, Kevin would do his best to get some action from each of them. Despite going to rehab numerous times, he said that he loved living on the edge.

Like other high-maintenance clients, Kevin would call numerous times with a request for me to increase his limit. Given our long history, and his supposed ability to pay, I agreed.

Kevin Washington had a way of making everything seem larger than life. It was part of his charm. Tall, fit, and good looking, he had all the trappings of wealth—the watches, the cars, the palatial homes, and the ego. And that was part of his problem. When he called me about the debt he owed, and a bet he wanted to place, I could sense the manic energy in his voice. He didn't ask if I was available or if it was a good time to talk—he just launched into his pitch with the fervor of a man possessed.

"Matty, listen," he said, his words tumbling over each other. "I've got a proposition for you. You're going to love this."

I already had a sinking feeling in my stomach. "Kevin, you owe me $2 million. Let's settle that debt before you bring propositions to me."

He laughed, a harsh, mirthless sound. "Let's settle it all in one go, with a single bet. We'll clear the slate, or you'll make a fortune."

I knew I wasn't going to like what came next.

"I want to put $2 million on the Warriors to win the series. If they win, we're square. If they lose, I'll owe you $12 million. Simple, right?"

The Warriors and Cavaliers were scheduled to play Game 3 in the best-of-seven finals series, for the 2016 NBA championship. The Warriors were up 2-0, and heavily favored to win the nba title.

My silence must have spoken volumes, because Kevin rushed on. "Stephen's on fire, and I think the Warriors are a lock. This is a way for us to wipe the slate clean and move on."

"I don't want to take that bet, Kevin," I said firmly. "You owe me $2 million. Let's handle that first."

"Check it out," he said. "If you don't take the bet, I'm not paying you anything. You can sue me, or do whatever you want, but I'm not paying you shit. If the Warriors win, you wipe my debt clean and we start fresh. Otherwise, we're finished ."

I could hear the desperation in his voice, but I also knew his type too well. "Kevin, the Cavaliers are 5-1 underdogs. If they lose, you're on the hook for $12 million. You understand the risk?" Although I knew he was a problem, I also had memories from my buddy Anthony, who eventually came into some money and made me whole on the $600,000 that he owed

"I understand, Matty," Kevin responded, his voice taking on an edge. "And I'll take care of it. You know I've always paid you. I've got properties, businesses. I'll sell something if I have to."

"If you won't pay me the $2 million you already owe, why should I expect you to pay $12 million?"

"Because you know I'm good for it. I've paid you more than $2 million over the years. Don't act like you don't trust me now."

I was pissed, knowing that he had backed me into a corner. I didn't operate like other bookmakers. I didn't use enforcers or muscle to collect. I worked on an honor system, and Kevin wanted to exploit my generosity in accommodating him. "I'm not happy about this, Kevin, but you're not giving me any choice. I'll take the bet. But let's be clear, if the Warriors lose, you owe me $12 million. Do I have your word as a man on that?"

"You've got my word Matty. We'll have a fresh start after this."

To everyone's shock, the Cavaliers after being down 3-1 in the series, led by LeBron James and Kyrie Irving, pulled off a stunning upset over the Warriors.

I called Kevin the next week after the dust settled. "Matty, Matty, Matty," he said before I could get a word in. "We both know that's just monopoly money. Eat the loss and let's move on, clean slate."

"Kevin, you owe me $12 million. We had a deal."

He laughed again, that cold, empty sound. "Matty, Matty, Matty. You like taking my bets. Do what you've got to do, but I'm not paying this time. We'll start with a fresh, clean slate."

With big-money degenerate gamblers, we win sometimes, we lose sometimes. But we've got to keep pushing forward. I'm in a game of risk, of trust, and sometimes, betrayal. Even with those losses, I came out ahead. As Kevin acknowledged, I'd won millions from him in the past. And with the luck that Nicole brought, I multiplied those resources as we traveled from one casino to the next.

During those first several years of our relationship, Nicole and I rarely spent more than 10 consecutive days in our home. Despite living in a resort-style property, getting away to exotic locations couldn't have been easier. With casino hosts constantly offering to coordinate private airfare from Orange County, we were always on the go. In those days, before legal problems complicated my life, casino hosts knew that I would routinely gamble millions of dollars per hour, and they welcomed me with open arms. With Nicole by my side, I frequently came out a winner.

After two years of being inseparable, I proposed. Without a doubt, I wanted to spend the rest of my life with her. She brought me more happiness than I'd ever known, and we wanted hundreds of friends to join our wedding celebration. We chose The Resort at Pelican Hill for the wedding and reception. As one of the premier wedding destinations in Orange County, overlooking Newport Coast, we'd have to wait a year to get a date. Wanting to celebrate sooner, we started traveling to various destinations looking for the perfect spot to host friends for our bachelor and bachelorette parties.

Steve, my casino host, who always went above and beyond when booking gambling excursions for me, suggested that we visit casinos at the Baha Mar Resort in Nassau. He coordinated travel arrangements and a $1 million credit line. Like all resorts in the Bahamas, the Baha Mar feels like a tropical paradise, with lush gardens, pristine beaches, and an extraordinary water park. We enjoyed a few days of gambling, and checked out before dawn, eager to make a flight that would get us back to Miami before 8:00 am.

The casino had extended me credit, I used the credit successfully, and in the end, cashed in my chips. Ordinarily, I would've considered it a successful trip. The casino kept clear records, recording all my winnings and losses. During our brief stay, I'd won approximately $160 grand, which would become part of the tax records for the Bahamas. As far as I knew, the income wouldn't be recorded in the United States. When leaving the Bahamas, I didn't see any reason to bring attention to the cash I'd be carrying home. My tax accountant would be in a better position to decide how to declare those winnings.

As I requested, the Baha Mar cashier provided my winnings in tightly-banded stacks of $10,000 each. I divided the currency evenly into our luggage and backpacks, believing that we'd make it back home without any problems.

Unfortunately, I miscalculated the aggressiveness of US Customs, which all American citizens had to pass through before leaving the Bahamas. I filled out forms for both Nicole and I, which required us to declare whether we were carrying any fruits, vegetables, or currency valued at more than $10,000. I checked no on all boxes, hoping to get through.

We passed the forms to the agent, along with our passports. The agent assessed the documents, then looked us over, checking computer screens that we could not see. He told us to go into another line for additional screening. Despite the agent saying it was random, I felt targeted.

"Your form indicates that you don't have anything to declare." The agent glared at me.

"What's that?" I tried to feign ignorance. "Forgive me. We're a little hung over. I just checked no to everything."

"Is that true?

"Look, we just flew over here to check out venues for our wedding. Like I said, I'm a little hungover and didn't read it closely. I just checked no to everything."

That's a problem," the agent said. "Do you have more than $10,000?"

"I do."

"How much currency are you carrying?"

"I don't know." I scratched my head. "I've been here for a few days. I was gambling a lot. I got lucky at the casino. I don't know how much I won. Maybe it is 150 or 160 thousand."

"You lied to us. You declared that you weren't carrying more than $10,000. That's a crime in the Bahamas."

"I'm not lying to you. I don't know how much I have. I won some money in the casino. I don't know how much."

"If you can't tell me how much currency you're carrying, within $500, I'm turning you over to the Bahamian police for further processing."

"Just say it's $170,000. I know it's not more than that."

The agent didn't want to converse further. He used his radio to call the Bahamian police. They came for us and led us to a holding area. Nicole started to panic, and I felt awful for what I had done. Trying to persuade them to cut her loose and spare her the indignity of what was to come, I told them that I had filled out the forms and I was responsible.

I hoped that they'd simply take the money and let us go. Instead, after leaving us waiting in the holding cell for a while, the officers returned and told us to stand so they could cuff us. Nicole started to cry. I asked if they'd let me speak with someone from the US embassy. They got someone on the phone, but he didn't offer any help, saying it wouldn't be any big deal. The next thing I knew, the officers directed us to get into an old van, and they drove us from the airport to a Bahamian police station.

I spoke with representatives at the US Embassy, but I neither got answers to my questions, nor any sense of confidence that they wanted to help us at all. When we got to the station, they locked us into holding cells. I shared the space with a Canadian citizen, and I could hear how terrified Nicole was when they led her into a cell that held another woman who claimed to be high on crack. We waited in those cells for a few hours, without any news. I heard men who were in cells adjacent to Nicole jeering at her, and I felt helpless to protect her from a problem that I'd created.

After several hours, the officers escorted us out of the jail and led us to a police van. After driving for about 20 minutes, we pulled into a prison. The warden came out to see us and I tried to talk with him, letting him know what happened. Nicole stood beside me shaking, crying, and hyperventilating with anxiety. The warden seemed to have some sympathy for us. He said that he was only doing his job, and that he had to lock us up. I asked for his consideration, saying that Nicole didn't have anything to do with it, as I had filled out the paper.

He scratched his chin, then asked her, "Ma'am, do you think you're in danger of harming yourself?"

Seeing that the warden was trying to help her, I nudged her to say yes. She got the message, then acknowledged that she felt weak and might try to hurt herself.

The warden then said he couldn't hold her in the prison, and instructed the officers to take Nicole back to the precinct, where she could wait in a single cell with a couch.

He locked me in a cell with a concrete floor, which I shared with three other guys. It didn't have a bathroom. I stayed there all night, unable to sleep a wink, worried about Nicole. We were detained on a Sunday morning, which meant that we'd have to wait until Monday afternoon to get in front of a judge who could release us.

The next afternoon, the guards came for me and put me in shackles. They drove me to the courthouse for an initial appearance. I exhaled when I saw Nicole. We were both dirty, and exhausted, but grateful to see each other.

The judge called us up and asked us what happened. I explained that we were hungover and trying to board a flight that would take us home. Citing my hangover as an excuse, I apologized for not reading the declaration form closely, and not acknowledging the cash I was carrying.

"Don't lie to me," the judge said. "I'm not new to the bench and I know when someone isn't being truthful. You tried to hide money, which is unacceptable. You need to hire an attorney. If you don't have an attorney, there are two attorneys in the back of the courtroom who can help you."

I spoke with the two attorneys. If we paid a $5,000 fine, and agreed to forfeit the money I didn't declare, they could persuade the judge to dismiss the case. Their fee for the service would be $5,000.

"Just to be clear," I said, "i'll need to pay $5,000 to the court, and $5,000 to you, and we'll be able to leave the Bahamas today?"

When the attorneys confirmed, I asked if I could pay with my American Express card.

Neither the attorneys, nor the court, would accept American Express.

"If I can't use my credit card, the only way that I can pay your fee, and the court's fee, would be if you allowed me to get back to the casino, where I can draw against my line of credit. Is that possible?"

The attorneys went to speak with the judge and the judge agreed. The attorneys then coordinated officers to drive me back to the Baha Mar Casino. Nicole had to wait at the courthouse. While I was away, she would use my credit card to book tickets for us to fly home. If I didn't make it back with the $10,000, we'd have to spend another night locked in the jails. Time was ticking. Because the judge said I had to be back in court before the court closed, at 5:00 pm.

I give all credit to the officers for their driving skills. I'm used to driving fast, but they were absolutely reckless, racing through one-lane roads that were dotted with potholes. I bounced around the backseat, with my wrists in handcuffs.

They got me to the casino, and feeling disgustingly dirty and sweaty, I walked straight to the cashier. She recognized me, but didn't comment on my appearance. I told her that I would need to tap into my credit line to withdraw $12,000.

Despite the wretchedness of my appearance, the cashier greeted me by name and spoke sympathetically. "I'm really sorry Mr. Bowyer. I cannot give you $12,000 in cash. We know you're good for it, and you have a sufficient credit line. Our policy doesn't allow guests to withdraw cash against their credit line. I can give you chips to gamble, but that's it."

I knew the rules, but had hoped she would make an exception. Without time to argue, I asked her to give me the marker. I explained to the officers that I'd have to go to one of the tables and place a bet. Once I won, I could convert the chips to cash, and we could resolve the matter.

The officers shrugged, and escorted me over to a Baccarat table. I put down a bet for $12,000, which would be sufficient for me to pay the court and the lawyers, and leave Nicole and I $2,000 to get home.

The bet did not go my way. I then signed a second marker for $24,000 and I put that down. I lost again. I signed another marker, and I put down a bet for $48,000. Again, I lost. Within ten minutes, I had lost $84,000.

I can't overstate the stress I felt at that moment. My wife was sitting in a Bahamian jail cell, and if I didn't win the cash we needed, I wouldn't have any way of getting us out of there. It felt as if I were carrying the world on my shoulders, but even in that moment, I knew that I had to keep my composure, focus on the game, and come out a winner.

Alex Pareinte, the president of the casino then came to my table. He asked what was going on. I told him the entire story and he agreed to help, saying I wouldn't have to gamble any more. He walked me over to the cashier and instructed her to give me $12,000 in cash. I signed the marker for $96,000, confirming that I would repay the $84,000 that I'd lost, and the $12,000 in cash that I borrowed.

We made it back to the court just in time. I paid the attorney, and paid the court, and the Bahamas Department Of Immigration officers then drove us back to the airport, where we boarded a flight to Miami, happy to put the ordeal behind us and go on to better times.

CHAPTER 12
The Wedding of a Century

The uncertainty accompanying my current complications with the DOJ is troubling, but it pales in comparison to the sheer terror and helplessness I felt when Bahamian officials led Nicole away in handcuffs. Memories from that night in a foreign country's jail haunt me like a persistent nightmare, an invisible weight that still drags me down. Regardless of how many years pass, thinking about that experience drains my energy.

When they separated us, I felt powerless. I made the foolish decision to lie on a customs form, which dropped us into that predicament. Had I been honest about my winnings, the officials wouldn't have taken us into custody. The irony is that my winnings from the Baha Mar Casino didn't have much bearing in my life. With gambling, I'd go up and I'd go down, always moving onto the next adventure. My line of work exposed me to risks and potential problems, which I understood. But I had a duty to protect Nicole, and my lapse in judgment put her at risk—which I still regret. She trusted me, and I pledged that I'd never let her down again.

Before I proposed to Nicole, I felt almost invincible, at the top of my game. Together, we enjoyed an incredible hot streak in casinos from

Las Vegas to Monte Carlo. Whether betting on the Super Bowl, playing high-stakes Baccarat, or placing winning bets at the Blackjack table, it seemed like I just couldn't lose. My bankroll swelled to unprecedented levels with her by my side, affording us the luxury of living the high-roller lifestyle without a care in the world.

It didn't take long before I knew that I wanted to spend the rest of my life with Nicole. She had become my good luck charm, my partner in every way, and my closest confidante. I started planning for a wedding that would be as extraordinary as she is, a grand gesture that would show everyone just how much she meant to me.

Before proposing, I had to find an exceptional ring, something unique and stunning. I reached out to my friend Phil, a professional jeweler and designer. Phil and I worked out at the same gym, and over the past several years we'd developed a good friendship. When I told him my plan of proposing to Nicole, and that I wanted an exceptional ring, he promised to design something spectacular. When he asked about the budget I had in mind, I told him that he shouldn't be constrained by budgets. I wanted Nicole to have an extraordinary wedding ring, and I asked him to use his judgment.

Phil gave me a stack of picture books so I could get an idea of different styles. He explained the different cuts and colors and weights. We agreed on a breathtaking, five-carat emerald cut diamond of exceptional quality.

"I'll make this a masterpiece, Matt," Phil said. I'll have it for you in a few weeks. "When you put it on her finger, she'll be absolutely stunned," he promised. I paid him $150,000, which would be one of the first expenditures for the unforgettable wedding I wanted to celebrate with her. It would be her only wedding, I wanted her to remember it for a lifetime.

Nicole had grown accustomed to our frequent international travels, so she didn't blink when I told her that I'd planned a two-week trip to Europe. Although she thought we were going so that I could gamble, the only plans I had for that trip was to woo her in various romantic cities and at the end, propose to her in Paris. We'd start in Italy.

I had to figure out how I'd transport the ring to Italy without her seeing it. We packed our luggage together, and I didn't want any possibility of her seeing the ring. With limited options, I decided to hide the ring in my underwear during the flight. The jet would be in the air for more than 13 hours, and I knew that keeping her jewels alongside my jewels wouldn't be too comfortable. But it would be the safest way to ensure she didn't find the ring.

As we approached security, I realized that I hadn't considered the detector. Thankfully, I walked through without setting off any alarms. The discomfort of having a diamond ring pressed against my sensitive parts became unbearable. Even while reclining in the comfortable first-class seats, I had to shift and adjust constantly, hoping she wouldn't notice.

We landed in Venice in the late evening, checked into our hotel, and then started walking around the historic city. By then I abandoned my original plan of proposing in Paris. I couldn't imagine trying to hide the ring from her for another day. Instead, I resolved to propose that very night, our first night on the trip.

We walked around San Marcos Square, marveling at the ancient architecture and the shimmering canals that stretched out before us. The city was a living, breathing work of art, with every building and bridge steeped in centuries of history and romance. It was nearly 11:00 in the evening, and we were famished, but the local restaurants were closing. We spotted a charming restaurant nestled between stores along the narrow cobblestone streets. Staff were beginning to turn off the exterior lighting that brought attention to blooming flower boxes cascading down the walls, adding a splash of color to the ancient brickwork.

When we walked inside, we smelled the aroma of Italian cuisine, and admired the warm ambiance of the cozy interior. Venetian artwork covered the walls, showcasing scenes of gondolas gliding through the city's iconic canals and picturesque views of Venetian landmarks. It was elegant, with rustic wooden tables draped in crisp white linens adorned with flickering candles that waiters were blowing out. It was an intimate atmosphere, one that could not be better for the romantic, unplanned dinner I had in mind.

As the owner watched me admiring his restaurant, he said in heavily accented English, "I'm so sorry, but we're just closing down for the night. Come back tomorrow, please."

I pulled him aside discreetly and pressed five crisp $100 bills into his hand. "We've traveled all the way from California," I explained, my voice low and earnest. "This is a very special night for us. I'm planning to propose to my girlfriend. I know it's late. But is it possible for you and your staff to prepare a memorable meal for the two of us? I promise to take care of all your staff."

The owner's eyes widened with understanding, and he quickly pocketed the money. "Congratulations," he whispered. "We're happy you chose Venice to propose to this beautiful lady. No worries. It will be our pleasure to create a dining experience you'll never forget."

He led us to a beautifully set table overlooking the canal that hadn't yet been cleared. The flickering candlelight casting a romantic glow across Nicole's face. The attentive staff catered to our every need, presenting us with a multi-course feast that showcased the very best of Italian cuisine. The owner and his team had truly delivered, creating a culinary masterpiece for our special night.

As we finished our meal, I told Nicole I wanted to wash my hands, and went to the men's room. While there, I put the ring in my inside pocket, looking forward to the perfect moment when I'd put it on her finger.

After more than two hours, I thanked everyone profusely for staying with us so late and tipped them well. We strolled out, hand-in-hand, wandering through the labyrinthine streets, alive under the starlit sky. A soft, ethereal light bathed the grand buildings and ancient statues of San Marcos Square. It was after 2:00 am and Nicole wanted to get back to our hotel. But I led her to a secluded spot in the square, took a deep breath, and dropped to one knee.

Nicole's eyes widened in shock as she realized the significance of the moment.

I reached into my pocket and pulled out the ring. "Nicole," I began, my voice filled with emotion, "I never dreamed of loving a woman as much as I love you. You've brought so much joy and light into my life, and I can't imagine spending another day without you by my side. Marry me, please. Will you be my wife?"

Nicole gazed upon the stunning diamond ring that Phil had crafted specifically for this moment, a sparkling symbol of our love. "Yes," she whispered, her voice choked with emotion. "Yes, I'll marry you."

I slipped the ring onto her finger. Surrounded by the timeless beauty of Venice, I was the luckiest man in the world.

The next day, we hired a photographer who accompanied us back to San Marcos Square. We recreated the proposal so he could snap photographs that would become a permanent part of our story. Nicole had given me a storybook relationship, and I wanted to pass our memories down to our children, and to our children's children.

It felt like the most magical engagement ever. We stayed in the best hotels anyone could imagine, traveling from Venice to Florence, Rome, and Naples. Although I had planned to finish our trip in Paris, we were so enchanted with Italy that we spent our entire trip there, and I'll never forget it.

After we returned, we wanted to dive headfirst into the extensive planning for our wedding. First, I showed Nicole that she'd always have security. On our dining room table, I set out bundles of $100 bills, in $10,000 stacks. I put them in rows of 10, or $100,000 per row. We had 20 separate rows, or $2 million in cash.

"We're going to bury this cash in our backyard," I told her. "We'll put it out of our mind for the next 10 years," I said. "We'll get life insurance, and other types of financial security for you. But if anything should ever happen to me, anything at all, you'll be able to access this money. It won't solve all problems, but $2 million can get a person over most humps in life."

From Walmart, I ordered several metal boxes that I could lock. For extra security, we put the cash in zip-lock bags. Then, in a space beside our outdoor barbeque, I dug a hole about three feet deep. I laid down a tarp, placed our boxes of cash on the tarp, and then began to fill the hole in with dirt. I replaced stepping stones on top, making it look as if the area had been undisturbed. The cash would remain hidden unless Nicole or I had to retrieve it. I felt better knowing that I'd set aside that security for our future. I hoped that we'd never need to dig it up again.

With our futures somewhat secure, we began visiting the top venues of Southern California. Our top contenders for the wedding included the Fairmont Grand Del Mar, with its sprawling grounds and elegant ballrooms, the Montage in Laguna Beach, boasting stunning ocean views and luxurious accommodations, and Pelican Hill in Newport Coast, a breathtaking resort perched atop a bluff overlooking the Pacific.

Pelican Hill was a sight to behold. The resort's Italianate architecture, with its sweeping arches and graceful columns, seemed to transport us back to the romantic streets of Venice. The lush, manicured grounds were dotted with fragrant olive trees and vibrant gardenias, creating a serene and picturesque setting. The view truly took our breath away. From the resort's vantage point, we could see the vast expanse of the Pacific Ocean stretching out to the horizon, with the rugged coastline of Newport Beach below, promising an unforgettable backdrop for our special day.

We knew instantly that the perfect place to exchange our vows and celebrate our love with family and friends would be Pelican Hill. We'd have a massive undertaking to reserve the resort and prepare for our wedding and reception, requiring us to wait almost a full year before we could marry. We intended to host just over 250 people, and we wanted to ensure every aspect of the celebration would be extraordinary, regardless of cost. The wedding planner required a $250,000 deposit, and warned that it could be twice that amount before we finished, depending on what we chose for the reception. Some people spoke about brides acting like princesses, but Nicole said that my demands went way over-the-top of anything she'd ever seen.

Besides the resort fee and wedding planner services, I contracted with numerous vendors to create an exceptional experience. I hired a main band, a separate band for the cigar room, and I brought a Las Vegas DJ to spin records when the bands weren't playing. We ordered a stunning creation of lace and silk for Nicole's custom wedding dress, as well as a custom tuxedo for me. We invited 50 people to our rehearsal dinner at Javier's, a chic restaurant overlooking the picturesque Crystal Cove beach.

As we sat with the wedding planner making our final plans, a thought struck me. "Have you seen the movie *Meet Joe Black*?" I asked.

She nodded, smiling as she encouraged me to continue.

"Do you remember at the end of the movie, where an orchestra played as Anthony Hopkins walked away?"

"I do," she replied.

"I'd like you to hire an orchestra of that caliber to play for us right after we're pronounced man and wife."

The wedding planner laughed, then tried to reel me in. "Are you sure? You've already got a lot going on here. To hire an orchestra and set up, you'd have to budget another $100,000—on top of everything else."

All in, our costs had already ballooned to more than $600,000 for the celebration. I was prepared to go for it, but Nicole gave me a gentle nudge, suggesting that perhaps we'd already gone above and beyond. I agreed to relent.

I refused to skimp on preparations for our first dance as a married couple. Nicole, an exceptional dancer, had been on the salsa dancing team at USC. Part of the reason I fell head-over-heels in love with her was the graceful way she moved the first time I saw her dance. As a white guy, I typically danced like a white guy—and not like Patrick Swayze. But Nicole's combination of sexy elegance mesmerized me.

Although I didn't expect to match her skills, I was determined not to embarrass her by dancing like a club-footed imbecile during our wedding dance. To practice, we went to clubs and danced into the night every time we traveled to Las Vegas. Besides that, we signed up for 12 lessons with a professional choreographer who helped us master our steps.

Nicole selected a song that began slowly, drawing us together in a tender embrace. We waltzed closely, and I held her as she dipped, her long golden hair flowing as we spun in circles. After about 60 seconds, the dj switched the song and the beat picked up to a lively salsa rhythm, and she wowed me with her moves. Her body moved with the rhythm, hips swaying, feet gliding effortlessly across the floor. She was like a flame, captivating and hypnotic, and I could feel our guests being equally mesmerized. Although demure and quiet in most settings, when she danced, she was an artist, painting vivid strokes of passion and grace with every movement.

We practiced relentlessly, driven by a shared determination to perfect our dance. Our rehearsals were intense, and it got to the point where, at just the right moment, I would lift her over my shoulders and spin her around the room to the beat like a helicopter blade. The exhilaration on her face and the seamless grace of our movements filled me with confidence.

With every practice session, our synchronization and chemistry grew stronger. I knew we'd be ready to dazzle our guests with a performance that showcased not just our skills, but the deep connection and love we shared. On our special night, our wedding dance would be nothing short of spectacular.

I couldn't wait to see Nicole walk down the aisle, to pledge my eternal devotion to her in front of our family and friends. But several months would pass before our wedding day. While waiting, I'd continue running my business, which sometimes required that I focus on matters that weren't always pleasant—like dealing with people who didn't know how to control their gambling, and gamblers who didn't always act honorably.

In marrying me, Nicole accepted that I'd bring her around all sorts of Vegas-type characters, like Michael and Marcia. They weren't in our inner circle, not close enough to warrant an invite to our wedding. But they were typical of the type of characters I interacted with regularly in my line of work.

Besides all the glitter of Las Vegas, the atmosphere brings out a lot of degenerates and dangerous people. I met Michael through Patrick, a notorious, scumbag gambler. He stood out as a breed apart from the other degenerates—a walking, talking embodiment of everything rotten in the gambling world.

Patrick wasn't just a gambler. He lived like a force of chaos, leaving a trail of unpaid debts and shattered promises. His eyes glazed over from too many nights of getting high, smoking, and drinking.

As a master manipulator, Patrick wove a web of lies with practiced ease, ensnaring unsuspecting victims into his deceitful schemes. I learned the hard way not to trust Patrick after he stiffed me for 100s of thousands. Once I cut him off, he said he'd try to make things right by introducing me to Michael. He promised that he could help boost my business in some way, and that Michael would be a good connection for me to have.

Patrick described Michael as a powerful figure in the world of bookmaking, an honorable man who had connections to one of the well-known crime families in Boston. I checked around with other people I knew, and I heard that Michael was legit. He wasn't a full-blooded Italian, so he didn't have his button as a made-man. That didn't make him any less dangerous, Patrick said, and the family always backed him up as an affiliate, an earner.

Like me, Michael earned a living as a sports book. With Patrick's introduction, I started placing all my baseball bets with him. Michael pledged that he could handle all the action I sent his way. With Nicole as my good luck charm, I continuously increased the size of my bets, building a steady stream of winnings, which Michael didn't like.

After I'd already won more than $500k, Michael said that he wanted to meet me. I had a great weekend, requiring him to settle up with me. We'd never met before, so I was surprised when he said that he wanted to fly out from Boston to meet. Patrick had told me that I should be careful around Michael, because he was a semi-violent guy, and he always reminded me of Michael's connections to soldiers in organized crime.

But I didn't see any reason to worry. I'd placed bets. And I won. I expected to get paid.

We sat on a hotel patio, drinking espresso. I could feel him sizing me up. He was taller than me, well built with a swarthy complexion. He wore expensive clothing, an East Coast type, with slicked back hair, gold-rimmed sunglasses, dark lenses.

Between puffs on his cigar, he asked how I had gotten such an edge. He wanted an explanation for my consistent winnings.

When I told him that I simply did my homework, he shrugged, as if he didn't believe me.

"Well, I'm not paying you. You can forget about that," he said.

I kind of admired him for having the audacity to fly all the way out from Boston just to look me in the eyes and tell me that he wouldn't be paying me.

"Why not? You took the bets. I won. You owe me the money, straight up."

He shrugged. "I don't got it, and I'm not going to get it." In his facial expression, I could see that neither my money, nor his statement about not paying me, concerned him in the least.

I considered my options, but his reputation and connections to the mob weren't lost on me. My operation had always been clean, free of any involvement with the underworld types. I sat there looking at him, in silence. Then he continued.

"That doesn't have to mean you're not going to get your money," he tugged another puff on his cigar. "I'm just not going to be the guy who's paying."

It sounded as if he wanted to propose something, and I asked what he had in mind.

"I know a lot of deep-pocket guys," he said. "You pick the teams, let us know who you like, and we'll place the bets with our people in Vegas. They'll give you a cut of the winnings. You can get your money that way, without taking any risk of losses. How's that sound?"

"If I can't trust you to pay me the $500k that you owe me, why should I think that they're going to pay me?"

"Because I told you they will," he said. He took another puff on his cigar, while staring into me.

I wasn't in any position to go to war with a connected guy, and I didn't want to. I didn't really have a choice. If I wanted any hope of getting my money, this would be the only shot I had of getting it. The alternative would have been to walk away, chalk it up as a loss and move on. The greed in my mind had other ideas, not to mention, I was always intrigued by the mob and the balls of this guy.

I agreed, and we started working out the arrangements. To my surprise, as I won, his team started to chip away, kicking me back my cut each week. Despite what he'd done to me, I admired his audacity and fearlessness. We started hanging out together. As he swaggered through the casino, anyone could see that he demanded respect. In many ways, he embodied the archetype of a gangster straight out of a Martin Scorsese film, complete with a Joe Pesci-esque charm that belied his ruthless nature.

During one of our escapades in Las Vegas, Michael introduced Nicole and me to Marcia, a woman whose reputation preceded her. Marcia was a force, a seasoned gambler who had earned her stripes at the tables of the Bellagio. Her raspy voice and no-nonsense demeanor hinted at a lifetime spent in the gritty underbelly of the gambling world, always with a cigarette dangling from her parched lips.

She didn't have any shame. Within minutes of meeting her, Marcia was asking about my background and how much I earned. When she learned that I'd once worked in commodities, she said that decades earlier, she worked at the Chicago Mercantile exchange. She told Nicole and me that she'd once been the mistress of a wealthy man who staked her with $12 million, which she lost playing craps for high stakes. "I married the felt and the dice," she said. In any given year, she said, she wouldn't miss more than four or five days without shooting dice.

Then, out of nowhere, I heard her say "Give me some money," her gravelly voice cutting through the smoky haze of the casino. She didn't ask, she simply demanded, like a Las Vegas hustler.

"What's that," I asked, taken aback by her bluntness.

"I need some money."

"Why do you need money?"

Marcia shrugged, her eyes glittering with a mixture of desperation and defiance. "Help me out," she rasped. "Just give me some money, I'll get you back."

Nicole, ever the compassionate soul, urged me to comply. Laughing at the encounter, I reached into my pocket and pulled out a stack of hundred-dollar bills, and peeled off ten for her. As she counted the money, she regaled us with tales of her past, her life intertwined with the highs and lows of the gambling world.

I don't think that I saw Marcia a single time when she didn't ask me for money, but I always handed over what I had in my pocket—not out of charity, but because she'd become an invaluable source of clients. As a premier independent hostess that catered to whales, she knew every whale that came through Vegas. Through her, I met a slew of high rollers, many of whom opened accounts with me and bet astronomical sums.

Although I've rarely needed to borrow money from banks or institutions, I've heard that banks were willing to lend money when people didn't need it, and they were stingy with their loans when people needed the loans. Ironically, casinos were the same way. Although the best casinos now prohibit me from stepping foot onto a gambling property, depriving me of my livelihood, when I was at the top of my game, they all courted Nicole and me, offering anything and everything to get me to gamble with them. I wouldn't have had that status without the seedy relationships I made over the years, including people like Patrick, Michael, and Marcia.

The more casinos heard about my reach, the more invitations I'd receive from the casino hosts. Although I could afford to travel independently, covering my costs without a problem, why should I when my people at the casinos would take care of me. We flew private from Orange County to Miami, and then took a sea plane to Atlantis, one of our favorite hotels. After gambling there for a few days, another private plane flew us to Panama. From there, our family flew to the Dominican Republic, and from the Dominican Republic, we boarded a private jet and flew to Foxwoods, in Mashantucket, Connecticut. Each place we stayed, gave me a credit line in excess of $2 million. I could travel without a dollar in my pocket, just going from one casino to the next, knowing that nothing was out of reach for us.

One of our best and most memorable trips before our wedding, included a private flight from Orange County to the Dominican Republic. Nicole and I, along with her parents, my mom and stepdad, my brother Shawn and his wife, and eight of our closest friends joined us for the unforgettable trip. The jet's opulent interior, with its plush leather seats and attentive service, made the flight an experience in itself.

When we landed in Punta Cana, a convoy of luxury SUVs were on the landing strip. They whisked us away to the Hard Rock Hotel & Casino, a sprawling resort with its captivating blend of tropical beauty and rock 'n' roll glamor. The hotel grounds featured lush gardens, sparkling pools, and stunning ocean views. The tropical resort included world-class restaurants, vibrant bars, and an impressive collection of music memorabilia that paid homage to rock legends.

As a highlight, the casino arranged for our group to sit in the front row for a private concert by Andrea Bocelli. They set up the concert venue on the resort grounds, in an open-air amphitheater that allowed the warm Caribbean breeze to enhance the magical atmosphere, setting the perfect mood for the evening.

Bocelli took the stage and instantly mesmerized the audience with his powerful voice, filled with emotion, creating an unforgettable experience. I felt so grateful that Nicole's parents were able to share in the evening, as I wanted them to know that I'd always take care of their daughter.

Besides the concert, I had a great experience in the casino, along with my friends Sean and Cody. These guys were the epitome of nerdy brilliance— sharp minds and keen eyes, perfect for our shared passion for gambling. As experts in hole carding, they were invaluable assets during our casino escapades. Banned from most casinos, they had to go to casinos in other countries where they haven't been yet. Hole carding, for those unfamiliar with the term, is a technique where players catch glimpses of the dealer's hole card, the face-down card in blackjack. That insight could give me an edge, allowing me to make a more informed bet.

We devised a simple plan that required precision and coordination. Once Sean and Cody identified a lazy dealer who was sloppy enough to flash the hole card, we'd set our strategy into motion. At the blackjack table, we'd strategically position ourselves: Cody on one end, at first base. Sean sat on the other end, at third base. I sat in the middle chair. We didn't show that we had any relationship to each other.

While the dealer pulled a card from the shoe, Cody would flip her a small tip, distracting her. It made the dealer a little less cautious, allowing Sean, who sat at third base, to see the hole card. He'd then give me a sign, allowing me to know what the dealer had in the hole card. It gave me an edge. Sean and Cody placed insignificant bets, but I was betting three hands between anywhere from $15,000 to $75,000 a hand, paying attention to the signals that I got from Sean and Cody.

As a professional gambler, I relied on these moments to maximize my advantage. The signs were discreet—a tap of a finger, a scratch on the nose, signals we had meticulously rehearsed. With the knowledge they provided, I skewed the odds slightly in my favor, enough to walk away with $1.4 million, which we split three ways. It wasn't the most I'd won in a weekend, but being able to give our family and friends a taste of that magnificent life made for an unforgettable memory, just before our wedding.

Finally, after more than a year of waiting, we married on July 22, 2018. Everything went exceptionally well, with the highlight being our dance. Nicole amazed everyone, and all the practice paid off, because the crowd cheered each time I twirled her around. One of our guests recorded our wedding dance on her iPhone, then uploaded it onto her YouTube channel. Within days it went viral, it got 12 million views, prompting a call from a producer of the Ellen DeGeneres show, asking permission if she could publish it.

We felt so grateful to begin our marriage with such an unforgettable memory, and glad that 255 or our closest friends and family could celebrate with us. Without exception, the people told us it was the best wedding they'd ever seen. Our best times, I knew would be ahead of us.

CHAPTER 13
High Roller

Being married didn't slow down my business at all. Nicole and I had already been traveling together for several months. By the time we married, she'd accompanied me on trips across the globe, and I didn't have any reason to believe those times would ever stop. After all, it wasn't as if I was footing the bill for all the good times.

There's an irony to it all. Whether it's gambling or business, when people are succeeding, others welcome you with open arms and all types of doors open wide. When people struggle, on the other hand, a person can't get through a door with a crowbar. For example, if a person needed capital to fund a venture, or to get over a hump, banks would not be so eager to step up and help. But if a person was flush with cash, the bank invited the person to borrow, increasing the limit.

With casinos, the hosts would do more than lend money. They encouraged their best customers to go on lavish vacations, near and far. Traveling with the Lakers or getting front-row seats to a concert with Andrea Bocelli were once-in-a-lifetime opportunities. With all their properties, however, casinos could make things happen in many locations, building exciting opportunities routinely. Sometimes we'd travel to the other side of the world; other times, we'd travel to the other side of the state.

One such opportunity arose when Caesar's Palace invited me to participate in the celebrity golf tournament at Harrah's Casino in Lake Tahoe. American Century Investments sponsored the televised event, known as the American Century Championship. American Century Investments saw the event as a chance to align their brand with the prestige and excitement of a high-profile tournament, gaining extensive exposure through television broadcasts and media coverage.

The sponsorship allowed American Century Investments to showcase their commitment to supporting major events and to reach a target audience that included high net-worth individuals and celebrities. The event provided American Century with the perfect platform to network with influential personalities, potentially leading to future business opportunities.

Since the leadership at Caesar's Palace considered me one of their biggest gamblers, eager to keep me playing at their tables rather than losing me to the competition, they rolled out the red carpet, offering perks and amenities that were hard to refuse, such as the invitation I received to play at Harrah's.

My host at Harrah's, Angie, called me with hopes that I'd spend more time at her casino. I could tell from her tone that she had something special to offer.

"Matt, we have a fantastic event coming up at Harrah's in Lake Tahoe," Angie began. "It's the annual celebrity golf tournament, and we'd love for you to join us. You'll get to play alongside some big names. It's a great way to enjoy a weekend and maybe even make some new connections."

Angie knew how to pique my interest. "Sounds awesome, sign me up!" I told her. "What do you need from me?"

"Just bring your usual bankroll. We're asking participants to bring a minimum of $500,000. Based on the amount they bring to wager, they'll get to choose which celebrity will be on their tour. Go big or go home."

I didn't hesitate. "I'll bring two million. Tell me the options and I'll let you know which person is right for me."

Angie sent me a list of celebrities who would be playing in the tournament. I could choose from Sean Payton, a legendary NFL coach, known for leading the New Orleans Saints to a Super Bowl victory, Travis Kelce, a star tight end for the Kansas City Chiefs, Adam Thielen, who was a great wide receiver for the Minnesota Vikings, Joe Pavelski, captain of the Dallas Stars, and a leading figure in hockey, Golden Tate, an NFL wide receiver, known for his time with the Seattle Seahawks and New York Giants, and Derek Carr, who quarterbacked for the Raiders, or Charles Barkley.

The choices were great, but without hesitating, I chose to play with Charles Barkley, the former NBA star known for his time with the Philadelphia 76ers, Phoenix Suns, and Houston Rockets. I admired his outspoken personality and humor, and felt as if we could have a great time together.

Caesar's Palace and Harrah's both operated under the umbrella of Caesars Entertainment, a massive entity in the casino world. This ownership structure allowed for seamless experiences across different properties, creating a unified front that would cater to high rollers like me. The hosts at Caesars Palace knew that keeping me happy meant ensuring I had the best experiences, whether in Las Vegas, Lake Tahoe, or anywhere else.

Harrah's Lake Tahoe was no different. They pulled out all the stops to ensure their celebrity golf tournament was the highlight of the year, inviting celebrities from all walks of life. The casinos used the celebrities as bait to lure big gamblers and hopefully, build better relationships with them. Each person invited had to commit a significant amount to wager, making it a lucrative event for the casino, hopefully one that would last.

The casino sent a limousine to pick up Nicole and me from our gated community in Orange County. The drive to John Wayne Airport was smooth, and we boarded a Gulfstream jet with a luxurious interior, plush leather seats, a fully stocked bar, and a spacious cabin that allowed us to relax in style for the one-hour flight.

Upon landing, a Rolls Royce awaited us on the tarmac. The drive to the casino offered stunning views of the lake and surrounding mountains. When we arrived at Harrah's, however, the hotel looked like a dump, at least as compared to the other hotels that have hosted me and invited me to play. I was only there for the money, so I put up with it.

The next morning, we headed to The Edgewood Tahoe Golf Course. With thousands of fans and media buzzing around the course, the atmosphere felt electric, as if we were on an authentic PGA tour. The immaculate greens and breathtaking views of the lake and mountains made it a perfect setting for the tournament.

Charles Barkley was a force of nature. He stood 6 feet 6 inches and weighed around 280 pounds, a physical powerhouse. His golf game, though not as legendary as his basketball career, was still impressive. Charles had a unique swing that drew as much attention as his commentary on sports shows.

"Hey Charles, great to finally meet you," I said as we shook hands on the first tee. "I've been looking forward to this."

"Likewise, Matt. Heard a lot about you," Charles replied, his smile wide. "Are you ready to make some money on the course?"

I laughed. "We'll see about that. Let's just enjoy the game."

As we played, our conversation flowed naturally. We talked about everything from sports to life outside the spotlight.

"You know, Charles, I've always admired your game. But I also know you're quite the gambler. I look forward to seeing whether you can live up to your reputation at the casino later this evening," I said casually, not wanting to press too hard.

Charles chuckled. "Yeah, I've had my fair share of bets. But I'm here to play golf today."

"Same here. Let's have a good time."

Playing with Charles was a highlight. Each year, I looked forward to this event, not just for the game but for the conversations and connections made.

Walking with athletes or celebrities to every hole made one thing clear. They were just like anyone else, people who enjoyed camaraderie and competition. I also got to connect with entertainers like Ray Romano, Steph Curry, and

Justin Timberlake. Each interaction felt genuine, free from the pressures of the casino floors.

After the game, we reconvened in the high-limit room, which the casino sectioned off for celebrities and high rollers. The games there differed from golf, with higher stakes. Charles sat at the Blackjack table, and when he spotted Nicole and I walk in, he gave me a nod. "You in," a glint of challenge in his eye.

I smiled. "Always, Charles. Always." I bought in with $100,000 and began the game.

The tournaments weren't only about the golf or the gambling, as I appreciated an opportunity to forge new relationships, to build new memories. Every year, I returned to Harrah's, not just as a gambler but as someone who appreciates the finer things in life and the people who made those experiences unforgettable. Given the legal clouds hanging over my head, this will be the first year in many that I am not going to join the tournament in Lake Tahoe.

Besides golf outings, the casino also opened opportunities for Nicole and me to watch some of the most anticipated sporting events of the year, such as when my host at Caesars Palace invited me to attend the popular fight of Floyd Mayweather against Conor McGregor. Since I pledged to bring more than $2 million to gamble, my host coordinated tickets for me to enjoy the fight with six friends.

The tickets showed a face value of $7,500 for the ring-side seats, but had I wanted to cash them in, with all the buzz around that fight, our seats would have easily brought more than $50,000 each on the open market.

For months, the media had built up that fight, which was dubbed "The Money Fight." Analysts and fans alike were divided, with some praising Mayweather's boxing prowess and others rooting for McGregor's unconventional style and sheer confidence. The hype was further fueled by a multi-city tour where the fighters exchanged heated words and engaged in dramatic face-offs, each trying to outdo the other in showmanship.

In the months leading up to the fight, coverage of "The Money Fight" saturated the sports channels and websites. Both fighters embarked on a multi-city promotional tour that included stops in Los Angeles, Toronto, New York, and London. Each event was more theatrical than the last, with the fighters building up the hype with their intense verbal sparring.

In Los Angeles, McGregor took the stage in a flashy suit, immediately criticizing Mayweather's financial troubles and calling him out for his conservative fighting style. "He's running away all the time," McGregor taunted, waving his arms dramatically. Mayweather, never one to back down, responded by flaunting a $100 million check and reminding McGregor of his perfect boxing record.

The Toronto event was even more explosive. McGregor mocked Mayweather's age and height, calling him a "little man" and making fun of his outfit choices. The crowd, largely in support of McGregor, roared with laughter and applause.

Mayweather, in response, promised to knock McGregor out and repeatedly called him a "quitter," referencing McGregor's last UFC fights.

By the time the tour reached London, the animosity was palpable. Both fighters refused to back down, and their exchanges grew increasingly personal and aggressive. The press coverage was relentless, with every media outlet capturing the escalating drama and building anticipation for the fight.

We arrived in style, courtesy of a private jet that whisked us from Orange County to Las Vegas. As we touched down, the casino coordinated a fleet of limousines to transport us to our suites at the Casino. At fight time, they transported us to the T-Mobile Arena. Las Vegas always had a buzz, but that night we especially felt the tangible excitement as we drove through the brightly lit streets of Vegas, the city buzzing with fans eager for the spectacle.

The T-Mobile Arena, packed to the brim, had its own energy, thick with anticipation. The lights dimmed, and the massive screens flickered to life, showing the fighters in their dressing rooms. The crowd erupted as Conor McGregor made his entrance, accompanied by *"Foggy Dew,"* an Irish folk song that set the stage for his dramatic walk to the ring. Draped in an Irish flag, McGregor exuded confidence, his eyes locked on the ring.

Mayweather's entrance was equally theatrical. To the beat of "We Will Rock You," he made his way to the ring surrounded by an entourage of bodyguards, trainers, and celebrities. Dressed in a shimmering gold robe, he walked slowly, soaking in the mix of cheers and boos. His face was a mask of concentration, his eyes never leaving the ring.

As the fighters stood face-to-face for the final stare down, the tension in the arena reached its peak. The lights focused on the ring, with the announcer drowning out the crowd's noise into a low rumble, as the moment finally arrived.

Our ring-side seats offered an unparalleled view of the action. Celebrities around us added to the glamor of the event. LeBron James sat just a few rows ahead, his presence causing a stir among the crowd. To our left, Jennifer Lopez chatted animatedly with her entourage, while Leonardo DiCaprio and Charlize Theron sat nearby, their eyes glued to the ring. Demi Lovato, who had just performed the national anthem, took her seat, exuding star power.

As the fight began, the arena erupted in cheers and applause. Mayweather, the undefeated boxing legend, danced around the ring with his trademark defensive style, while McGregor, the brash UFC champion, attempted to land powerful blows with his unconventional stance. The tension was high, with each round bringing the crowd to their feet, cheering and shouting in support of their favorite fighter.

The immense stakes weren't only high for the fighters, but for everyone involved. The fight generated staggering amounts of money, with pay-per-view sales breaking records and the live gate raking in millions. I read reports that the fight generated an estimated $600 million in revenue, with pay-per-view buys alone contributing around $450 million. Tickets for the live event sold out within minutes, with secondary market prices soaring to over $20,000 for the mediocre seats. Ringside seats went much higher. The live gate at the T-Mobile Arena brought in another $55 million, setting a new record.

Most analysts and fans expected Mayweather to win, given his unblemished record and unparalleled defensive skills. However, McGregor's unpredictable style and knockout power had many believing he could pull off a monumental upset. Experts predicted the fight would last several rounds, with Mayweather's technical precision pitted against McGregor's raw aggression.

As the fight progressed, it became clear that Mayweather's experience and skill were too much for McGregor. In the 10th round, Mayweather landed a series of blows that forced the referee to stop the fight, declaring Mayweather the winner by technical knockout. The crowd erupted in a mix of cheers and boos, the excitement of the evening reaching its peak.

After the fight, we made our way back to the casino, the thrill of the evening still coursing through our veins. The high-limit room was buzzing with energy as celebrities and high rollers mingled, recounting the night's events and placing their bets. Nicole and I went to play Baccarat, and Mark Wahlberg joined the action beside me.

"That was some fight," Nicole said, her eyes still wide with excitement.

"Unbelievable," I replied, shuffling my chips. "Mayweather really knows how to put on a show, and McGregor did great against the champion."

Memories from the fight would last a lifetime, but on the flight home, we had more fireworks.

Our friends had all flown home the day after the fight, but Nicole and I decided to stay a few extra days. We would board a commercial flight home rather than fly private.

While at the casino, I didn't only get to enjoy the fight, but I won just under $200,000. Before checking out, I asked my host to meet at the cashiers cage so I could bring my winnings home in cash. I brought 20 tightly packed bundles of $10,000, all stacks of crisp $100 bills. Stacked beside each other, they were the size of several bricks. I signed the cash transaction reports for the casino, as required by law.

Nicole and I traveled with a suitcase we would check, but also with a large designer duffle bag that she carried. She put our cash in the duffle bag, assuming that it wouldn't be a problem. When Nicole put her bag on the conveyor belt that went through the airport's scanner, it caught the agent's attention.

I could look over the rail of the conveyor belt and see the same screen that the agent was studying. He kept looking at the large mass inside the bag, trying to decipher what it was. He flagged the bag, sending it to another agent for further inspection. He called us over. When he saw she was carrying US currency in tightly wrapped stacks, he asked about it. I told him that I had won the cash at the casino, and I had put the cash inside.

He asked to photograph me, and I agreed. Then he gave us the bag and allowed us to go on to board our flight. I didn't think anything further of it.

When we landed in Orange County, I stood by the conveyor belt at baggage claim, waiting for the bags to come down. Nicole was a few feet away from me, looking at messages on her phone. Two males approached me. They were looking at something on their phone, and then looking at me, as if comparing a photograph to me. They asked if I was Matt Bowyer.

I nodded to confirm.

The agents then showed me their badges, from Homeland Security. They asked where my girl was.

I shrugged.

When I could see that they weren't looking, I caught Nicole's eyes and gave her a head nod. We were close enough that we could communicate with such gestures, and she understood that I wanted her to get the hell out of there. Without hesitating, she turned around and walked out. She had her carry-on over her shoulders, and the cash was safely inside.

The officers again asked where my girl was and I simply shrugged, as if I didn't know what they were talking about. One of the officers assumed it was an attractive girl standing a few feet away from me. He approached and told her that she'd have to come with him after her bags came down the chute.

She looked at him strangely and asked why. He flashed his badge. I didn't have any idea who she was, but they assumed she was traveling with me. While they spoke with her, I sent a text to Nicole, telling her to get in a cab and go home.

Finally, the bags we checked slid down the chute.

They kept me separate from the other girl they detained. Then they led us both into a private area. They opened my suitcase and began going through the luggage.

"Why do you have women's clothing in your luggage?" the agent asked me.

"Anything goes in Vegas," I joked.

"Where's the money?"

"Am I under arrest?" I asked.

The agent said no.

"Great," I told him. "I boarded a plane, I got off the plane, and now I'd like to go home with my bags. I'm not answering any other questions."

I could hear the girl they apprehended in the room next to me. She was freaking out, claiming that they didn't have any reason to be harassing her. They kept asking her where the money was. Obviously, she didn't know what they were talking about, and told them that she'd never seen me before in her life.

Realizing that they'd screwed up, and that Nicole was long gone with the money, they let us both go on our way.

It wasn't that I had anything to hide from the agents. I'd won the money in the casino and I'd signed the requisite forms the government required. But by then, I knew how the government operated. The agents likely would've relieved me of the money, then started new investigations, saying they were going to seize the currency until I could prove the origins of the funds I had used to win $200,000.

I didn't see any reason to go through that harassment.

Nicole was already home by the time I walked through the door. We shared a laugh over the whole ordeal, thankful that we had managed to avoid what could have been a very inconvenient situation. It was just another reminder that in the world we navigated, it was always better to stay a step ahead.

It wasn't only the casinos in Las Vegas that tried to lure me with the promise of attending epic sporting events. We even took some trips out to less desirable casinos, such as the Foxwoods Resort Casino in Mashantucket, Connecticut. While it didn't have the same glamor and allure as the casinos in Las Vegas, it offered its own unique charm and experiences.

Compared to Las Vegas, Foxwoods felt a bit dingy. The sprawling complex featured six casinos, making it one of the largest gambling venues in the world. While impressive in size, Foxwoods lacked the polish and opulence of Las Vegas. It had dim lighting, and a constant hum of slot machines. For the most part, people didn't dress to impress, not even for the high rollers rooms, giving it a different atmosphere.

Still, the casino was determined to win my patronage.

A host reached out to lure me to Foxwoods for a weekend of gambling. I wasn't all that interested until he offered to fly my group in a private Sikorsky helicopter to Boston for a Red Sox game. David Ortiz, one of the star players for the Red Sox and all of Major League Baseball, was going to retire, which promised to make the game exciting.

I invited my friend Mike Imech and his fiancée, Rachel, who had introduced me to Nicole. The four of us prepared for an adventure that promised both high stakes and high excitement.

I wired funds to the casino, and I also gave Mike funds so that he could play beside me, as part of my team. We arrived at Foxwoods, where the host greeted us with enthusiasm. Although I always looked forward to winning some money at the Baccarat table, my real purpose in making the cross-country trip was the upcoming helicopter ride to Fenway Park.

The Sikorsky helicopter waiting for us was a sight to behold—sleek and luxurious, promising a flight as memorable as the destination. When it came to interior comfort and elegance, the interior of the Sikorsky rivaled a Gulfstream jet. The plush leather seats arranged in a spacious cabin that was the size of a small living room, allowed us to stretch out and appreciate the memorable ride. Through the large windows, we enjoyed panoramic views of the Connecticut countryside as we lifted off, the rotor blades slicing through the air with a smooth, steady rhythm.

The flight from Connecticut to Boston was swift and scenic. As we approached the city, the urban landscape came into view, with its iconic skyline and the winding Charles River. The helicopter landed at a designated helipad near Fenway Park, where ground transportation awaited to take us to the stadium.

The limousine pulled into a private entrance at Fenway Park, likely reserved for dignitaries and the casino. We stepped out and walked to the private box that the casino had reserved for us, immediately enveloped into the energy and excitement of the crowd. It was my second time in the historic stadium, which I'd seen a hundred times on television, with its distinctive green facade and the famous Green Monster in left field. Boston fans donned Red Sox jerseys and caps, waving signs and cheering for their beloved David Ortiz and team.

David Ortiz, affectionately known as "Big Papi," was a legend in Boston. His retirement marked the end of an era, and the city wanted to celebrate. Ortiz had been a powerhouse for the Red Sox, known for his clutch hitting and larger-than-life personality. His contributions to the team and the city had cemented his status as a local hero.

Born in the Dominican Republic, David Ortiz immigrated to the United States and began his professional career with the Minnesota Twins. He joined the Red Sox in 2003, Ortiz quickly made his mark, becoming a fan favorite and a key player. Over his 14 seasons with the Red Sox, he helped lead the team to three World Series championships, breaking the "Curse of the Bambino" in 2004. Known for his clutch hitting, Ortiz delivered some of the most memorable moments in Red Sox history. Big Papi's larger-than-life personality and leadership on and off the field endeared him to fans and teammates alike.

As we settled into our seats, the pre-game festivities were in full swing. The crowd roared as Ortiz took the field for the last time, waving to the fans and acknowledging their adoration. The stadium was packed, every seat filled with fans eager to witness this historic moment.

The game itself was a thrilling spectacle, against the Toronto Blue Jays. The Red Sox played with passion and determination, fueled by the energy of the crowd and the significance of the occasion. Ortiz delivered a memorable performance, reminding everyone why he was such a beloved figure in the sport. The Red Sox, determined to send their hero off with a victory,

305 / www.MathewBowyer.com

played a hard-fought game, but ultimately, they lost to the Blue Jays with a final score of 2-1. Despite the loss, the focus remained on celebrating Ortiz's incredible career and the impact he had on the team and the city.

Leaving Fenway Park, we felt a mix of exhilaration and nostalgia, with the luxury and comfort of the Sikorsky providing a perfect setting for Nicole and I to enjoy with our friends Mike and Rachel. With the game behind us, we were ready to dive into the gaming tables. Although the Red Sox didn't win, Mike and I cleaned up at Foxwoods, leaving with more than $400,000 than I wired before I left California.

Another one of the less-celebrated venues that recruited me was the Ameristar Casino in East Chicago, Indiana. Al, a host and friend from Ameristar, had been urging me to visit the casino and gamble, knowing that I played big. To sweeten the deal, Al promised me six seats for Game Three of the World Series in Chicago. It was the first time the Chicago Cubs had played in the World Series since 1945. The Cubs had not won the World Series since 1908, so it was a big game. Nicole and I invited my daughter Lauren to join us. We also brought our friends Mike and Rachel, and my host Al also joined us.

The Ameristar Casino was not located in the best part of town. The area around it felt industrial and rough, a stark contrast to the opulence of Las

Vegas. The casino itself had an air of wear and tear, with an ambiance that would have benefited from an upgrade. The carpets were worn, and the strong smell of stale smoke hung in the air like a cloud. The patrons were mostly locals, dressed casually, as if they'd just gotten off a shift at an industrial plant, adding to the less formal atmosphere.

Knowing the girls would feel unsafe, I booked us some suites at a more upscale hotel in Chicago. After checking the girls in, Mike and I returned to the Ameristar, where my host had set me up with a $1 million credit line. The casino's high-limit room, while not lavish by any stretch, still offered the thrill of big stakes. I used the line of credit, but unfortunately blew through the majority of the credit line losing 800k in literally just a few short hours.

Given the high-crime area surrounding the casino, the management took extra precautions with their high rollers. The casino sent security guards to escort Mike and I out, ensuring our safety as we made our way back to Chicago, which was only a short drive to our hotel. The presence of the guards was a stark reminder of the casino's location, and we appreciated the professionalism.

As with visiting Fenway Park for the first time, the real highlight of this trip was visiting Wrigley Field. I had some history in Chicago from back when I worked with Micky, trading commodities and setting up his office. It always felt good to be back.

I wouldn't say Chicago was my kind of town, like Frank Sinatra sang, but there was some nostalgia there, and I enjoyed going over some of the spots with Nicole, my daughter, and our friends.

Wrigley Field, with its iconic ivy-covered brick walls and manual scoreboard, exuded a timeless charm. The atmosphere around the stadium was old-school baseball, filled with fans who had waited a lifetime to see the Cubs in the World Series. My casino host had gotten me desirable tickets at Gate F, Suite 14. These seats, with a face value of $650, were in high demand.

Given the excitement across the country for the Cubs, it didn't surprise me when I saw offers in the aftermarket for $10,000 for seats in the area where we would watch the game. The money didn't interest me, as I wanted our group to enjoy a fabulous time there, eating hot dogs and munching on peanuts while we sang with the crowd, "Take me out to the ball game."

Even though the Cubs lost Game Three, 1-0, the experience of being at Wrigley Field for such a historic event was unforgettable. The excitement, the hope, and the sheer joy of the fans created an atmosphere that we'd never forget.

The Cubs may have lost Game Three, but they came back to win the series in Game Seven, ending a 108-year championship drought. We were glad to be a part of their journey.

Nicole and I will miss those adventures, but thankfully, we have awesome memories, not only from Harrahs, Caesar's, Foxwood, and Ameristar, but also from the much more glitzy casinos of Monte Carlo.

CHAPTER 14
A World Apart

I am grateful to my friend Steve, a casino host who always treated Nicole and me well. Steve opened relationships with numerous casinos, arranged for me to have high credit lines and unbelievable perks. Although my problems with the criminal justice system have put those perks out of reach, I still have great memories. Some of the best memories that Nicole and I cherish are from our visits to Monte Carlo.

Steve arranged for Lufthansa to provide us with two first-class tickets, with lay-down seats, at a retail value of $30,000. The flight experience was only the start of the luxury that awaited us. Before going on our first trip to Monaco, Steve instructed me to wire $1 million in Euro to the casino, which the casino matched, providing an additional $1 million in credit that I could draw upon. With $2 million in chips at my disposal, and all the confidence in the world, I stood ready to test my skills in the most opulent casino of any city in the world. He booked us a suite at the Hotel Hermitage Monte-Carlo, a world-class hotel, well known for its elegance and breathtaking views.

Monte Carlo wasn't anything like Las Vegas or the other gambling venues I'd visited in the

United States or the Caribbean. The casinos were quiet, almost serene, devoid of the blaring music, glitter, and flashing lights. Regardless of the VIP treatment Vegas casinos gave to other high rollers and me, anytime we walked outside of our suite, we got sucked into an atmosphere that pulsed with energy, fueled by the bells of slot machines and the chatter of excited tourists who were excited to get away from small towns like Topeka or Akron or Talladega. They didn't care much about appearances there—fat people in cutoff jeans, tank tops, and cowboy hats shuffled through smoke-filled casino floors, pulling slot-machine handles beside people who looked like gangbangers from an inner city street corner. People focused solely on the next thrill.

I'm not saying there was anything wrong with people who preferred comfort as they liked it over style and elegance. Vegas offered hot-dog eating contests and all-you-could eat buffets, which some people liked. Everyone could find their fun, no matter their background. As the motto held, what happens in Vegas stays in Vegas.

Not so in Monte Carlo, which felt like a different universe altogether. Elegance was the norm, not the exception. The men who walked through the gilded doors of the casinos dressed in tuxedos or impeccably tailored suits, while the women dressed in designer gowns, accented with expensive diamonds and gold jewelry that sparkled under the chandeliers.

People came to the Hotel Hermitage looking for the epitome of luxury. Perched on the edge of the Mediterranean Sea, every room offered panoramic views of blue waters, dotted with extraordinary yachts. Our suite was plush, with a private balcony overlooking the harbor. The scent of fresh flowers and the saltiness of the sea breezed in through open windows.

Each morning, we'd head to the top-notch hotel gym. During one of my workouts, I met two Russians who frequented the hotel. They were young, and powerfully built. Being competitive, I kept up with their training routine. They may have been bigger, younger, and stronger, but I had the energy to make sure they wouldn't outwork me. I liked them both, and felt comfortable kicking it with them.

After our workout, we agreed to meet again on the casino floor. When we finished our exercise, they walked out to board a superyacht—a vessel so large it seemed to dwarf the other yachts around it. The yacht had some notoriety, the kind that appeared in glossy magazines with a price tag of more than $300 million. They didn't make a show, but as I watched them step aboard, I could see that Monte Carlo was home to a level of ostentatious wealth that few people could imagine. I hoped to learn more about them while we tested our skills against the dealer at a Baccarat table.

Nicole and I dined at Le Grill, a phenomenal restaurant perched atop the Hotel De Paris. Besides great cuisine, it gave us an amazing view that took our breath away. From our table, we could see the glittering lights of the city below, with the Mediterranean stretching out into the dark night. We both felt as if we were in a James Bond movie.

After dinner, we headed to Jimmy'z, one of the most exclusive nightclubs in Monte Carlo. It's known for being packed with royalty, celebrities, high rollers, and international jet setters from around the world. People who partied in the VIP section at Jimmy'z expected to drop more than $10k for a night of dancing and drinking and being seen. The club's cutting-edge lighting and vibrant dance floor created a charged atmosphere, another perfect spot for Nicole and I to build memories. Dancing with her, especially in a place like Jimmy'z, always made me feel as if I were the luckiest guy on earth.

As a person who spent his life in casinos, I knew the value of luck. Everything seemed to be going my way while we were there, with the general manager opening every door and making us feel as if we were VIPs. At the casino, I put $2 million in chips to work. By placing large bets with each hand, I wagered more than $10 million every hour. I didn't see the two Russians I met earlier when we were working out in the gym, but there were other high rollers putting down $100k worth of chips on each hand. Win or lose, we all kept playing until the sun came up.

By the end of our trip, not only had I reclaimed the money I wired, but walked away with an additional $1.4 million. As a treat, I splurged on Nicole, taking her shopping through all the designer stores. We blew through more than $200,000 on clothes and handbags alone , and as parting gifts, I bought matching platinum Breitling watches, a symbol of our unforgettable first trip to Monte Carlo.

Unfortunately, when the FBI raided my home in October of 2023, they confiscated my Breitling—a painful reminder that the government could easily tarnish my most precious memories. I thought I'd lost the watch forever. Fortunately, after several months of judicial proceedings, prosecutors surprised me by calling me for a return to their office. They handed over a box containing many of the belongings the agents had seized from my house. When I opened it, I felt glad to see our Breitling watches, which will bring back memories from our visits to Monaco, and which I look forward to passing down to my son Kingston.

For our second and third trip, Steve booked us at the Hotel De Paris, which we admired so much after walking through the hotel on our first trip, when we dined at its rooftop restaurant, Le Grill. Our second trip, the bets didn't go my way and I lost somewhere around $200k at the tables, which was simply an expected part of the ups and downs of my chosen vocation. Fortunately, we made up for the losses on our third trip, when I walked out with winnings of roughly $260k. Our trips to Monte Carlo were both memorable and profitable.

In retrospect, had it not been for the relationships I'd built on our first two trips, the third trip could've been a disaster. As I'd done on the first two trips, I prepared for the third trip by sending a wire for $1 million from my trust account to the casino before leaving the United States. Steve had assured me that the casinos would offer a credit line that matched the funds I sent in advance.

Neither of us knew that the banking laws in Monte Carlo had changed at some point between my second and third visit.

Thinking that I had money waiting for me when I'd get there, I only carried pocket change of about $3,000 in US currency for the flight. I didn't anticipate needing more, because I expected that the casino would allow me to draw upon the funds I had sent in advance. We arrived at the Hotel De Paris, looking forward to a great time. While we were checking in, however, the general manager told me that the casino wouldn't accept the $1 million wire transfer that I'd sent.

"Why not?" I asked. "It hadn't ever been a problem before."

The manager told me that laws in Monte Carlo had changed since my previous visits. Casinos could only accept wire transfers from individuals who had complied with the anti-money laundering and know-your-customer laws, and they could not accept funds from anonymous trust accounts.

"How come you didn't tell me before I left the United States?" I asked.

If I had known that there was a problem, I could have made different arrangements, or completed the necessary paperwork. "The casino had sent wiring instructions, and my bank confirmed that it sent the money." I told him.

He apologized profusely, and offered to help. We called my bank together. My bank confirmed that the funds had been transferred back into my account, because the wire did not go through. I asked the banker to transfer the funds from my trust account to my personal account, then wire from my personal account. The banker confirmed that he could make the transfer, but the bank would not authorize him to send a $1 million wire transfer to the casino unless I appeared in the bank personally to sign for the wire transfer in person. Since I was already in Monte Carlo, that wasn't a viable option.

Fortunately, the general manager at the Hotel De Paris did his best to make things right. Even though I could not send funds until I returned back to the United States, he authorized $200,000 in casino credit. With that advance, and my lucky charm by my side, I played the tables well enough to walk out with nearly $260,000 after paying all expenses.

The criminal case put a stop to those kinds of experiences. At least I had the memories, and the hard assets that I'd been able to put together. Others were not so fortunate.

When the federal authorities began pulling strings at the Las Vegas casinos, trying to build criminal cases against anyone who did not comply with anti-money laundering laws, know-your-customer laws, and other laws pertaining to the gambling industry, they found Wayne Nix, one of the most prominent bookmakers in Los Angeles. The investigation spread, bringing me into the web of problems. Then the agents went after other bookmakers, such as my friend Damien LeForbes.

I met Damien back around 2014, almost ten years ago. By then, I had hundreds of accounts that, cumulatively, booked more than $50 million in bets annually. Damien had a similar book-of-business, and our paths frequently crossed. We'd hang out, enjoy the perks of a gambling life, such as going to poker games together, and before I met Nicole, hanging out with Vegas women together.

Like me, Damien didn't only book bets, he also gambled heavily, fancying himself a professional poker player, or high-stakes gambler. As I had done, Damian got started in bookmaking because of his personal affinity for gambling. Some guys were truly professional poker players, earning a living by participating in high-stakes tournaments.

Damien wasn't really that kind of professional. He booked a lot of bets, and anyone who booked a lot of bets generated cash flow. The cash flow allowed him to bet high stakes in poker tournaments. A professional poker player would likely have the discipline to walk away if he lost. A good bookmaker like Damien had the cash flow to buy more chips, to stick around and keep betting until the cards started to go his way. If they didn't, it wouldn't be the end of the world, because money would continue coming in through his bookmaking operations.

Following the Wayne Nix scandal, the authorities started questioning any casino workers they could find, which led them to Damien. When authorities arrested him, Las Vegas newspapers sensationalized the event, saying that he lost more than $12 million at Resort World alone, and that authorities had already accounted for more than $150 million worth of wagers through his bookmaking business. If a person didn't understand bookmaking, those numbers sounded extraordinary. People in the industry, however, knew that those numbers were misleading, suggesting that a bigger crime had taken place.

By the time I met Damien, he had already taken all the steps to modernize his bookmaking operation. He'd gone to Costa Rica, set himself up with a sports gambling website, and started doing business. Both his clients and his agents could log into his website and begin setting up accounts; Damien simply paid a fee on a per-head basis.

By participating in poker tournaments, playing craps, blackjack, or shooting dice, Damien got to know other people who lived on the edge. First, they got their fix for excitement by placing their sports bets with his service, and then they started to supplement their income by working as an agent, inducing all their friends to also book sports bets with Damien's service.

He worked with the same kind of clientele that bet with me. They were real estate agents, stock brokers, contractors, business people who didn't want to travel to Las Vegas to place bets. They could get all the excitement they needed by logging onto his internet site. Damien had a great reputation for paying on time, and his business grew to include hundreds of people. Cumulatively, they'd wager millions of dollars each week.

Although they'd win or lose sporadically, overtime, Damien would always come out ahead— just as any good bookmaker would do. Getting to $150 million worth of bets wouldn't take long, because a typical gambler would bet five games, ten games, or more over a weekend during football season. Each of those bets would be in the thousands of dollars. The numbers added up quickly.

Being as much of a degenerate gambler as me, Damien put his cashflow on the line, over and over again. He had big balls and I respected him. The problem was that he blew through everything, never putting enough aside to purchase hard assets that would stand the test of time.

He was married, and together with his wife, he had two sons. Since Damien had massive cash flow, he lived in a multi-million dollar home in an expensive beachfront community. Rather than keeping his money tied up in real estate, he rented. That decision had the advantage of keeping him liquid, but as Damien found, that liquidity could also be a disadvantage.

The FBI agents raided Damien's home a few months after they hit me. At my place, the agents walked away with cash, casino chips, gold coins, some jewelry, handbags, and other trinkets of the trade. In today's market, the home I lived in with Nicole and our son Kingston would easily fetch $5 million—but a trust owned the home, offering some level of asset protection. During the raid at Damien's house, the agents got most of his liquidity, which exceeded $3 million in crypto and US currency.

Although the government agreed to return watches and handbags that they took from my place, Damien understood that it would be unlikely that he'd ever see stacks of hundred-dollar bills that they carted out of his house. When he called me to commiserate over our shared troubles, he told me that he'd lost everything in that raid, and didn't even know how he'd be able to pay the rent.

Those losses sent him into an emotional tailspin. He lost his mind, even had to be hospitalized after attempting suicide. As a friend, hearing this made me sick to my stomache. Only a person who has been through a federal indictment could truly understand what pain and suffering comes with it.

As bookmakers and gamblers, we should always remember our place, and our status in the game. We had to use the same kind of critical thinking that would give us the confidence to put down millions of dollars on a single bet, as I had done numerous times.

I could put those resources on the line because I had already planted some seeds of stability, with real estate, investments, gold, and businesses that would carry on with value regardless of how the wager turned out. As bookmakers, we had to remember that we were not the same as our clients. Damien did not take such precautions.

He gambled as if he had the same fallback as the billionaires who used our services to place bets with us.

Jeffrey Schotenstein, for example, placed millions of dollars worth of bets through my system. His father, the billionaire founder of American Eagle Outfitters and a major figure in commercial real estate, could help Jeffrey dig himself out from any kind of hole. When Jeff started using my website to bet, he urged me to give him a $1 million credit line, and asked me to authorize him to bet up to $100k for each game.

I agreed.

But I had to look at his account constantly. The guy would bet on anything and everything, without any pattern. I'd review his account in the early afternoon and see that he was up $1 million. A few hours later, by the end of the betting day, he'd be down $600k.

He'd go up and down. When his losses got too big, he'd try to settle at a discount, offering me trinkets—but the kind of trinkets that the son of a billionaire collected. He once paid his debts by giving me two Richard Mille watches, telling me that he paid more than $300k for each of them. Another time, when his father had cut him off, or put him on some type of restricted spending, Jeffrey tried to scam his own family. He told me that his family had an account at a high-end jewelry store. If I visited the store, I could charge anything I wanted if I applied the value to his debt. It's the reason that Nicole got a second wedding ring, with a six-carat yellow diamond. It cleared out Jeff's debt, and Nicole got two wedding rings, which I thought she deserved, because she's beautiful!

Unfortunately, Damien never collected those kinds of assets. He wanted liquidity. It gave him the firepower he needed to put everything on the line each time he visited a casino, but it also gave the FBI agents a windfall when they raided his home. He couldn't even appreciate the memories like those that Nicole and I cherished, such as those from our visits to Monte Carlo. In his view, life wasn't worth living any longer.

I weathered the storm of a raid by the FBI easier than Damien, perhaps, because I understood and accepted the risks of the vocation I chose. Regardless of what happened, I believed that I would land on my feet, okay, ready to fight another day.

I didn't have a billionaire father to fall back on like Jeffrey. Instead, I had the greatest mom in the world. She may not have had financial resources to cover for the many errors I would make, but she gave me many gifts, helping me to build confidence. People who met her would tell me that she was the nicest person they'd ever met. Her life had a lot of ups and downs since my father abandoned us when I was a child, and I'm grateful that she found Mark, my stepfather, a retired fire battalion chief, who has built a great marriage with her over the past 30 years. She lost a great deal, with my brother's death, my younger brother's challenges with substance abuse and imprisonment, and with the crazy life that I've lived.

Growing up with those challenges helped me appreciate the need to prepare for the rainy days—because I always expected them to come. If it was just me, I could live on the edge, with total confidence that I'd be able to recover from any setback. But I knew that it had never been "just me."

From the time I was a teenager, I felt a deep sense of responsibility to do anything possible to help out my mom—which led to my developing great skills in door-to-door sales. One of the great victories of my life was when I saw her break down in tears of joy as I told her that by signing up more accounts than any other paperboy, the Orange County Register rewarded me with an all-expense paid trip to Hawaii. I was 14. I was very happy to give those tickets to my mom.

Since then, the responsibilities kept growing. By marrying young, I knew that I had to get things together quickly, and found my groove while waiting tables at a Mexican restaurant, and then making myself indispensable in Micky's brokerage business. The more children I had, the harder I had to work to build a moat around me, creating something of meaning that I could always count on as protection—so that I'd never sink into those waves of emotional turmoil that threatened to drown out Damien's spirit.

Those efforts I made to set a net beneath me in case I fell didn't always work out. It wasn't too long ago that my friend Ryan Boyajian told me about his friend Andris, an amazing entrepreneur who had built a $20 million home in Newport Beach. Andris was about my age, Ryan said, and he'd had an amazing career. While a student at the University of Maryland, he spotted an opportunity by chance to create a new industry in debt settlement.

With less than $5,000, Andris set up his business with a phone line and a series of newspaper ads. The ads, he said, were quite simple: "Got debt? We can help. Call 1-800-EndDebt." From the day he started running the ads nationwide, his phone rang with prospective customers.

Andris said he charged his customers a sign up fee of about $100, along with a nominal fee of $5 per month for each credit card. Once they became customers, Andris would take over, calling huge credit card companies like Visa, MasterCard, Discover Card, and others. He'd tell them that he had a client who was going to discharge the debt in bankruptcy unless the company renegotiated the terms. The customers were paying extortionate interest rates that exceeded 30 percent per year, and they were financing purchases that they'd made to eat in restaurants, or to buy throw-away consumer items.

The credit card companies didn't have anything to repossess. If the customer filed bankruptcy, they'd lose everything. Without exception, the credit card companies agreed to new terms. To continue receiving payments on the debt, the credit card companies agreed to lower the interest rate, and to stretch out the terms of the loan, provided the customer kept paying toward the debt each month.

Andris grew his company quickly, eventually building a customer base of more than 500,000 people, each of whom was paying $5 per month for each credit card. Before he had turned 30, Andris had built a business that brought in an average of more than $10 million in monthly revenues.

Andris leveraged the wealth he generated to launch other businesses, including an international property development company. He purchased an oceanfront plot of land that was as large as the island of Manhattan in a central American country. When he bought the property, it was all jungle that abutted white-sand beaches of the Caribbean. He built a community with more than 1,000 homesites, and then began selling those homesites to Americans who wanted to retire overseas.

The more my friend Ryan had told me about Andris, and the housing development he built, the more enthusiastic I became. Andris and I became friends, and I considered his development to be a great opportunity to build another safety net. We came to an agreement, where I'd give him $2 million. He could use it for anything he deemed necessary to advance his development, including building houses or other structures that would generate monthly income. I viewed it as a great way for me to build a steady flow of monthly revenues.

As agreed, I provided him with $2 million that my gambling and bookmaking operation generated. Then, within six months of investing, an agency of the federal government sued Andris, alleging that he had violated laws pertaining to fair trade. The net result, in an instant, the overseas investment I made with hopes of building a safety net to catch me if I fell, turned out to have a gaping hole. The investment turned out to be a total disaster, resulting in a 100 percent loss, which I couldn't even deduct on my taxes.

Fortunately, Andris had relationships with other high net worth individuals who gambled heavily. I admired his honesty. He immediately came to see me, explaining all that had happened. Alleging that he violated fair-trade laws, our government seized more than $150 million worth of his assets, including his amazing house in Newport Beach. Despite all those losses, he told me how he intended to make me whole. "I can't give you back any money," he said, "because the government took everything I have. But I know people who bet heavily on sports. I'm going to introduce you, and through the bets they place, I hope you'll recover over time."

He certainly did his part. Over the course of a few months, those bets resulted in nearly $1 million in earnings that I otherwise wouldn't have received.

Less disciplined bookmakers blew their money gambling, buying cocaine, or paying hookers. I did my share of profligate spending. But I also made sure that I built equity, investing in hard assets that I hoped would spare me the total washout that Damien described.

Those preparations helped me stay focused in the long months that led me to the late summer of 2024—more than ten months since the FBI raided my house. But in August, my life took another drastic turn, forcing me to confront the formal judicial process. This journey would come in steps, my attorney Diane Bass explained, beginning with an initial appearance where I'd enter a not-guilty plea. Later, I'd have a change-of-plea hearing, where I would shift my plea to guilty under the terms of our agreement.

Diane had negotiated the deal, and we believed it would lead to home confinement. Yet, like any deal, it wouldn't be real until every party signed, agreed, and, ultimately, the judge delivered a sentence.

To take those next steps, Diane drove me to the Ronald Reagan Federal Courthouse in Santa Ana, doing her best to prepare me for what I'd face. As we approached the courthouse, the building loomed over us, its sleek stone and glass exterior reflecting the sun's sharp glare. Inside, the blast of cold air-conditioning hit my skin, an abrupt change from the California heat outside. I tried to steady myself, but the marble floors and towering ceilings added weight to each step. Everything felt oversized, and I was like one of many puppets walking through its halls. Those of us facing criminal charges would await decisions that others made to reshape our life.

Diane and I passed through security, the clatter of the scanner and the low murmur of voices in the lobby adding to my tension. When we entered the elevator, I felt the weight of the silent crowd packed inside. The hum of the elevator felt deafening as my mind raced, replaying conversations with Diane, with Nicole, with anyone who had tried to reassure me. I tried to imagine what lay ahead, but every scenario seemed worse than the last.

The elevator stopped with a slight lurch on the sixth floor. As the doors slid open, we stepped out to see Rachel, the prosecutor, waiting for us. She greeted us with a polite nod, her face calm, professional. She led us to a conference room, where other cases were also on the docket that day. I could feel my palms dampen, my breathing shallow as I anticipated the next steps.

After a brief meeting, a pretrial services officer came to meet me, saying she would prepare a report to give the judge insight into my character and, ultimately, my eligibility for bail. She looked at me with an unflinching gaze, clipboard in hand, asking a series of questions that felt designed to peel back layers I would have preferred to keep hidden.

She asked, "Have you ever used drugs? Cocaine, acid, ecstasy?"

"No," I said, shaking my head. "Only alcohol. I've never used illegal drugs."

Her questions shifted, drilling into the details of my gambling history. "What's the largest single loss you've experienced?"

I did my best to speak casually, as if the memory were nothing. "Two million," I said, almost under my breath. "On a football game."

With each answer, she made notes, her face a mask of impartiality. When she was done, she recommended several conditions for my pretrial release: regular drug tests, participation in Gamblers Anonymous, and, to my surprise, mental health counseling.

The first two didn't faze me. I'd never used drugs, so peeing in a cup seemed irrelevant, and I was used to hearing about Gamblers Anonymous. But the idea of mandatory counseling for mental health—that bothered me. I didn't want any record suggesting I needed mental health help. I looked at Diane, my discomfort, and she agreed to challenge that part of the recommendation.

Before we reached the courtroom, we learned of an error. Someone in the clerk's office had mistakenly posted my case on the public docket, drawing a swarm of reporters who were now gathered outside. Diane and the prosecutor scrambled to explain the mistake to the magistrate judge, hoping to avoid a media circus. After a brief consultation, they reached a compromise: my appearance would move to a different floor, in a quieter courtroom, hopefully away from any cameras.

When the time came, I pulled open the heavy doors and stepped into the sterile, quiet space. The walls, plain and unadorned, felt like they were pressing inward, emphasizing the gravity of each movement, each breath. Across the room, a probation officer sat at a table, her expression unreadable. To her, I was likely just another name on a docket, one of many facing judgment.

Beside her sat an IRS officer, a silent reminder that my finances, my transactions, every dollar that had passed through my hands was under a microscope. He had a notepad in front of him, though he barely looked at it, his eyes fixed on me with an unreadable scrutiny. Next to him was an FBI agent, exchanging quiet words with the IRS officer. I felt their combined gaze like a weight on my shoulders.

Diane and I took our seats. Her calm presence was my only comfort, a steady reminder that, in this room, I was not alone, even if everything inside me felt otherwise.

Each passing minute felt stretched, warped, as though time itself resisted moving forward. I tried to focus, to stay present, but my mind drifted. The quiet hum of the air conditioning, the echo of footsteps in the hall, the faint rustle of papers—it was all I could do to keep from falling into a spiral of regret and dread. Soon, I would be someone else entirely: a man formally charged with a crime, no longer free, bound by whatever terms the court imposed.

Finally, the bailiff's voice broke the silence, instructing us to rise. The magistrate judge entered and took his seat, his gaze sweeping over the courtroom with a practiced detachment. My stomach tightened as he read out the charges against me: operating an illegal gambling business, money laundering, and filing a false tax return.

"How do you plead?" he asked, his voice echoing.

"Not guilty," Diane answered for me, as she had already explained for me that it was temporary, just a formality before I would accept a plea agreement in anticipation of sentencing.

The judge accepted the plea, then began detailing the conditions of my release. I saw his lips move, but the words felt like a foreign language. It was all I could do to nod in vague agreement as he spoke about the restrictions I'd face, including limits on spending my own money, all tied to the money laundering charge.

Diane assured me she'd explain later, but the message had become very clear that things had gotten serious. This wasn't some negotiation or theory anymore. I was here, in a courtroom, facing my future. The judge's voice became a distant drone until he asked if anyone had anything further to say.

Diane stood and formally objected to the mental health counseling recommendation. The judge's lips broke into a smirk, as if to say, Anyone who wagered $2 million on a single football game could probably use counseling. He denied the objection.

And with that, it was over. My future now rested in the hands of a judge, a calendar, and a courtroom I was only beginning to understand.

CHAPTER 15
Guilty

As Diane and I left the courtroom, I felt a strange mix of exhaustion and unease. We walked in silence through the courthouse lobby, where the cold air still clung to my skin, though outside, the late-summer heat was ready to swallow me up again. On the drive back to San Juan Capistrano, I finally broke the silence, glancing at Diane as she gripped the wheel with that same determined look she always had when the stakes were high.

"What do you think?" I asked, but before I could get the words out, she was already shaking her head, her face tight with frustration.

"The magistrate judge was just... difficult today. He shot down every argument I made about avoiding the programs. Usually, he's more reasonable," she said, sighing as if she was the one facing what lay ahead. "But remember, Matt, he's not the one with the final say on sentencing. That'll be a different judge entirely."

I nodded, though my mind was swimming with more questions than clarity. "So what's the difference? I mean, between the magistrate judge and the sentencing judge?"

Diane took a breath, slowing down as we turned onto the highway, and explained the distinction as if it were supposed to be obvious. "A magistrate judge handles preliminary matters, sets bail conditions, rules on some legal motions—administrative things, basically. The sentencing judge, however, will hear the full case, weigh the evidence, and ultimately decide your sentence."

I absorbed the explanation in silence. *It's just a formality*, I told myself, but it didn't feel like that at all. Sitting in front of that magistrate judge, I'd felt exposed, as if every decision from here on out was a card played with the deck stacked against me.

Yet, despite the frustration of it all, I knew my path was set. Bail or no bail, judge or no judge, this was my reality. I had to follow the rules, comply with the conditions, and hope the pieces eventually fell into place. There was no doubling down, no bluffing or talking my way out of this one. I had no choice but to play it straight.

As Diane continued her usual back-and-forth with the intricacies of court procedures, I found my thoughts drifting, oddly enough, to a sculpture I'd seen in Europe several years before. It had struck me then—a bronze block, just a simple, solid base of metal at first glance, with a powerful man chiseling himself free from it.

He held a hammer in one hand, a chisel in the other, each blow carving out the contours of his muscular form, as if he was giving birth to his own strength. He was literally breaking free of his limitations, sculpting himself into something more.

The image stuck with me, and in moments like this, it almost felt like a calling. Maybe that was what I was meant to do now—redefine myself, chisel away the layers of a life that no longer served me. I couldn't be the man I was before, even if I tried. Those days were over. I had to find a way to build a new life out of this mess, one that didn't leave me vulnerable to scandal, supervision, or the headlines of another Ohtani story gone wrong.

At least the magistrate judge hadn't required prison or detention just yet. But I could feel the weight of his conditions. Reporting to a probation officer? I hadn't seen that coming. The idea stirred something inside of me, and unsettled me, as if I'd been dropped back into a game where I didn't know the rules.

The drive home was quiet after that. Diane dropped me off, offering a few final words of reassurance. But all I could think about was that statue, the hammer, the chisel, and the man emerging from a solid block of bronze. If I was going to rebuild, I'd have to break free piece by piece, following this path through the court system, probation, and whatever lay on the other side.

All I knew was that I had to start chiseling now, even if I didn't yet see the form I was supposed to take.

When I walked into the house, the weight of the day hung over me like a heavy coat I couldn't shrug off. Nicole was in the kitchen, sipping coffee or tea at our kitchen counter while watching Kingston, our son. The sight of her brought relief and a reminder of all the ways my decisions were now rippling through our lives. She turned toward me as I set my keys on the counter, her expression a mix of curiosity and concern.

"How did it go?" she asked, setting her mug down. Despite her calm voice, I knew her well and could tell that she was bracing herself for whatever news I had.

I leaned on the counter, holding my hand to my face. "It went... okay, I guess. Diane argued her best, but the judge laid down some restrictions that I didn't expect."

"Whatever the restrictions are, we'll work through them together."

I told her that the judge ordered me to undergo mental health counseling, to undergo drug testing, and to participate in Gamblers Anonymous, and that a probation officer would have to oversee me. I also told her that, basically, as a person charged with a crime, I had to give up the rights that we previously took for granted. I had to submit to a monitoring system that would allow authorities to "mirror" my phone—which means that they could see every call, and every text. They could monitor my financial accounts. Further, both probation officers and US Marshals said that they intend to surprise us with random and unexpected home visits., or demand that I participate in video calls so they could check my location. Finally, I wouldn't be able to leave California without their consent. It was a bit much for Nicole to take.

"Probation officer?" Nicole squinted in surprise. "What does that mean? Are they going to be monitoring you all the time?"

"I don't know yet," I admitted. "I have to call the probation department tomorrow. Diane gave me the contact information. The clerk at the court handed it over on my way out. I'll figure out more when I talk to them."

Nicole crossed her arms, leaning back against the counter. "This is a lot, but we'll get through it, whatever comes."

"I know," I said, meeting her eyes. "One step at a time, okay. We've still got each other, and we'll get to the other side of this fiasco."

She didn't say anything for a moment, just gave a small nod and stepped closer, resting her hand on my arm. "I know we will," she said softly. "I just wish it didn't have to be this way."

So did I, but there was no point in saying it. We both knew the situation for what it was. After a quiet dinner, I sat alone in my office, trying to refocus my mind on the manuscript I'd been chipping away at. Writing had become my way of staying grounded, a place to channel anxiety and uncertainty. Even as I typed, the looming call to the probation officer lingered there in the back of my mind, like an itch I couldn't scratch.

The next morning, after my usual routine—fitness, cold plunge, sauna—I dialed the number. A reception person put me on hold. My heart was steady, my voice even, but I couldn't help feeling a flicker of apprehension when a curt, professional voice answered.

"This is Officer Kressler," she said.

"Good morning, Officer Kressler. My name is Matt Bowyer," I began, keeping my tone polite and measured. "My lawyer, Diane Bass, directed me to contact you as part of my release conditions."

There was a pause before she responded. "Yes, Mr. Bowyer. Thank you for calling. I'll need you to come to my office for an initial meeting. We'll discuss the terms of your supervision and next steps."

"Of course," I said, forcing a tone of cooperation. "When would you like me to come in?"

"Tomorrow morning, 10 a.m. My office is at the federal courthouse in Santa Ana. Please bring a government-issued ID."

"Understood. I'll see you then," I said, jotting down the details before we ended the call.

I wasn't thrilled about going back to the courthouse. Just being there felt like stepping into quicksand. But there was no use dragging my feet. If this was the next hurdle, I'd face it head-on.

The following morning, after my routine, I dressed for the meeting. Typically, I wear athleisure clothes, as my life is pretty carefree. For this visit, I wore slacks, a blazer, and a button-down shirt, wanting to make a better impression, giving off the vibe that I respected the culture of a federal government office. I hoped Officer Kressler would see me for who I am, and not just another case number. As I drove to Santa Ana, I kept my mind focused, replaying the mental scripts I'd used in gambling halls and high-stakes negotiations. Stay calm. Stay polite. Stay confident.

When I arrived, the courthouse felt just as imposing as before. I steeled myself as I walked through security and followed the directions to the probation office. The receptionist barely glanced at me as she gestured toward a sign-in sheet, and I scribbled my name before taking a seat.

"Mr. Bowyer?" a voice called a few minutes later.

I stood and turned to see a woman in her early forties, dressed in a crisp blazer with a professional air that bordered on intimidating. "Officer Kressler," she said, extending a hand. She struck me as someone who would want to stay all business, impervious to my charm.

"Nice to meet you," I said, offering a firm handshake. "Thank you for seeing me."

She nodded, her expression neutral, and led me to a small, plain office. As I took a seat, I told myself to stay steady, to let none of the tension show. This was just another game, another opponent, and I had to play it smart.

"I'll explain the expectations for your supervision," she began, her tone formal and efficient. As she spoke, I nodded along, careful to listen, to show respect. But in the back of my mind, I was already calculating. Could I win her over? Could I ease the edges of this process, make it smoother for both of us? If I handled this right, maybe she'd see me as someone cooperative, someone who wasn't trying to make her job harder.

I smiled at the thought. If nothing else, I'd learned the value of a good first impression.

As I sat in Officer Kressler's small, windowless office, I felt like I'd stepped into an alternate reality. It wasn't the drab walls or the sterile air, but the sheer weight of the conditions she laid out—each one adding another link to the chain that would now bind my life.

She didn't waste any time getting to business. After handing me a stack of forms, she asked me to detail every aspect of my life: finances, monthly expenses, income streams, and even projections for how I'd cover my bills going forward. I filled out the forms as thoroughly as possible, explaining the balance between my income, Nicole's contributions, and the savings we'd rely on to stay afloat. Kressler scanned the papers, her pen scratching notes in a way that felt almost accusatory.

When she finally looked up, her expression was neutral, but her tone carried the weight of authority. "Your finances show a shortfall between your income and expenses," she said. "You show anticipated earnings of roughly $16,000 per month, but household expenses of $30,000 per month. How do you plan to address your shortfall?"

I explained that by working harder, I could increase my income. The forms also showed that I had roughly $150,000 in savings, which would help me to bridge the gap. I assured her I had plans to increase my income, to work harder, to find a way. Her face didn't shift, no acknowledgment, just a curt nod before she moved on. But I also felt judged, as if she didn't approve of my monthly expenses, or more likely, she resented me for spending so much.

"Under the conditions of your release, you'll need to submit detailed monthly financial reports," she said. "Bank statements, credit card statements—any account you have signing authority over. On behalf of the court, I will monitor your spending. Conditions of your release require you to get advance approval before you make any single transaction that exceeds $15,000. You'll also need to disclose cash transactions and ensure all expenditures are directly related to household needs. Do you understand?"

"Yes," I said, keeping my tone measured. Inside, though, it felt like my world was shrinking, one restriction at a time. She then asked me to initial a form to confirm my understanding. It felt as if she was trying to trap me, or laying the groundwork to come after me later.

Her next instruction hit me like a punch to the gut. She told me to download forensic software that would track every call I made, every website I visited, and every text I sent or received. My initial reaction was disbelief. This wasn't just supervision. It was invasive, constant surveillance.

"I'll need you to install this forensic software on all your devices," she continued, her tone unyielding. "Your phone, computer, iPad— everything. Your family members must also secure their devices with passcodes and confirm they won't let you use them. The court needs to ensure you're complying with the conditions of your release. Do you understand?"

I nodded, though my stomach churned. "Yes, I understand."

She looked me square in the eye. "This is not optional. If you'd prefer not to comply, the alternative is custody."

"I'll comply," I said quickly. There was no question—I couldn't afford to put my freedom at further risk. But as I sat there, agreeing to software that would strip away any remaining sense of privacy, I felt the full weight of my situation. I signed the forms where she requested, to confirm my understanding. Then I followed her instructions to download the software on my phone. She again made sure that I understood that the court prohibited me from using any phone or computer that did not have the forensic software.

Her instructions then turned to Gambler's Anonymous meetings, asking for some type of confirmation that I attended the meetings regularly, at least twice each month. Random drug tests would begin immediately after our meeting concluded. Then, she told me that I'd have to hire a licensed mental health therapist, who would provide weekly counseling, at my expense. The therapist would need to send reports on my participation directly to her. Basically, going forward, she made sure that I understood she would be responsible for monitoring, tracking, and scrutinizing every aspect of my life.

"It's not me putting these restrictions on you," she said, trying to soften the blow. "The court imposed these orders. My job is to ensure that you're complying with the court orders. Do you understand?"

The entire meeting had gone very different from what I had expected, but I acknowledged my understanding. She said that she would make an appointment to visit my home for an initial visit. She asked that my wife and family be at the house when she visited, because she wanted them to confirm that they understood conditions of my release, and that I was not authorized to use any digital devices that did not have the forensic tracking software.

"Following that first scheduled visit," she said, "all visits would be random and unannounced."

It became clear there would be no escape, no reprieve. My life, once filled with private jets, luxurious hotel suites, and high-stakes bets, had been reduced to this: justifying every dollar I spent and every step I took to someone who viewed me as a file, a case number, a potential threat.

When she finally asked if I understood, I nodded. "I understand," I said, though the words tasted bitter. I told her she could count on me to comply with every condition, to do whatever it took to stay in line.

"Good," she said, closing her file. "Then we're done for now. Report to the front desk and let them know that you're ready for your first drug test. I'll be in touch to schedule the installation of the software at your house."

With that, the meeting ended. I shook her hand and thanked her for her time, trying to project an air of cooperation. But inside, I felt drained, hollowed out by the reality of what my life had become.

As I stepped out of Officer Kressler's office, the receptionist pointed me toward a hallway where I'd take my drug test. The line stretched out ahead of me, a mix of people who, by appearance, could not have been more different from me. Most of them wore baggy clothes or stained shirts, their arms inked with gang tattoos or prison stamps. A few seemed barely awake, nodding in and out of consciousness as they shuffled forward. I felt entirely out of place in my designer clothes and polished shoes, standing there with my expensive watch catching the fluorescent lights.

When my turn came, a male officer stepped out of a nearby doorway and called me over. He led me into a small, bare bathroom with a toilet and a mirror bolted to the wall above it. The setup made it clear: the mirror was there so he could see my junk, ensuring there'd be no tricks or tampering. My stomach tightened.

"Go ahead," he said, handing me a plastic cup. He stood a few steps behind me, his eyes fixed on the mirror.

I stepped up to the toilet, holding the cup, but nothing happened. My body refused to cooperate. My mind raced, every second stretching longer, the weight of his gaze making it impossible to relax.

"I can't go," I said after what felt like forever.

The officer sighed and turned the faucet on and off, as if the sound of running water would somehow fix things. "You've got two more minutes," he said curtly.

"What happens if I can't?" I asked, my voice edged with frustration.

"You'll have to leave and come back," he said. "But let's see if you can make it work."

With the clock ticking and my anxiety mounting, I managed to squeeze out enough to fill the cup with pee. I handed it over, relieved to be done, but the officer held it up to the light and frowned.

"It's too clear," he said. "This won't work."

"What do you mean? You were standing right there. I just did what you asked."

"It's diluted," he said flatly. "You need to come back when it's not."

"I'm an athlete," I protested. "I hydrate a lot—I drink tons of water."

He wasn't interested in explanations. "Go downstairs, eat a bagel, drink some coffee, and come back when you can give us a proper sample."

Humiliated, I left the room and followed his instructions. I sat in the cafeteria, staring at the bagel and coffee I didn't want, the absurdity of the situation grinding at me. When I returned, I managed to give him the "yellow pee" he wanted. He ran his test and, after a few minutes, cleared me to go.

The entire experience left me feeling stripped of dignity, as though I'd been reduced to a box on someone's checklist. But I reminded myself that this was the price of freedom, however conditional. At least I had the liberty to go home.

As I walked out of the courthouse and back to my car, the contrast between my past and present hit me with brutal clarity. I thought about the times I'd sat in Monte Carlo casinos, millions of dollars in chips at my fingertips, the rush of high-stakes games, the freedom to make my own rules. And now, here I was—tracked, monitored, and surveilled, living under the watchful eye of the government. My liberty hung by a thread, one misstep away from unraveling completely.

I sat in my Range Rover for a moment before turning the key, staring at the dashboard as if it held the answers I needed. There was no way around it—this was my life now. I'd have to adapt, to navigate these new restrictions, to prove I could stay within the lines they'd drawn for me.

As I drove home, I thought again of that bronze statue in Europe, the man chiseling himself free. The image had inspired me before, but now it felt like a mandate. I had to keep chiseling, carving out a new version of myself, no matter how confined I felt. Because the alternative wasn't just losing my freedom—it was losing who I was entirely.

When I got home, the weight of the probation officer's instructions still hung over me. I knew I couldn't waste time, so I pulled out my laptop and started googling mental health professionals. It was humiliating—sitting there, typing "mental health counseling near me" into the search bar like some lost soul. I didn't feel like I needed therapy. But what I thought didn't matter. The court required it, and I had no choice but to comply.

Scrolling through the options, I found Dr. Berger, a psychologist with an office just a few blocks from my house. The proximity seemed like fate, or at least a small convenience in a sea of complications. I called her office, and she answered on the third ring.

"Dr. Berger," I said, trying to sound composed. "My name is Matt Bowyer. I'm facing federal charges, and as a condition of my release, I have to undergo mental health counseling. I'm hoping you might be able to help."

Her voice was calm and professional, which put me slightly at ease. "I understand, Mr. Bowyer. I've worked with others in similar situations. I'm familiar with what the courts require."

I explained my circumstances and asked if she'd take me on as a client. She agreed, outlining her fees—$200 an hour for our sessions and for the time she'd spend writing reports for the probation office. It stung, knowing I'd have to pay out of pocket for something I didn't even want. Ordinarily, spending a few hundred dollars wouldn't phase me. I'd typically tip a valet that much just for parking my car, and give a matching tip when I left the restaurant. But I wasn't in that position any more, and didn't want to take on unnecessary expenses. Yet I didn't see any other choice.

If I refused to pay, or even objected, Officer Kressler would likely give me a choice, saying that I could either comply with the court's order, or she would declare me noncompliant, which could lead to my going into custody.

We scheduled an initial appointment for later that week. When I walked into her office, I completed the standard intake forms and then sat down in a quiet room with her. For a moment, we just looked at each other. It felt awkward, surreal. Finally, I broke the silence.

"I feel like Tony Soprano sitting here," I said, forcing a smile.

Dr. Berger tilted her head, curious. "Do you see yourself as a gangster, like Tony Soprano?"

"No," I said quickly. "I just don't know what I'm supposed to do."

She nodded. "Why don't you tell me what's going on in your life?"

For the next hour, I told her everything—my legal troubles, the conditions of my release, the probation officer's demands. It was clinical, detached, like talking to someone who was cataloging my words for a file. As I left her office, I couldn't help but think how strange it was that this would now be part of my weekly routine.

But the strangeness didn't end there. My next hurdle was Gamblers Anonymous. I didn't want to go, but again, what I wanted didn't matter. I showed up at the meeting on a Thursday night. The room was small, the fluorescent lights harsh, and about 17 people sat in a loose circle of folding chairs. Their slouched posture and downcast eyes told me everything I needed to know—they were people who had been beaten down by life, unable to escape their habits.

The moderator, a man named Enrique, passed out a list of 25 statements. Each person was supposed to read one, then share how it applied to their life. It reminded me of Bible study sessions I'd been dragged to as a kid. One by one, the group members spoke. A guy who worked at Best Buy talked about losing $50 bets, which had added up to more than $1,200. Another shared how his gambling had interfered with his job and made him feel worthless. Each person's story sounded like a confession, heavy with regret and shame.

I cringed as I listened, wondering how I'd fit into this group. My turn was coming, and I had no idea what I was going to say.

When Enrique finally called on me, he welcomed me to the group, his tone warm but firm. He looked like someone who worked outdoors as a gardner—strong hands, sun-worn skin, and a demeanor that hinted at years of hard work. "Matt, since this is your first meeting, why don't you introduce yourself and share a little about why you're here?"

I hesitated for a moment, then decided to tell the truth. "I've been a bookmaker for years," I said, glancing around the room. "I'm here because the court requires it, but honestly, I don't see myself as a compulsive gambler. I've made my living from gambling—high-stakes bets, private jets, million-dollar clients."

The room shifted. For the first time all night, people sat up straighter, their eyes locked on me. The quiet murmurs stopped as they leaned in, hanging on my every word. I responded to their questions about the lifestyle I'd lived, the glitz of

Monte Carlo, the thrill of million-dollar bets, and the roster of celebrities who had been my clients.

As I spoke, I could feel the energy in the room change. Even Enrique got into it, asking more questions. The stories before mine had been filled with regret and despair, but mine was something else entirely. It wasn't a tale of caution—it was an adventure, a glimpse into a world they'd only dreamed about. I could tell by their expressions that they were captivated, and I could sense the impact I was having. Although I didn't need to be there, maybe they did. My story could potentially pull them back into the very world they were trying to escape.

Enrique thanked me for sharing. "I hope this group can help you as much as it's helped the rest of us."

I nodded, but in truth, I didn't think he or any of the people there could help me with anything. Although I knew I had a gambling addiction, I didn't belong there. Gamblers Anonymous was supposed to be about recovery, about moving forward. I wasn't sure how to reconcile their experiences with mine.

But I would do what the court required.

In September, about a month after my initial appearance, I reached the next phase of my judicial proceedings: the change-of-plea hearing. Diane had explained the process in detail, but no amount of preparation could have readied me for what was to come. Unlike the initial appearance, this hearing would be public, and Diane warned me that the media would be out in full force.

"They'll be firing questions at you," she said the night before, her voice firm but sympathetic. "Don't answer. Don't touch the cameras or microphones, no matter how close they get. Just look down and keep walking until we're inside the courthouse."

Nicole, Diane, and I rode together in a car I'd hired, the atmosphere tense as the driver navigated the streets toward the federal courthouse. As we approached, I could see the crowd gathering—about 50 reporters, cameras slung over shoulders, microphones clutched in eager hands. I took a deep breath as the car slowed to a stop.

"Ready?" Diane asked, her tone suggesting the answer didn't matter. We had no choice but to face it.

I stepped out first, followed by Nicole and Diane, and immediately the swarm closed in. The reporters walked in front, beside, and behind us, firing questions I couldn't even process. The flashes from their cameras were blinding, and the microphones hovered inches from my face. Each step felt heavier than the last, and though it was only about a 50-yard walk, it stretched into an eternity. I kept my head down, as Diane had advised, focusing on putting one foot in front of the other until we finally stepped through the courthouse doors.

Inside, the chaos of the media melted away, replaced by the cold, sterile stillness of the building. I glanced at the bulletin board near the entrance and felt my stomach drop. There, in bold letters, was my name: United States of America v. Mathew Bowyer. It wasn't a private matter anymore; it was public, and the whole country was coming after me. Seeing it written there, for everyone to see, made me feel dirty, as though my name had been permanently stained.

We entered the courtroom, where my family and friends were already seated. Diane had suggested they come, thinking it might offer me some comfort. But knowing they had seen my name on that board, that they were here to witness this moment, only deepened the pit in my stomach.

The hearing began with US District Court Judge Holcomb entering, his presence as formal and intimidating as the room itself. He would be the man who would decide my fate, and whether to honor the plea agreement that had led me to believe I'd get home confinement.

After everyone stood and he took his seat, he announced the purpose of the hearing: my change of plea. He then began reading every charge in the indictment, one by one, each word a blow to my already fragile composure. At Diane's suggestion, my family sat in the courtroom, as a sign of support. I didn't like that they had seen the bulletin board with my name on it, as a criminal defendant.

"Do you understand these charges?" the judge asked after he read details of each count against me.

"Yes, Your Honor."

He continued to ask about the charges in multiple ways, ensuring I was fully aware of what I was agreeing to. "Are you under the influence of drugs or alcohol? Has anyone coerced you? Do you understand the maximum penalties for these charges?"

I answered each question as required, my mind racing as he laid out the stark reality: ten years for money laundering, five years for filing a false tax return, and three years for illegal bookmaking. A total of 18 years was on the table, and he made it abundantly clear that no one—not Diane, not the prosecutor—could promise me anything about what he would decide. They could make recommendations, he said, but the judge wanted me to acknowledge that he alone would determine my sentence.

"I understand," I said, though the words felt like swallowing glass.

He went on to outline the broader consequences of my plea. As a convicted felon, I would lose the right to vote, to own a firearm, and to enjoy the liberties I'd once taken for granted. The gravity of it all hit me like a freight train, but there was no turning back now.

The prosecutor then stood to present the government's case, focusing on the volume of bets I'd handled. He cited one client, Ippie Mizhuhara, Shohei Ohtani's interpreter, and announced that I had taken more than $326 million in bets from him. The number reverberated through the courtroom, a figure designed to shock and outrage.

I wanted to object, to explain that the number was misleading, that it represented gross bets placed across countless games, most of which offset each other. The net loss was a fraction of that—a more accurate $40 million. But none of that mattered now. The number was out there, and it would be the number in all newspapers and television reports that everyone remembered.

The hearing dragged on, the judge repeating questions to ensure I understood every aspect of my plea. The courtroom, with its high ceilings and imposing atmosphere, seemed to close in on me. My name, my actions, my failures—everything was laid bare for all to see.

After what felt like an eternity, the judge finally spoke the words that would change my life forever. "The court accepts your guilty plea." He kept the conditions of my release in place until my sentencing hearing, which he scheduled for the spring of 2025.

And that was it. In that moment, I became a convicted felon. No matter what happened next, that label would follow me for the rest of my life.

The hearing had lasted 90 minutes, but it felt like four days. As I walked out of the courtroom, the reporters were waiting again, cameras flashing, voices shouting. Outside the courthouse Diane gave a brief statement to the media. She spoke about the guidelines and answered questions while I stood by her side, not saying anything, which wasn't really in my character.

In that circus, I saw constant flashes, and I heard a barrage of questions. In a sense, all the drama overwhelmed me. All the attention may have been appropriate for a case like OJ Simpson, who had been on trial for murder. I just kept my head down, and tried to keep rolling with the tide as I climbed back into the car. Nicole squeezed my hand, but I couldn't bring myself to look at her, as I felt a lot of weight on my shoulders at that moment.

The drive home was silent, the gravity of my new reality pressing down on me. I thought again of that bulletin board, of my name beneath the words United States of America. The comeuppance, or reckoning, would be something I'd have to deal with, to recalibrate.

As I reflect on this journey, I find myself returning to the statues that have inspired me—symbols of resilience, reinvention, and contemplation. There's the statue of the self-made man, chiseling himself out of a block of bronze, a metaphor for my own efforts to break free from the life I've lived and reshape my future. Then there's The Thinker, a statue depicting one of the ancient Greeks, resting his chin on his fist, a man deep in thought, grappling with life's vicissitudes. It reminds me of the necessity of recalibration—of meeting the world as it is, not as we wish it to be.

I can thank Micky Dhillon for helping me understand this process. Micky gave me my start in the commodities business, teaching me lessons that shaped my professional life. After the federal agents raided my house, I met Micky for breakfast, laying everything out on the table—the investigation, the charges, the uncertainty of what lay ahead. He listened carefully, then offered the kind of advice that only a mentor like Micky could provide: "Recalibrate," he said. "Understand how you got here. Write it all out. Then make a plan, and execute that plan day by day."

He was right.

Writing this book has been my way of recalibrating. By recounting everything that brought me to this moment, I've gained clarity about where I've been and where I want to go. Now, as I wait to see what sentence Judge Holcumb imposes,

I'm thinking about the future. Whether it's home confinement or something more severe, I'll be ready. The key is to keep chiseling, to keep thinking, and to keep moving forward.

I've begun laying the groundwork for the next chapter of my life. With the help of friends like Scott Johnson and Justin Paperny, I've started learning the power of social media. It's a tool I never dared use as a bookmaker, where secrecy was paramount. But now, it's time to bring my life into the light. This book is part of that process—a stepping stone that I hope will not only help me rebuild but also inspire others to recalibrate their own lives, no matter the challenges they face.

Recalibration isn't easy, but it's always possible. It starts with a decision to push harder, to write the next chapter even when the current one feels impossible to overcome. I've made that decision. I hope you will too.

If you want to see how I'm preparing for what's next, follow me on Instagram @matthewbowyer5 or any of the new social channels I'm developing. This is just the beginning. After Judge Holcumb hands down my sentence, I'll write the follow-up to this story. No matter what happens, I'll continue chiseling, recalibrating, and moving forward.

The only question that remains is: Will you?

CHAPTER 16

Epilogue: Recalibrated, But Not Finished

The weight of uncertainty feels heavier than anything I've ever endured. There's no way to soften the anxiety that consumes me. I'm confronting a harsh reality—one where a possible prison sentence awaits, threatening to separate me from my children, my family, and the life I've built.

Over the course of my career, I've paid out hundreds of millions in lost wagers, but no financial loss compares to the prospect of losing my freedom. I'm still haunted by the thought that I may not be able to provide for my wife, five children, and other responsibilities, at least for a while.

This is a true test of resilience, one that brings sleepless nights and an endless mental chess game filled with "what-if" scenarios. Anxiety and fear creep in, challenging the pride I once felt in my ability to overcome adversity. This situation is unlike anything I've faced before—more complicated than the time I was basically kidnapped in Costa Rica.

February 7 was meant to mark the end of a chapter—a day I had braced myself to accept. I stood ready to face the sentencing hearing and move forward, ready to accept whatever decision the judge made. Then my attorney told me the

Court had postponed the date until April 4—a day my family expected to celebrate my 50th birthday.

That change felt like a cruel twist of fate. Instead of celebrating a milestone, I'd wake up knowing that in a matter of hours, I'd be standing before a judge, waiting for a decision that could forever alter my life.

I finally wrapped my head around the new sentencing date. To foster optimism about a favorable outcome, my wife and I planned a 50th birthday celebration for that evening, hoping to also "celebrate" a sentence of probation or home confinement—the best possible outcome we could imagine.

But then, my attorney called with an update: the Court had postponed the sentencing hearing again.

Now, October 3 stood as the new date that would dictate my future, and potentially my liberty.

The constant delays, shifting timelines, and loss of control over my life have drained me. Yet, through it all, I've found peace in the simple truth: success isn't defined by what we earn or achieve, but by how we adapt when life takes away the things we once took for granted.

To adapt and overcome the challenges, I used the same strategy that worked for me many times before. From the time I started my life delivering newspapers or preparing to pass the exams I needed to sell commodities. I made a plan to move forward. I set new goals and committed to rebuilding, step by step. As I move into my life's second century, determined to support my wife and family, I'm focused on rebuilding, with a stronger foundation, making intentional decisions.

The Pre-Sentencing Process

As part of this process, I faced one of the most invasive and challenging aspects of the legal system: the pre-sentencing interview. This formal procedure, led by a probation officer—Officer Wang in my case—involves gathering information to prepare a recommendation for the judge. This recommendation plays a pivotal role in shaping the final sentencing decision.

A pre-sentencing interview is an in-depth, two-hour session where a law enforcement officer asks invasive questions with the intention of writing about every facet of your life. During this process, the officer asks about personal history, beginning with childhood and tracing your journey up to the present. The officer will inquire about the reasons behind past decisions, mistakes, and ask you to describe what you've learned from every experience that shaped who you've become over the course of your life. The questions go well beyond the specifics of your case. The probation officer wants to assess your character, lifestyle, family background, and even your attitude toward the charges you face.

I didn't like responding to her questions about my past financial decisions, or where I stood with assets, liabilities, income, debts, and expenses down to the last penny. The report would provide the government with a clear picture of my financial standing: including my ability to pay fines. Personal financial circumstances would influence the judge's decision on sentencing.

I understood the report would detail every bank account, investment, and financial commitment on record. And if I made errors or omissions in reporting, my lawyer warned that I'd run the risk of a sentencing enhancement, or even a new criminal charge, for obstruction of justice.

The experience was draining, leaving me exposed and vulnerable. Yet, the probation officer navigated it with clinical precision, brushing off the deeply personal questions as a necessary part of the process. According to her, the information was critical for compiling the Pre-sentence Investigation Report (PSR), a document he would submit to the judge along with his sentencing recommendation.

This report carried immense weight, shaping the judge's perception of me long before I set foot in the courtroom. In essence, this interview became the judge's lens for understanding the probation officer's assessment of my character:

> » Was I truly remorseful?
> » Did I show promise for rehabilitation?
> » Or did I come across as someone worthy of a harsher penalty?

That interview was one of the most surreal moments of my life. As I sat there answering each question to the best of my ability, I was acutely aware that she was analyzing my words, and that he would use them to write an official government report that would become a part of the permanent record, and destined to shape my future. Yet, like every other challenge on this journey, I faced it head-on, resolute in my determination to move forward, no matter what lay ahead.

Navigating Personal Chaos:

As if the legal battles, the uncertainty of my future, and the stress of the pre-sentencing process weren't enough, life dealt me yet another blow. Our home flooded, forcing us to move out for four long months in the midst of everything. It felt like one disaster was following another, especially when I learned that the cost of repairing our 6,800 square foot home would exceed $600,000, because the flood had destroyed the entire first floor of the house.

Losing our home and belongings during the upheaval brought an overwhelming wave of stress. We found ourselves juggling the chaos of insurance claims, coordinating with contractors for repairs, and striving to create some semblance of stability for our family during the months it would take to rebuild our lives.

Uprooting daily routines for such an extended period would challenge any family, but it became even more disturbing to face it during one of the most difficult chapters of my life. There were moments when the weight of it all felt unbearable. Our home has always been our sanctuary—a haven of comfort and peace. I purchased it for a few million, and over the years, poured millions more into it to make it truly our own. The unexpected flood stripped our comfort away, leaving us in turmoil.

Life seemed determined to test me at every turn, pushing me to discover how much I could endure.

To make matters worse, the banking system completely cut me off, shutting down every personal bank account and credit card I owned, despite my impeccable credit score of over 800.

Even Nicole, who didn't have any involvement in my legal issues, saw her accounts and credit cards frozen. This unjust action prevented her from processing payments for her small legitimate business that sold women's athleisure wear, Coco on the Go. We were American citizens, but we were going through direct assault on our ability to earn an honest living, jeopardizing our livelihood, our ability to pay bills, and the financial stability of our family.

The troubles didn't end there.

My jiu-jitsu studio, Rysk Brazilian Jiu-Jitsu, faced a major setback when anonymous administrators abruptly shut down our merchant account, leaving us unable to process student payments. It was a harsh reminder of how unforgiving the system could be.

Imagine striving to turn your life around—leaving behind gambling, building legitimate businesses, and working tirelessly to move forward—only to encounter door after door slamming shut. Even fulfilling obligations like repaying fines or taxes became an uphill battle, as the same financial institutions that once gladly took my money now refused to acknowledge our shared humanity, wanting nothing to do with me.

Meanwhile, the media refused to give us any peace. Japanese reporters and local news outlets relentlessly hounded us—showing up at our home, flooding our Instagram with messages, and even contacting our friends and family in search of details. Some showed up with cameras to my jiu-jitsu studio. The intrusion was constant and unending.

Owning My Story

Instead of letting the decisions of others define me, I took control of my narrative, against all advice from my attorneys. I kept putting myself out there—through podcasts, interviews, social media—any platform where I could share my story on my own terms. It was empowering to have a voice and use it to share my story with others. The exercise helped me build strength through a vulnerable time. Even though my lawyers didn't like my decision, I pushed forward, speaking openly to anyone who showed interest.

I enjoyed my collaboration with Mark Laita's Soft White Underbelly. Mark has built a platform with millions of loyal followers. He draws viewers in with raw, unfiltered stories of humanity. Several times a day, his show profiles individuals navigating life's harshest realities, offering a window into their struggles and resilience.

When Mark invited me to share my story, we spent over two and a half hours filming. Afterward, he described our session as one of the best interviews he's conducted in five years. Hearing this from someone who has spoken with people from every corner of life—Skid Row survivors, former cartel members, mafia hit men—lifted my spirits, reaffirming my sense of purpose. Even amid chaos, we could find meaning and value in the changes that life brings.

After our conversation ended, Mark asked if Nicole would be willing to share her side of the story. People would want to understand what she had endured. Though hesitant at first, Nicole agreed—an enormous step for someone who had previously shied away from the spotlight. Nervous but determined, Nicole spoke into the camera, facing the challenge head-on. I felt grateful we could navigate the experience together. Mark assured us he wouldn't publish the story until after the sentencing hearing, a gesture I deeply appreciated. Nicole and I eagerly awaited how audiences would react.

I also had the chance to sit down with Big Herc, who had launched a platform on YouTube called *Fresh Out*, which brought more attention to people who went through the prison system and the life they lived after incarceration. While it's not a world I'm personally familiar with, given the potential of prison in my future, Big Herc showed interest in learning from my perspective on how to adjust after a legal setback that could, potentially, take my liberty. I enjoyed our intense conversation, and responded honestly to his raw questions.

I also had the opportunity to interview with ESPN's Tisha Thompson, though I must admit, it wasn't the most enjoyable conversation. She flew out from the East Coast to visit me in my home. After some softball questions about the architecture of our home, and how she liked the design, I could see her agenda. From her questions, I could see her intent to highlight the connection between Shohei Ohtani, Ippei Mizuhara, and Mathew Bowyer. She would portray me as a morally compromised individual—a man seduced by the allure of luxury, indifferent to ethical boundaries, and blind to the theft and fraud occurring under my watch. The way she framed her questions and guided the discussion left no doubt that she would write a story that would get more eyeballs onto her television segments and blog, building an audience by trading on my name and the complexities of my unresolved criminal case.

Building Beyond the Headlines

Though my future felt uncertain, I refused to remain idle. I pressed on, responding to influential media figures who expressed interest in bringing attention to the career I built as a bookmaker, and the consequences that followed when authorities charged me with crimes related to my business.

One such opportunity was appearing on Craig Carton's radio show, which he called *"Hello, My Name Is Craig."* Craig's show focused on gambling addiction and awareness. Craig had a personal history with gambling, which added depth and authenticity to our conversation. We went into the highs, the pitfalls, and the journey toward getting over the problems. Craig's audience, coupled with his personal experience, made this a powerful platform to share my story and contribute to the broader conversation about how gambling could influence people's stability and their lives. In both of our cases, it could also influence our liberty.

I got to film with the *Digital Social Hour*, a fast-growing podcast Sean Mike Kelly hosted. Sean has cultivated a massive audience through candid, thought-provoking conversations with some of the most influential figures in business and culture. His meteoric rise in the media world showed the result of hard work, and it inspired me. I liked his unique approach to storytelling, which provided the perfect platform to share my insights on all aspects of sports betting, the business of bookmaking, and the life of a professional gambler.

When the acclaimed writer David Amsden reached out about preparing a feature for *Rolling Stone*, I knew that I would have to seize the opportunity. The magazine reached millions of people, and from that publicity, new opportunities could open. During our first conversation, David shared his vision for a 10,000-word, in-depth piece that would profile my life and the journey that shaped who I am today. Working with a writer of Amsden's stature—renowned for profiling some of the most complex and fascinating figures in modern culture—gave me complete confidence that he would take the time to tell my story with the depth and nuance necessary to bring it to life for readers.

As I've heard many times before, when one door closes other doors open. I've always believed that there are more opportunities in the future than in the past. Following my conversation with David, he told me that leaders at *Rolling Stone* had an interest in filming a documentary of the story, and they were prepared to invest up to $2 million to produce it. I wouldn't get any compensation for participating, yet by reaching more people, I hoped to launch the next phase of my career. While I await the outcome of my sentencing hearing, my entertainment lawyers are working out the details for that documentary. As a result of all the efforts I've put into memorializing my story, Hollywood big shots reached out. And in July, 2025, I signed a "shopping" agreement with "The Cut," an amazing team that produces award-winning documentaries for networks such as Netflix, Apple, and Amazon Prime.

We have to engineer our success, and that will always involve some level of risk. My defense attorney, Diane Bass, warned me of the risks of talking to reporters openly. She was doing her job. But I had to remind her that I was the client, and I would sink or swim by the decisions I made. She was doing her job, and I was doing mine, continuing to speak out.

An opportunity opened for me to collaborate with Doghouse Productions, an innovative media project with Eric Gagne, Bob Nightengale, and Tim

Ring. Their show was laid-back, mixing storytelling with behind-the-scenes moments—think golfing, dinner table conversations, cocktails, and candid, unfiltered dialogue. I liked the unscripted approach, offering their audience a genuine glimpse into the personalities behind the headlines.

Another project I went for came with an ongoing commitment to work with "The Confidence Quotient Podcast," with Michael Carrillo and Zane Kaufman. Instead of focusing on the controversy of a criminal charge, Michael and Zane asked questions that would help an audience understand more about how to engineer resilience, or to recalibrate when the life of a professional gambler and risk taker took an unexpected turn. We discussed the strategy I used—against legal advice—on how to overcome adversity, build mental strength, and create something meaningful even in the midst of uncertainty. Diane didn't like that I spent my time writing a manuscript, or being so open when speaking to the media, but I persisted, always pushing forward.

Sometimes, a man has to embrace the age-old saying and take the bull by the horns. New opportunities aren't created through timidity. Take the life of President Donald Trump, for example. Regardless of how you feel about his politics, it's hard to deny that he's a decisive figure—a man who charts his own course.

Even when faced with over 90 felony charges, he refused to back down. While lawyers and pundits urged him to stay quiet, he crafted his own strategy, recognizing that no one else would be as instrumental in shaping his path to victory. Instead of retreating into defense, President Trump took the offensive—and triumphed.

In a way, I can identify with President Trump's story. After all, we share some experiences in common. We've both been fingerprinted, stood for a mug shot, and have chosen to rebuild our own way, despite felony convictions.

What was that song Frank sang? *I did it my way*.

Giving Back and Paying It Forward

While focusing on rebuilding myself, I've also done my best to give back—through public speaking. I wanted to help others understand the consequences of bad decisions, and inspire them to make better choices. One of the most memorable experiences was speaking at USC's Marshall School of Business, in Hoffman Hall. Addressing a group of bright college students under the guidance of Professor Leonetti, we explored the theme of accountability and the far-reaching consequences of poor decisions—sharing how missteps could unexpectedly change the course of life.

I introduced them to the 10-10-10 Rule—a simple but powerful way to approach every major decision which I learned from Suzy Welch. Before making a choice, ask yourself:

» How will this decision impact my life in the next 10 minutes?

» How will it affect me in 10 months?

» And where will it leave me in 10 years?

Shifting your mindset means looking beyond the present moment to consider the long-term impact of your choices. Had I embraced this perspective earlier, my life might have taken a different path. But rather than dwelling on what could have been, I choose to use my experiences to guide others and help them avoid the same missteps.

The Next Chapter

My story is far from over—the next chapter is mine to create.

Life is a journey of twists and turns, marked by setbacks, triumphs, and moments that demand change. The real question isn't whether challenges will arise, but how you will face them when they do. So, if today signaled the end of one chapter in your life, how would you begin writing the next?

After my judge sentences me, I'll write the next chapter of mine. Regardless of whether he grants leniency, with probation or home confinement, or he is stringent, taking more of my liberty, I'm determined to push forward, creating new opportunities along the way.

With this epilogue, I stand on the edge of the unknown—preparing to face my judge for sentencing. My mindset has never been stronger. Regardless of what adversity may come, I know I'll meet it head-on. I've learned how to recalibrate, which is why I chose this title.

Through my line of work, I've learned that many lack the discipline to dig deep and find that extra gear when life gets hard. Truly successful people — the ones who rise above — are those who own their mistakes, stop making excuses, stare crisis in the face, and move forward, knowing that more opportunities will come. No matter what. People fall, they rise, and they keep rising.

I hope my story has challenged you to think differently, to fight harder, and to build upon that never-quit mentality we're all capable of developing.

If you take one thing from this book, remember that when life knocks you down, RECALIBRATE!

PHOTO GALLERY
Images from the Journey

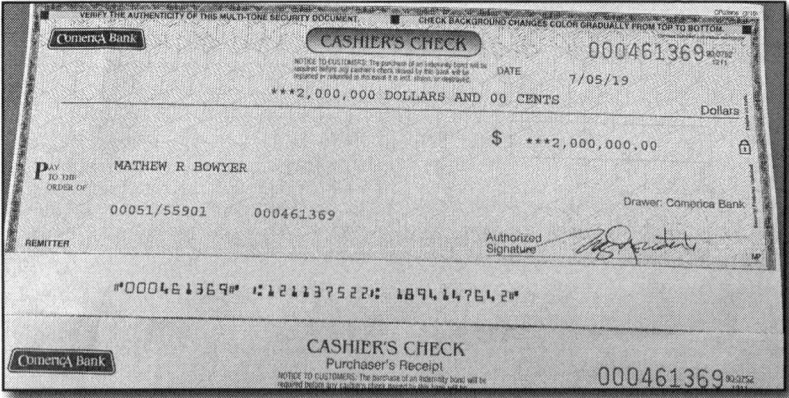

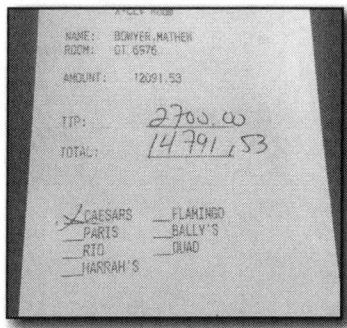

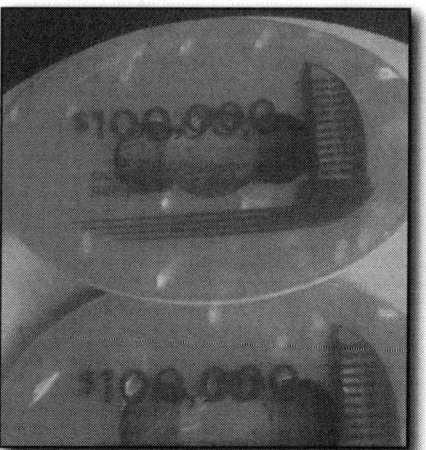

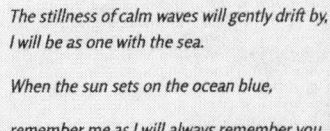

The stillness of calm waves will gently drift by,
I will be as one with the sea.

When the sun sets on the ocean blue,

remember me as I will always remember you.

As the sun rises...go live life as full as can be

Made in the USA
Columbia, SC
11 September 2025

da10ec84-9a6c-4963-b57d-65ff7ae67439R01